Musicking TikTok

New Approaches to Sound, Music, and Media

Series Editors:
Carol Vernallis, Holly Rogers, and Lisa Perrott

Forthcoming Titles:
Musical New Media by Nicola Dibben
David Bowie and the Transformation of Music Video by Lisa Perrott
Popular Music, Race, and Media since 9/11 by Nabeel Zuberi
Busby Berkeley at Warner Bros.: Ideology and Utopia in the Hollywood Musical by James Phillips
Climate Change and Audiovisual Media edited by Alexis Bennett, Annette Davison, and John Richardson
Tyler the Creator's Remaking of Hip Hop by Gustavo Souza Marques
Visual Music: A History and Theory of the Abstract Moving Image by Henry Balme

Published Titles:
Transmedia Directors by Carol Vernallis, Holly Rogers, and Lisa Perrott
Dangerous Mediations by Áine Mangaoang
Resonant Matter by Lutz Koepnick
Cybermedia: Science, Sound, and Vision edited by Carol Vernallis, Holly Rogers, Jonathan Leal, and Selmin Kara
The Rhythm Image: Music Videos in Time by Steven Shaviro
YouTube and Music: Cyberculture and Everyday Life edited by Holly Rogers, Joana Freitas, and João Francisco Porfírio
More Than Illustrated Music: Aesthetics of Hybrid Media Between Pop, Art and Video edited by Elfi Vomberg and Kathrin Dreckmann
Remediating Sound: Repeatable Culture, YouTube and Music edited by Holly Rogers, Joana Freitas, and João Francisco Porfírio
David Bowie and the Art of Music Video by Lisa Perrott
Haunted Soundtracks: Audiovisual Cultures of Memory, Landscape and Sound edited by K. J. Donnelly and Aimee Mollaghan
Traveling Music Videos edited by Tomáš Jirsa and Mathias Bonde Korsgaard
Vincenzo Bellini on Stage and Screen, 1935–2020 edited by Emilio Sala, Graziella Seminara, and Emanuele Senici

Kahlil Joseph and the Audiovisual Atlantic: Music, Modernity, Transmedia Art by Joe Jackson
Aesthetic Amalgams and Political Pursuits: Intertextuality in Music Videos edited by Tomasz Dobrogoszcz, Agata Handley, and Tomasz Fisiak
Musicking TikTok: A Musical Ethnography from a Glocal Austrian Context by Juan Bermúdez

Musicking TikTok

A Musical Ethnography from a Glocal Austrian Context

Juan Bermúdez

BLOOMSBURY ACADEMIC
NEW YORK • LONDON • OXFORD • NEW DELHI • SYDNEY

BLOOMSBURY ACADEMIC
Bloomsbury Publishing Inc
1385 Broadway, New York, NY 10018, USA
50 Bedford Square, London, WC1B 3DP, UK
29 Earlsfort Terrace, Dublin 2, Ireland

First published in the United States of America 2025

Cover design: Louise Dugdale
Cover image © Oriana Lendechy, 2022

Library of Congress Cataloging-in-Publication Data
Names: Bermúdez, Juan (Ethnomusicologist), author.
Title: Musicking TikTok : a musical ethnography from a glocal Austrian context / by Juan Bermúdez.
Description: New York : Bloomsbury Academic, 2025. | Series: New approaches to sound, music, and media ; vol 15 | Includes bibliographical references and index.
Identifiers: LCCN 2024023561 (print) | LCCN 2024023562 (ebook) | ISBN 9798765112182 (hardback) | ISBN 9798765112229 (paperback) | ISBN 9798765112199 (ebook) | ISBN 9798765112205 (pdf)
Subjects: LCSH: TikTok (Electronic resource) | Music—Performance—Technological innovations—Austria. | Music—Performance—Social aspects—Austria. | Music and technology—Austria.
Classification: LCC HM743.T55 B47 2025 (print) | LCC HM743.T55 (ebook) | DDC 302.30285—dc23/eng/20240626
LC record available at https://lccn.loc.gov/2024023561
LC ebook record available at https://lccn.loc.gov/2024023562

ISBN: HB: 979-8-7651-1218-2
ePDF: 979-8-7651-1220-5
eBook: 979-8-7651-1219-9

Series: New Approaches to Sound, Music, and Media

Typeset by Newgen KnowledgeWorks Pvt. Ltd., Chennai, India

To David and Emilia

I was never alone in this journey, and I would not have been able to complete this project without the support of fantastic people who were for me in every moment, in every joy, in every instant of doubt and desperation. This book holds a piece of each and every one of them.

Contents

Figures

Introduction[1]

It all began on a day like any other. Waking up as usual in the same place as usual. The warm sunlight shines through into an ordinary living room while a little boy runs around an old couch. In the middle of this infantile whirl, an old man holding a colorful storybook sits down. The child sits next to his grandfather. Together they turn the pages of the book. The toddler smiles and points to an image, and then tries to zoom it hectically by opening and closing his thumb and index finger. On the other side of the room, his parents smile and exchange familiar looks just before they burst out laughing. Disconcerted by their reaction, the grandfather asks with a stern tone of voice: "What is there to laugh about?" For a short moment, a slight breather, these words freeze in the air, and a second later the sound of the laughter fills the air. The child keeps on trying, but this time he is upset, crying …

This story is one of many personal experiences that have made me aware of the role that new technologies and media play in shaping the everyday lives of our children. The child in the anecdote interacts with an image in a way that is natural for him, but the reaction provoked by his fingers on the page of the book is different from the one he expects from his experience with smartphones, drawing him to an alternate reality. Meanwhile, his grandfather, who is unfamiliar with this digital native behavior, is far from understanding the reaction of the parents. Although we share a common lifeworld, it seems that we differ in the ways we perceive reality, and in the same way in which our children understand the world differently from how we adults do, the current state of ethnographies is different from those experienced in their origins. The research I conducted on musical practices around the smartphone application TikTok—formerly known as Musical.ly—is an example of how ethnographic realities have changed.

[1] This research was funded within the uni:docs fellowship of the University of Vienna and the process of writing and editing of the book was funded within the Post-DocTrack Pilot Program of the OeAW. Also, extensive parts of this work were translated from Spanish to English by Natalia Neira Nieto. The author is grateful for her assistance throughout this process.

The year was 2017. It was an autumn morning when I came across my colleague Bernd Brabec in the hallways of the university. After deciding to go for a walk together, Bernd took out his smartphone and showed me a couple of videos of that very interesting thing his daughters were doing in an application called Musical.ly. Before that moment, I had never heard anything like that—it seemed I was too old already to know about these new trends. The screen showed a couple of young people dancing and lip-syncing using their smartphones, performing different dances and different musical pieces. This was an unknown way of musicking to me. I was fascinated by those dances and lip-sync practices. I thought of it as a beautiful manifestation of creativity and the diversity of human musicking. Driven by both fascination and curiosity to know more about these practices, I soon downloaded Musical.ly onto my smartphone.

Broadly speaking, Musical.ly was a smartphone application purposed for creating and sharing short videos. Officially launched in August 2014 as an educational platform (MOOC), it would soon be geared toward music creation (Carson 2016), providing an interaction space for different music and video practices. During the fall of 2017, Musical.ly had little visibility in the global cultural imaginary, even though it already had around 200 million users. Meanwhile, this application was completely inexistent in ethnomusicological scholarship. However, the practices and visibility of Musical.ly would change in 2018, after Musical.ly was acquired by the Chinese company ByteDance and transformed into the application we know today as TikTok.[2]

TikTok is currently one of the most downloaded apps on the globe with approximately one billion users worldwide.[3] Its visibility has transcended borders, becoming a phenomenon that has undoubtedly established itself in the global cultural imaginary. But back in that fall, Musical.ly was still unknown, not just to me but also to most of my colleagues and friends. Nevertheless, the performative world of Musical.ly did not let me escape. Unwittingly, I found myself involved with this application and conducting explorative research. A couple of weeks later, I had my first conversations with Musers[4] and colleagues to help me concretize my research project. And well, this is the context in which my journey to understand Musical.ly—and subsequently TikTok—began.

[2] For a detailed analysis of the transformation of Musical.ly into TikTok, see: Kaye et al. (2021); Savic (2021); and Kaye et al. (2022).

[3] See Sensor Tower, https: //sensortower.com. State from December 2023.

[4] Muser was the name used for Musical.ly users, combining both of these words.

From the beginning, it was clear to me that many aspects of this project were going to be very different from my previous work about the diatonic *marimba sencilla* in Chiapas, Mexico (see Bermúdez 2021a). Among many other differences, my object of study went from being apparently tangible and concrete to intangible and abstract. The interaction with my informants and the consequent relations of power would be marked by new intersectional contexts. Additionally, the apparent inexistence of physical locations and interactions for observing and/or participating made me think about where and how I was going to carry out my fieldwork. In short, it was clear that investigating a kind of deterritorialized multimedia musicking, such as Musical.ly, offered many theoretical implications while possessing practical and theoretical challenges. Up to this point, everything seemed manageable to me, but what I did not anticipate was the resistance and/or rejection that my topic would receive from many of my colleagues.

One would think that those old—but not less objectionable—stories of white men secluded in a faraway land discovering *virgin* and *exotic* worlds would today be nothing more than romanticized images of a long gone past that does not exist in ethnomusicology anymore. However, the reactions and comments I received from many colleagues showed me otherwise. These images turn out to be an insisting "curse" that in many cases still determines the way ethnographic work is comprehended. More than once my research was confronted with academic resistance due to its strong opposition to those normative images. In other words, I was told that what I was doing, my object of study, my research, was not ethnomusicology.

But, why not? Had I misunderstood something during my years of study? Perhaps I did, perhaps I didn't. I was and still am convinced that ethnomusicology, as I understand it, is not defined by a specific object of study. Ethnomusicology does not refer to the research of a specific type of "music" or the music taking place in a specific territory, but rather to human musicking as a whole. From Japanese *gagaku* up to Lady Gaga, from yodeling to Mexican mariachi, from Beethoven to the TikTok app, ethnomusicologists should be able to explore all musical practices in the world with ethnographic methods and from a culture-relativistic perspective. Yet, some ethnographies still generate a similar image to the one created by the forebearers of ethnomusicology, as already pointed out some years ago by Bruno Nettl (1983: 4). That said, while exploring a kind of musicking like the one existing on Musical.ly or TikTok did not represent an epistemological problem, it did demand developing a more critical reflection of some of the underlying assumptions of our musical practices, a need confirmed by observing the reaction my research topic provoked on some colleagues.

Indeed, my selected topic was not always greeted with (perhaps naive) enthusiasm by my colleagues. Yet, it occasionally did lead to some quite "prudent" questions. There were three main matters that were thematized in those criticisms. In the first place, (1) concern about the performance I wanted to study. Some of the most frequent questions I received included: "What do you plan to research if no one is making music?" or "Which performance are you talking about?" But I ask myself, what *is* music? Most of these colleagues implied that there was one "true" kind of music, and whatever happened in Musical.ly was clearly not perceived as such. Moreover, (2) I was also asked about deterritorialization, as well as the "falsehood" of performances in digital media: "Where do these performances take place?" or "Juan, these are just representations, you should research *real* performances." These questions made me realize that the digital and the physical were perceived by some colleagues as two opposing concepts. On one side, there was "our real world," the place in which we meet and interact, where performances take place, and (true) music is created. On the other side, there was the so-called "cyberspace," "the internet," and "the media," that weird thing located in "nowhere land" where *only* representations, discourses, and texts about what's *real* are possible, and therefore no "true" performances take place. Is it really true that we can only perform in "real life" and "just pretend" in the digital world? Finally, (3) I was asked about the feasibility of ethnographic methods, and therefore, my capacity as an ethnomusicologist to research such a topic. It was obvious that the opinions of these colleagues and my own radically differed.

Receiving this kind of criticism made me think about issues and problems that otherwise I would have probably not been able to observe so early in my project. This helped me realize the importance of this investigation, as well as reflect on my profession as an ethnomusicologist. Though the rejections and criticism were not always pleasant, they indeed marked the path for my project. It was clear to me that in a world where interactions are increasingly taking place beyond physical contact, ethnomusicologists—or anyone who works with ethnography for that matter—are forced and encouraged not only to broaden their fields of activity but also to widen their approach and techniques in order to adjust to these new multimedia realities.

What Is Musicking TikTok About?

This book is about different ways in which musicking is manifested in TikTok from a glocal Austrian context. This study illustrates how some TikTokers encountered and began interacting with TikTok. It also reviews some of the different strategies these TikTokers employ to learn how to use the application effectively and develop their performances successfully. Throughout this study, I discuss how TikTok practices take place across multiple interconnected platforms, and I examine how localities are articulated and negotiated in these contexts. Furthermore, this study illustrates how TikTokers appropriate the platform to make their music. Above all, in this ethnographic work, I aim to add on and build upon ethnomusicological assumptions, theories, and methods for the study of musical practices in digital spaces.

At the beginning of 2018, research about musicking in the Musical.ly app was very scarce. After searching thoroughly for any kind of scholarly information on this topic, it seemed that back then no music scholar had written anything about this subject yet. Musical.ly did not seem to exist in the ethnomusicological literature. Although scholarship concerning TikTok[5] is rapidly growing and diversifying today, at that time, my research was delving into an area that had been little explored not only in musicology but also in other disciplines. In this context, I embarked on this project with a broad question: how and why is the musicking of the smartphone application TikTok, formerly Musical.ly, historically constructed, socially maintained, and individually created and experienced by diverse actors from a glocal context?

In order to satisfactorily approach an answer to this question, this study explores different thematic areas with their own specific questions, seeking to overcome some of the existing deficiencies in the ethnomusicological literature on Musical.ly/TikTok, as well as some of the questions and objects of criticism that I have encountered along the way during four years of ethnographic research. This thematic division, however, is only a theoretical construct. The topics dealt

[5] For a detailed exposition on the current research state of scholarship on TikTok and Short Video Studies, see: Zeng et al. (2021); Wei and Wang (2022). For examples of literature in relation to TikTok and music and dance, see among others: Abidin and Kaye (2021); Abidin, and Lee (2023); Bermúdez (2020, 2023b, 2024a, 2024b); Boffone (2021, forthcoming); Kaye (2020, 2022, forthcoming); Sánchez-Omos and Viñuela (2022); Vizcaíno-Verdú and Abidin (2022); Vizcaíno-Verdú and Aguaded (2022); Vizcaíno-Verdú et al. (2023).

with in it are interconnected and should not be understood as isolated in this delimited form.

The study is divided into five main foci. The first lies in developing new paths and points for reflecting and, therefore, creating the foundations for an interdisciplinary musical-ethnographic model (E^3thnography) for investigating multimedia and multilocal music practices. Secondly, this study focuses on TikTok performances: what kind of performances take place? How are these performances historically constructed, socially maintained, and individually created and experienced? What constitutes a performance? What performance possibilities do the technical conditions of the application allow? How do physical and cultural factors influence performances? When it comes to talking about performances, this work cannot ignore the performers. Regarding this aspect, I emphasize the questions: who performs and why? How does one become a performer? How does one learn to perform? How are performances prepared and carried out? How do performers interact before, during, and after the performance? Also, I seek to understand the way in which performers construct and experience their identity as performers; as TikTokers. For this, I ask: how does one become a TikToker? What does it mean for participating actors to be a TikToker? Which social images are reflected in these personae and how? What gender-specific roles are created, maintained, and experienced, and how does this happen? What characteristics are considered important for the creation of a TikTok persona? The fourth focus lies in the ideas of space and locality, as well as how these are constructed and experienced in TikTok. With that, I ask: in which physical and digital locations does this musicking take place? Which actors interact during musicking in the construction, experience, and maintenance of spaces of interaction? How are these spaces individually and communally created and experienced? And finally, with this study I seek to understand the ways in which TikTokers appropriate the platform for creating musical practices in and through it.

Embedding This Work

Overall, this book is the result of the circumstances of researching in a chaotic and changing world. But above that, it is the result of ethnographic research framed by three factors that, to different extents, influenced the what and how of this work: (1) the merge of Musical.ly and TikTok; (2) the COVID-19 pandemic;

and (3) my positioning as an immigrant cis-gender male scholar of color in his thirties investigating in Austria a musicking that is predominantly practiced by white female teenagers between thirteen and eighteen years old. This work is certainly the result of contexts, opportunities, and limitations that I as a person of color experienced during these last four years of research.

It was the beginning of 2018, and one of the most frequent criticisms I received about the research topic I chose was about the little stability and security that a smartphone application—such as Musical.ly—provided for developing a doctoral investigation. Considering that this project was supposed to last at least a couple of years, who could guarantee that Musical.ly would continue to exist during the whole project, and what would I do if Musical.ly suddenly vanished in the middle of my research? After some adventures searching for an adviser and institution that would accept my project, finally in the fall of that year, I officially started my doctoral studies on this topic at the University of Vienna. However, the joy would not be for long. This may seem like a cheap joke, but the day my dissertation topic on Musical.ly was accepted, the platform ceased to "exist." In the fall of 2018, the Chinese company ByteDance, which acquired Musical.ly the previous year, decided to turn this app into what we know today as TikTok.

It appeared that my colleagues were right: I had not even started my research when the application had already vanished. However, the merging of Musical.ly and TikTok ended up being more of an opportunity than a misfortune. The disappearance of Musical.ly and its consequent transformation into TikTok allowed me to understand and prove that the musicking of Musical.ly did not entirely depend on the application to exist. Just like in a bar, a concert hall, or an opera house, the smartphone application hosts a performance but does not constitute it in its entirety. People and their practices are the ones that keep a musical culture alive and existing, or would anyone ever assume that opera or jazz is gone or dead just because an opera house or a jazz club closed its doors?

Beyond this, another aspect that could not have been foreseen that greatly influenced my life and research, as well as TikTok's place in the global cultural imagination was the COVID-19 pandemic. Like many of you reading this book, overnight I was forced to abandon a symposium, go back home, lock myself up, reduce my interpersonal contact to a minimum, and move all my academic activities to digital grounds. The COVID-19 pandemic threatened the health of all citizens of the world and took control of their daily lives. At that moment, I found myself in the middle of my fieldwork about the musical practices regarding the TikTok application.

Like other musical traditions, musicking in TikTok has countless physical interactions between actors. Schools and parks become meeting places for TikTokers to watch, analyze, and learn different choreographies together; Meetups between TikTokers and their followers are held under different contexts; friendships and partnerships are taken beyond the platform into the physical world. Just like many fellow researchers, being locked up deprived me from observing and/or taking part *physically* in these practices. But the TikTokers I was researching were also locked up, finding themselves in a similar situation as mine. Although before the pandemic some of their practices (like performing, viewing, or sharing on the app) were already happening in digital environments, others (like Meetups) could no longer be executed as before. TikTokers were forced to carry on with their musicking from their homes, creating, transferring, and adapting old and new practices into this new lockdown context. In the same way, I would be forced to do research from a new context (see Bermúdez 2023a). After the pandemic ended, TikTokers could engage in physical activities again, and I could interact with them physically. By reflecting on my own experiences and position in this changing context, where I was co-present with the TikTokers, I could experience some of the performance possibilities and difficulties that TikTokers faced when articulating their musicking during and after the pandemic.

But beyond this, the pandemic changed the way TikTok was placed in the global cultural imaginary too. Even though TikTok was already heading to become one of the most downloaded apps in the world during the second half of 2019, the sudden break of the COVID-19 pandemic and the lockdowns that followed had a strong impact on the exponential growth of TikTok, even when the world seemed to stand in total stillness. People develop various aspects of their social lives through digital applications and platforms, for going to work, going to school, or gathering with friends and family. TikTok became one of the spaces in which social life during the pandemic took place. The visibility of TikTok spectacularly increased with the first lockdown. From being a relatively unknown application at the beginning of my research, TikTok became one of the most downloaded applications since 2020, a common topic and a referent in the current global cultural imaginary. Although not everyone really understands what it is, most people have at least heard the name somewhere, on television, in a movie, in the newspapers, or in a conversation with our children. TikTok has integrated into the practices and the imaginary of diverse social groups, and in a similar manner, members of these groups have developed their own practices and performative styles, expanding and enriching the musicking of TikTok.

However, the aspect that most influenced the development of my research was found in my own person. Although I had already spent half of my life in Austria, completed all my ethnomusicological studies in this country, speak the German dialect of the region I'm settled in, play in the music band of the village I live in, partake in many of the regional festivities, work and pay taxes in this country, having both of my children born here, and so on, I am not—and will probably not ever be—perceived as an Austrian man, not even as equally part of this country. The shape of my body, my features, and the color of my skin are always perceived as *FREMD*—foreign, alien—as the body of a stranger that does not belong here. Especially since the so-called "migration crisis" in 2015, I'm also perceived as an imminent threat. There is no doubt that all of this affected how my research developed. The following story is an example of this.

It was an ordinary morning in no particular place. I was excited to attend a Meetup organized by a TikToker. I arrived early, a couple of hours before it started so that I could observe the development of the encounter thoroughly. I also had the opportunity to introduce myself as a researcher to the participants from the very beginning. The followers began to arrive enthusiastically; most of them were teenage girls between thirteen and seventeen years of age who were accompanied by their parents. The girls began gathering in smaller groups, fired up in conversations about the host TikToker. The Meetup was about to start. Meanwhile, some members of the staff and journalists had already proceeded to take some pictures of the participants. I took my camera out as well to take some photos of what was going on at the event: the camera people, the staff, some participants, the venue, and so on. I approached some of the attendees for conversation, took another picture, and wrote some notes in my field journal. It was not long before someone came toward me and asked in English, "What are you doing here?" I then proceeded to explain in German that I was doing some research and what it was about. Time passed by, and more people started filling the place up. I had another conversation with the attendees, took another photo, and wrote more notes in my journal. Soon, another person approached me to ask why I was talking with the girls. Again, I explained I was a doctorate student doing some research and proceeded to explain the topic of my dissertation. The Meetup continued and these visits asking my reason for being there became more frequent. Time went by, and there were already a couple of people who took the task of keeping an eye on my activities. The Meetup with the TikToker began. I had some more conversations with the attendees, took more photos, and wrote down some more notes in my journal, perhaps the last ones. A police car parks outside the premises of the meeting. The next conversation took place outside the event. Again, I had to clarify what I was doing and explain what my research was about, this time showing proof of my legal residence in Austria and that I was working for the university.

It is probable that while reading this story some of you might have thought "Of course, I would also have my doubts if a male stranger approached my daughter." And yes, I get it, I would be suspicious too. But let us be honest: would your reaction be the same if that man was white instead of a person of color? And going back to the story, why did the police and the people who approached me not have any issues with the others who were also taking photos and talking to the girls? Regardless of the answer, the burden of colonialism and systemic racism is still present in our daily lives, and whether I like it or not, my body of color carries it. Access to my informants was biased in many ways by this fact. I must say that I was not always able to talk to TikTokers, and that organizing interviews was an even bigger problem. If speaking with them was often difficult, what could I say about making an "appointment" for a meeting afterward? With time, I began to develop strategies for "surviving" this unfavorable hierarchical relation between my informants and me, so that our conversations could become more feasible. But beyond this, the topic of privacy was an aspect that certainly influenced the development of my research. Even though after a while I found a way to talk to TikTokers, this did not ensure that they were willing to be recorded during an interview, a situation that led me to dismiss the use of a recording device during most conversations with TikTokers in the last years. Instead, I had to resign myself to focus on my field notes.

It should be noted that some of the deficiencies in documentation resulting from the previously mentioned aspects were set off thanks to the fantastic work of my students participating in the two research seminars I held at the University of Vienna during the summer semesters of 2020 and 2021. Thanks to their different sociocultural and generational backgrounds—and therefore their access to different groups of people—they were able to investigate and retrieve different aspects of TikTok individually and collectively that I would not have been able to approach in the same way. I'm certain that I learned much more from them than what I was able to impart. The materials gathered during these seminars led to fantastic bachelor theses (see Andruchowitz 2021; Cho 2021; Dornstädter 2021; Hintersteiner 2021; König 2021; Neuwirth 2021; Schrank

2021; Schrott 2021; Willenig 2021). Additionally, these materials helped me confirm many presumptions that I had developed in the previous years through my observations and conversations with TikTokers.

Methods and Frameworks

The arguments presented throughout this book are based on qualitative ethnographic research, considering the affordances of the platform, the performances carried out there, the experiences of the users, my experiences, and the many discourses related to the practices within TikTok. Therefore, together with the previously presented circumstances and contexts, this work draws from data from several complementary research approaches:

(a) Four years of participant observation on Musical.ly/TikTok between the spring/summer of 2018 and the summer of 2022. This was done both synchronously and physically, as well as asynchronously and digitally.
(b) Analysis of TikTok-related materials (including discussion boards created by users and by the industry), blogs, YouTube videos, Instagram Reels, TikTok advertisements, physical and digital youth magazines, press/media coverage about TikTok, player-produced TikTok tutorials, movies, and other audiovisual elements in popular culture thematized on TikTok, and so on.
(c) Analysis of TikTok videos compiled monthly from fall 2017 to summer 2022.
(d) Countless informal conversations with different TikTokers during Meetups and other informal situations during the four years of research, which due to access and/or legal-related issues could not be done differently.
(e) Two research stays in Hamburg during the TikTok Opera production "#FREE_Constanze" between September and October 2021.
(f) Fieldwork during multiple professional and amateur Meetups organized by TikTokers in different Austrian cities.
(g) A body of one hundred semi-structured interviews[6] with TikTokers within the framework of my seminar "Shadows in the Virtual Field: TikTok and the (Re)construction of a Multimedia Field" in the

[6] Many interviews were confidential. The names of interviewees are withheld by mutual agreement.

summer of 2021 at the University of Vienna, including interviews conducted by seminar participants.

(h) Reflections during four roundtable discussions between TikTokers and researchers during the spring of 2022 at the University of Vienna.

Chapter Overview

In the following pages, I aim to introduce the readers to the vast performative world of TikTok. I explore the existing musicking within one of the most used smartphone applications today and encourage readers to contemplate the possibilities of ethnomusicological (and ethnographical) research in a rapidly evolving world where physical and digital realms are increasingly intertwined. It should be made clear that with this work it has not been my intention or desire to produce a sort of "*the* book of." For this reason, the feeling of infidelity and even unfinishedness has not ceased to haunt me throughout the process of writing these pages. There are too many missing facets and too many historical and theoretical gaps. The study of the performative world of TikTok I assume and defend shows only the beginning of a journey toward a deep understanding of a global phenomenon that is to this day very little explored.

The structure of this book was thought of as a text that should be read from beginning to end because many of the arguments and ideas are presented, developed, transported, and/or converged throughout different chapters. However, this is done without forgetting to keep enough reflection points to be read individually without losing orientation. To facilitate the reading and understanding of the ideas presented here, each of the chapters focuses on a specific thematic axis, and the order of these chapters reflects in a general way my own journey to discover TikTok. Yet, it also reflects on some questions and objects of criticism that I encountered during these years of research together with numerous discussions about what researching the musicking of TikTok represents, as well as what this means for our ethnographic activities.

In Chapter 1, I briefly review the ethnographic model introduced by Alan P. Merriam (1964), as well as the additions made by Timothy Rice (1987) and Julio Mendívil (2016). On that basis, I continue by introducing the concept of E3 Internet by Christine Hine (2015) to this model to understand the internet and its (musical) practices as a daily, highly embedded, and embodied experience. With this, I make a critical reflection on the meaning of ethnographical work in the research of digital musical practices. I propose to understand musicking as a multimedia practice created and experienced individually by different actors in everyday synchronous and asynchronous, as well as physical and digital situations. In this chapter, I present an interdisciplinary musical-ethnographic model called *E³thnography* for investigating multimedia and multilocal music practices.

Chapter 2 is about the different ways in which participation is possible in the musicking of TikTok and the types of performances carried out through this application. In the first part of this chapter, I aim to understand the ways of interaction and interrelation present in this kind of musicking by discussing the elements that comprise the interface of TikTok, as well as the technical-performative possibilities provided by the application. This section was especially thought for those readers who are not yet familiar with the TikTok interface. After that, in the second part of this chapter, I examine the types of TikTok performances and develop a general categorization of these performances.

In the third chapter, I focus on the performers of the musicking of TikTok. In the first part of this chapter, I discuss how TikTokers became acquainted with and began using the application. After that, I go through some of the different strategies used by TikTokers to learn how to use the application and carry out their performances successfully. The second part of this chapter is dedicated to developing the concept of musical personae coined by Philip Auslander (2006, 2021). In this section, I analyze how performers go from being "common users" to TikTokers by developing and performing an identity I call TikTok persona.

Chapter 4 is about the musical geography of TikTok from an Austrian context. To understand the way in which localities in the musicking of TikTok are articulated and negotiated, in the first part, I will discuss the concepts of presence, co-presence, empathic co-presence, and non-presence as ways of critically reflecting on the ideas of "being there" or "being present," which are very important for ethnographic work. Additionally, I will introduce and discuss the concept of *musical geography through practice*. Following these reflections, the second part of this chapter examines and discusses how some of the TikTok practices can and did take place across multiple, interconnected platforms. For the third part of the chapter, I will analyze the different strategies that the TikTokers use for inhabiting, transforming, and making sense of the musical geography of TikTok.

The fifth chapter is focused on the performances held within the musicking of TikTok. Here I explore and analyze some examples of the ways in which

TikTokers appropriate the platform for creating musical practices in and through it. In the first part of this chapter, I discuss how TikTok is used as a digital stage for developing performances. In this section, I exhibit how TikTokers use the performative space and visibility provided by TikTok and turn it into a place, or more specifically, a *stage* for the development of their musical practices. The second part of this chapter is focused on the way in which actors of other already established musical traditions use TikTok for performative experimentation in new formats. In the final part of this chapter, I focus on how TikTokers develop musical practices that are characterized by their understanding of TikTok as a practice of its own and of equal performative value. In these musical practices, TikTokers look to borrow musics from other contexts, norms, expectations, and aesthetics of TikTok from a performative understanding particular to the platform through their performance, in other words, how TikTokers are TikToking musics.

This work is the result not only of numerous encounters, discussions, reflections, and surprises but also of misunderstandings, criticism, failures, and many moments of desperation and doubt, especially doubt. This is the result of the contexts, opportunities, and limitations that my person experienced during years of research and the pandemic. After all this, I'm convinced that the true aim of this work was not that of finding all answers but of creating new questions and points for discussion, of looking to set the floor for an interdisciplinary discussion about the why and the how of a multimedia musicking. I hope you enjoy this journey and this exploration of the performative world of TikTok as much as I did and still do.

1

Ethnographing TikTok[1]

Through the rise and expansion of the internet, as well as the development of new devices, new forms of communication, and new platforms, a vast number of interrelations between physical and virtual multilocal and multimedia spaces have been developed and established as an inseparable part of our daily lives. Especially younger generations, the so-called digital natives, perceive these interrelations as an extension of their own reality. We search for the closest restaurant in Google Maps while chatting with friends who could be across the street, in Germany, in Mexico, or in any other country. We *like* some pictures shared by our family or friends on Instagram, and we show our shopping tour or a concert we are at *live* via Facebook. In the same way that the use of digital media and devices transforms our daily lives, these technologies also influence our musical practices. Social media is commonly used by musicians to present and market themselves; however, there are other actors who also construct and participate in the discourses of these musical practices. As already seen in the past with the introduction of new technologies (see Enders 2013; Smudits 2002), the current appropriation of the digital worlds, as well as the development of new digital platforms (e.g., YouTube, Spotify) and devices have not only shaped the interaction between actors but also enabled and reinforced the adaptation and development of (new) forms of musical practices.

The study of multimedia musicking, such as TikTok, offers a large number of theoretical implications while possessing practical and theoretical challenges. In a world where interactions are increasingly taking place beyond physical contact, ethnomusicologists and other music scholars are forced and encouraged not only to broaden their fields of activity but also to widen their approach and techniques for adjusting to these new multimedia realities (see Bermúdez 2020, 2021b). In this chapter, I will briefly review the ethnographic

[1] Versions of the ideas raised in this chapter were originally published in a different or summarized form in Bermúdez (2020, 2021b, and 2024a).

model introduced by Alan P. Merriam in 1964, as well as the additions made by Timothy Rice in 1987 and Julio Mendívil in 2016. On that basis, I will continue by introducing to this model the concept of E3 Internet by Christine Hine (2015) to understand the internet and its (musical) practices as a daily, highly embedded, and embodied experience. With this, I will make a critical reflection on the meaning of ethnographical work in the research of digital musical practices. I propose to understand musicking as a multimedia practice that different actors create and experience individually in everyday synchronous and asynchronous, physical, and digital situations. I aim to develop new paths and points for reflection and therefore create the foundations for an interdisciplinary musical-ethnographic model for investigating multimedia and multilocal music practices.

A Model to Rule Them All

I understand ethnomusicology the way Timothy Rice defines it: "the study of why, and how, human beings are musical" (2014: 1). Therefore, I stand for a kind of ethnomusicology that does not lay stress on a musical object, but rather advocates pluralistic thinking and falls back on joint assumptions, methods, and theories, as well as on a political ideal. I stand for a kind of ethnomusicology that, in the words of Thomas Turino, aspires "to draw attention to different lifeways and modes of thought" (2008: 226) for (re)constructing its findings and perceptions. In connection with this thought, knowledge construction mechanisms and discussions of different music processes are viewed from a comparative and culture-relativistic perspective (see Nettl 2005: 13). This includes their *musicality* in its holistic course of performance and is not limited to auditory forms. I understand the term "musical" in the sense of the concept of *musicking* introduced by Christopher Small: "To music is to take part, in any capacity, in a musical performance, whether by performing, by listening, by rehearsing or practicing, by providing material for performance (what is called composing), or by dancing" (1998: 9). In consequence, ethnomusicology does not refer to the research of a specific type of "music" or of music taking place in a certain territory, but rather to human musicking as a whole. In this sense, I am convinced that the ethnographic method is suitable for investigating all forms of human musicking, including musical practices such as those developed in TikTok, but under specific assumptions and theories.

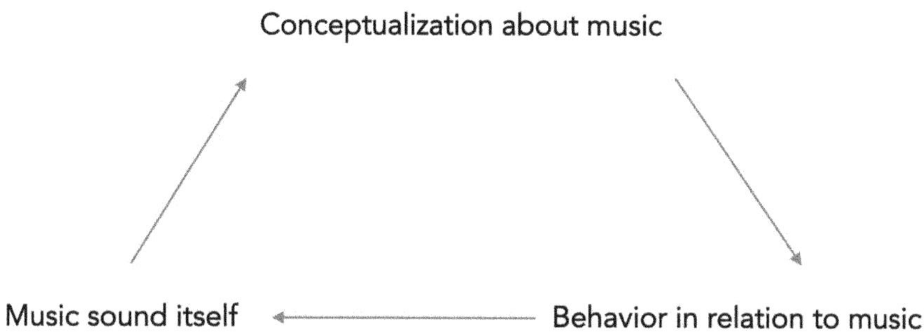

Figure 1 Merriam's model (1964), illustration by author.

In the book *The Anthropology of Music* (1964) Alan P. Merriam presents a model that would serve as a basis for ethnomusicological work (Figure 1). This model included the study of three analytic levels: *conceptualization about music*, *behavior in relation to music*, and *music sound itself.*

> The sound has structure, and it may be a system, but it cannot exist independently of human beings; music sound must be as the product of the behavior that produces it … But behavior is itself underlain by a third level, the level of conceptualization about music. In order to act in a music system, the individual must first conceptualize what kind of behavior will produce the requisite sound … It is at this level that the values about music are found, and it is precisely these values that filter upward through the system to effect [sic] the final product. (Merriam 1964: 32–3)

In the 1980s this model was expanded by Timothy Rice, influenced by the work of Clifford Geertz (1973). Rice added the focus on the individual and their experiences in the process of making music, as well as a diachronic perspective. When music is historically constructed and its experience is conveyed to the present, its social preservation is a logical fact. Music is constructed historically by people; it is socially maintained and individually created and experienced (Rice 1987: 469–88). Rice argued that:

> "symbolic systems … are historically constructed, socially maintained and individually applied" ([Geertz 1973:] 363–364). Instantly I recognized these as the "formative process" that I had been searching for. Here was a three-part model, analogous to Merriam's that was easy to remember and that seemed to balance social, historical and individual processes and forces in ways that seemed immediately and intuitively satisfying … Simply put, I now believe that ethnomusicologists should study the "formative processes" in music, that

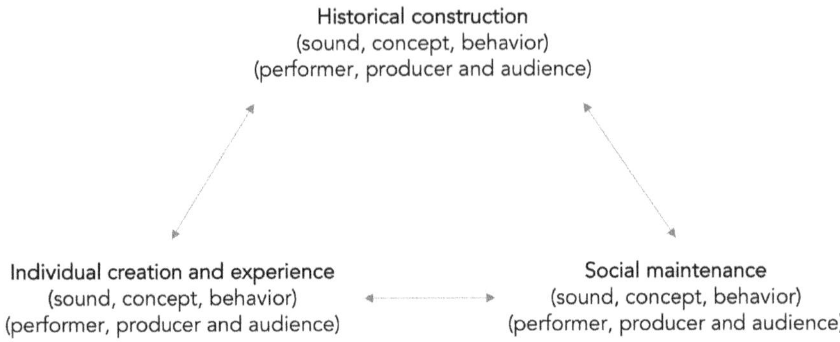

Figure 2 Merriam's model remodeled by Rice (1987) and Mendívil (2016), illustration by author.

> they should ask and attempt to answer this deceptively simple question: how do people make music or, in its more elaborate form, how do people historically construct, socially maintain and individual create and experience music? (Rice 1987: 473)

Rice's expansion conferred an additional dialectical level to Merriam's model by considering the role between the creation and the experience of actors of different musics even stronger.[2] This level focuses predominantly on the role of musicians and audience, but not on other actors that form part of the knowledge construction and negotiation. In 2016, Julio Mendívil drew attention to this limitation and proposed the introduction of the concept of *musicking*[3] introduced by Christopher Small (1998). He explains: "such an approach allows us to analyze the historical formation of sound's structures, behavior and concepts as a particular process in a given time and place, which involves all the actors *musicking* (not only playing and hearing, as Rice defines it)" (Mendívil 2016: 73).

With these two extensions (Figure 2), Merriam's model provided an excellent basis for the interdisciplinary research of musical practices, especially because with this approach we avoided "getting caught up in one facet or another of music—sociology without attention to sound, analysis of performance without

[2] Alan P. Merriam recognized the dynamism of musical practices, as well as the dialectical play between the creation and experience of the actors in his model. However, this dialectical level does not play a decisive role as is the case of the expanded model by Timothy Rice.

[3] Christopher Small defines musicking as "to take part, in any capacity, in a musical performance, whether by performing, by listening, by rehearsing or practicing, by providing material for performance (what is called composing), or by dancing" (1998: 9).

attention to social processes, the study of music that ignores movement, and so forth" (Seeger 2006: 229). Moreover, this model made it possible to explore the dynamic interrelations between different processes of auditive knowledge and the development of musical practices, as well as the creation and experience of this knowledge through the actors in a specific space over a certain period.

However, the analysis of multimedia musical practices, such as the practices in TikTok, requires more than a successful ethnomusicological model. The exploration of these practices demands methods and approaches that allow an analog and virtual conceptualization beyond the dichotomy (see among others Marcus 1995) and that are able to see digital media as practice (see Couldry 2010). For this reason, and to overcome these challenges, I propose to understand the internet and its (musical) practices, as postulated by Christine Hine: as an **E**mbedded, **E**mbodied, and **E**veryday experience—the E3 Internet (Hine 2015). She emphasizes that the internet,

> is embedded in various contextualizing frameworks, institutions, and devices, that the experience of using it is embodied and hence highly personal and that it is everyday, often treated as an unremarkable and mundane infrastructure rather than something that people talk about in itself unless something significant goes wrong. These three "Es"—for shorthand purposes, the E3 Internet—provided a backdrop for thinking about why it is difficult to apply ethnographic principles to the contemporary Internet, and how we might do so successfully. (Hine 2015: 32)

Through this shift to thinking in terms of the meaning of internet in the everyday life of the actors and their musical practices, as well as the recognition of internet as an embodied experience,[4] it is possible to expand Merriam's model with a new level, which reflects the realities of a deterritorialized and multimedia world.

In this way, I propose a new expansion to Merriam's model. This new model, which I call E^3thnography, prompts the research of *concepts, behaviors, and sounds that different actors of specific musicking (musicians/dancers, audiences, producers*[5] *and other actors musicking) historically construct, socially maintain, and individually create and experience in everyday synchronous and asynchronous multimedia situations* (see Figure 3). An E^3thnography enhances the possibility of exploring music cultures constructed through physical and digital interactions.

[4] It is important to emphasize that experience is influenced and determined by forms, discourses, times, objectives, and so on, and by the interactions between human and nonhuman actors.

[5] Here we can also talk about *produsers* (see Bruns 2008).

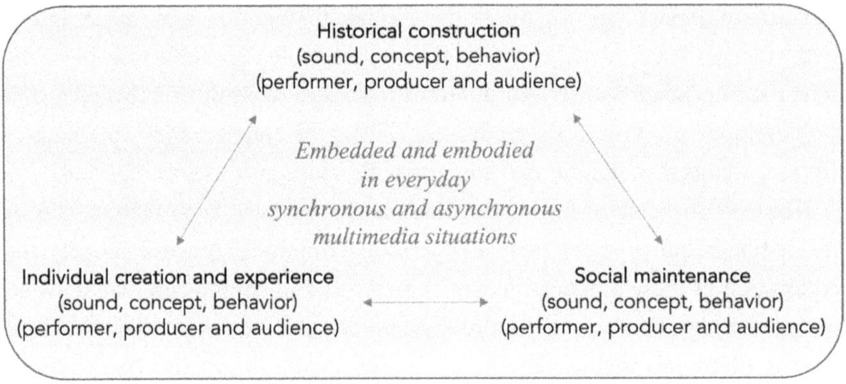

Figure 3 E³thnography, illustration by author.

Below, I will discuss a path leading to this interdisciplinary musical-ethnographic model for investigating multimedia and multilocal music practices.

Always Embedded, Embodied, and Every Day—Toward an E³thnography

E³thnography is based on the idea that the field is first constructed and negotiated once the constant multimedia interaction of physical and digital actors takes place, and that these practices can first gain a tangible and limitable "territory" after the (re)production and immersion in the musicking being studied (see Chapter 4). This makes it necessary to focus on the knowledge and experience of the actors and our experience as researchers while constructing and acquiring knowledge and studying these practices, instead of focusing on the physical place/space (see de Certeau [1984] 1988) where these practices are possibly happening. By focusing on what actors *do* under different circumstances and contexts *with* and *in* digital media, we can discover and observe the practices taking place in an asynchronous multimedia environment, and thus exemplify the interrelations produced by the field and its multimedia locations.

Musicking as Multimedia Practice

To explore mediatized musical practices, such as in TikTok, it is crucial to understand digital and analog media as practices that are created, negotiated, and experienced in everyday multimedia situations and contexts in a synchronous or asynchronous way. We need to focus on what people are actively doing *with* and *in* a mediatized environment, and herewith against a discourse that sees media exclusively as a communication or representation channel used by physical actors. I discard a discourse that ignores the active participation and discussion of living people who physically interact behind these multimedia interactions, and who also experience the multisensorial virtuality of this apparently passive practice while acting actively.

Although one can be in favor of the idea of multilocality in musical practices, assuming that a prevalent physical interaction exists in these practices can become a "problem" for research of music traditions with multilocal physical and virtual spaces of interaction, such as TikTok. The problem lies in the fact that researchers often still lean into thinking about the ethnographic field the way that Bronislaw Malinowski experienced and conceived it, namely, as consisting:

> mainly in cutting oneself off from the company of other white men, and remaining in as close contact with the natives as possible which really can only be achieved by camping right in their villages. It is very nice to have a base in a white man's compound for stores, and to know there is a refuge there in times of sickness and surfeit of native. But it must be far enough away not to become a permanent milieu in which you live and from which you emerge at fixed hours only to <do the village>. It should not even be near enough to fly to at any moment for recreation ... And by means of this natural intercourse, you learn to know him, and you become familiar with his customs and beliefs far better than when he is a paid, and often bored, informant. (Malinowski 1922: 6–7)

However, many of our contemporary musical practices show us a very different reality from the one that originated this ideal (see Cohen 1991). Clear examples of this phenomenon can be found in the research by Julio Mendívil on German Schlager (2008), Alejandro L. Madrid on Nor-Tec Collective (2008), Katherine Meizel on American Idol (2011), or Noriko Manabe on protest music in Fukushima (2015). Many of these practices either don't have a clear physical location or such location only exists as an abstract and imagined (see Anderson [1983] 2006) construct. Additionally, many of these practices don't need physical contact among actors to keep the mechanisms of production and experience of its auditive knowledge (see Mendívil 2008). In other cases, as Peter Wicke has noticed, these practices barely experience a specific location in the moment of its reception (2001: 25), processes that have made the synchronous experience of physical performance unnecessary for actors.

On the other hand, other musical practices show us a different understanding of what making music means. In the same way that the synchronous experience of performance seems to be superfluous in some musical practices, its synchronous sound production may also be superfluous. Creating, processing, and experiencing sound may occur in an autonomous way at different times and in different spaces. Practices such as DJing, remixing, mashups, or karaoke process and treat asynchronously prefabricated auditive products during their performances (see Brown 2015; López Cano 2018). Practices like air guitar or lip-syncing require an additional performance as an existing auditive product that is complemented by a mimic performance. Meanwhile, practices based on joint performances of a rock concert where musicians connected via the internet use plastic guitars, as in the case of Guitar Hero, show a different understanding of what it means to make music (see Miller 2012). In this sense, the musicking of TikTok is no exception. While we can find musical performances in a "classic" sense, in TikTok's musicking there are also duets, challenges, and other types of performances that show us different types of networked creativity and that go beyond a traditional vision of what "music" is, using the technical possibilities of the application to expand and/or create new forms of musical performance.

Through the interrelations between physical and digital multilocal and multimedia spaces and their enhanced involvement in everyday life, asynchronous multimedia and multilocal music practices such as TikTok multiply in today's global world. Although the role of digital media in musical practices is considered to be a widely studied topic in musicological scholarship, the premises of research have been limited to economical (see Flath 2016; Tschmuck et al. 2018) or discursive aspects (see Ayers 2006; Kärjä 2018). Moreover, there is an increasing interest in basic reflections on methodological challenges and possibilities of digital media in ethnomusicological research (see Marcus 1995; Barz and Cooley 2008). These reflections focus on the role of the media as a tool for ethnographic work (E-Fieldwork) as a communication and representation channel of physical reality (see Wood 2008; Hilder et al. 2017) or on the possibilities of virtual learning processes of physical musical practices (see Syed in Cooley et al. 2008). Research that sees new musicking practices primarily taking place in digital spaces as music of the same value as non-digital practices (see Lysloff 2003; Miller 2012; Boffone 2021) is a rare exception in the musicological discourse. In scientific practice, this often leads to a discourse where digital media is solely viewed as a communication or representation channel for physical actors, and the multimedia interactions and resulting auditory knowledge construction and exchange between their *cultural cohorts*[6] are pushed to a marginal position. This highlights the urge to see the paradigm of digital media "not as a text or production economy, but first and foremost as practice" (Couldry 2010: 35; see also Couldry and Hepp 2017).

Hence, as a result of the preference for a strict dichotomous separation between reality and virtuality, we build a discourse that does not perceive digital media as part of knowledge practice but rather as a passive representational practice. Under this paradigm, we risk reducing the experience of the users in digital media to simply obtaining information from the web. By doing so, we exclude the active creation and interaction processes of the actors who are physically acting behind these multimedia interactions and who experience the virtuality of this apparently passive practice with all senses while discussing actively, a trend that may lead to a new kind of armchair ethnomusicology.

A different approach to the relation between reality and virtuality can be found in scholastic philosophy: "In scholastic philosophy 'actual' and 'virtual' exist in a dialectical relation rather than in one of radical opposition: the virtual is not that which is deprived of existence, but that which possesses the potential, or force of developing into actual existence" (Ryan 1999: 88; see also Ryan 2015). Based on reflections about the difference between the possible and the virtual by Gilles Deleuze ([1968] 2014), Pierre Lévy (1998) invites us to think of the virtual not as something false or illusionary, but as "a fecund and powerful mode of being that expands the process of creation" (Lévy 1998: 16).

> The virtual is a kind of problematic complex, the knot of tendencies or forces that accompanies a situation, event, object, or entity, and which invokes a process of resolution: actualization … Actualization thus appears as the solution to a problem, a solution not previously contained in its formulation … It implies the production of new qualities, a transformation of ideas, a true becoming that feeds the virtual in turn. (Lévy 1998: 24–5)

That said, the virtual is not something lacking actual reality, but rather a way of being that produces "a change of identity" (Lévy 1998: 44) through a practice of actualization. This dialectical interdependence between the reality happening *at the current moment* and the *potential* or *imaginary* reality, meaning the virtual, has an influence on the perception of each of our cultural practices (see

[6] Turino defines *cultural cohorts* as "social groupings that form along the lines of specific constellations of shared habit based in similarities of part of the self" (Turino 2008: 111).

Lévy 1998; Bermúdez 2020). As the anthropologist Tom Boellstorff accurately observed: "our 'real' lives have been 'virtual' all along. It is in being virtual that we are human: since it is human 'nature' to experience life through the prism of culture, human being has always been virtual being" (2008: 5).

When the interrelation between real and virtual consists of a dialectical relation rather than of a dichotomic contradiction, our musical practices—which mainly take place in digital spaces—also experience a similar interrelation between experienced realities and potential or imagined realities. The interaction and interrelation between the actors of these musical practices also take place in a dynamic flow between the physical and digital worlds. A "non-media-centric approach"—the focus set on what actors do under different circumstances and contexts with and in digital media—is necessary because of "the ways in which media processes and everyday life are interwoven with each other" (Morley 2007: 20; see also Moores 2018).

Musicking as an Individual Experience

Secondly, an e^{3}thnographic approach requires a strong focus on the individual and their experiences as individuals or within the group in the process of making music. Yet, the focus shall also lie on the performative creation of individual musical personae and on the discussion of cultural behaviors related to them. Following Mark Slobin's idea that "we are all individual music cultures" (1993: ix), I agree with Timothy Rice when he speaks about "subject-centered musical ethnography" (2003; see also Abu-Lughod 1991). That said, I propose an e^{3}thnographic approach in which the individual and the physical and digital personae related to them represent the access and central point of our research. As a result of focusing on the people who create and experience the auditory knowledge of musical practice, it is possible for us to find and observe the dialectical interplays that occur as part of the implementation of musical practices in the interaction spaces beyond the physical world.

In a non-media-centric approach that perceives the interrelation of different media processes and our everyday life beyond the real/virtual or digital/analog dichotomy, interacting actors of these practices and their multimedia interrelations acquire a significant role in the generation of knowledge. The actors do interact not only in physical settings but also in digital or virtual interaction spaces. In the same way interactions can take place in spaces beyond the real/virtual dichotomy, interactions are not tied to a physical body, but instead to the many characteristics the actors hold in their identities. For multimedia musical practice investigation, the focus on a physical and synchronous interaction between actors represents the construction of a unilateral interaction picture that ascribes digital media as a passive representation practice and does not perceive it as a practice that generates knowledge. Contrary to this, the focus on "[the] *partial* selection of habits and attributes used to represent oneself to others by oneself and by others" (Turino 2008: 95) enables us to have a better understanding of multiple existing and potential identities of the performers beyond their physical bodies.

The interaction of these multiple identities of the actors encourages the development of specific performative identities, which may lead to the creation of a musical persona (see Auslander 2006: 102–4). These musical personae build a recognizable cultural construct beyond the concept of the body in the shape of an individual. In multimedia musical practices like TikTok, it is possible to observe a similar phenomenon: the performers, the so-called "TikTokers," try to create a recognizable musical persona through their performances, the so-called "TikTok(s)." Consequently, certain aesthetic properties, such as stylistic and performative characteristics of their performances, are put in constant dialectical interaction between performers, audience, and other invisible actors—including the algorithms, TikTok's business policy, content censorship, and so on—, to create their own *TikTok persona* (see Chapter 3). Similar to musical personae as defined by Auslander (2006, 2021), TikTok personae exist in different scenes and (digital) media, and not only in their usual environment or scene. This means that TikTok personae also perform outside the environment of TikTok, and they can be experienced in these other environments too.

Multimedia practices like TikTok are not only global and deterritorialized phenomena but are strongly connected with local realities (see Chapter 4). The creation and experience of a TikTok persona within a multimedia environment facilitates an increasing co-presence between the TikTok personae being perceived and their audience. This creates a certain *public intimacy* (see Pink et al. 2016) that suppresses the increasing deterritorialized and multimedia condition of interactions and interrelations of digital practices, a process that enables a performative construction and maintains a musical world, although it is not tangible. However, this co-presence is intensified by the inclusion of local realities in multimedia environments, as well as by a conscious and more physical togetherness. The spontaneous or organized gatherings of TikTokers and their audience aimed at constructing a more intensive embodied integration between the actors, which I refer to as *empathic co-presence*,[7] aside from economical aspects, play a significant role (see Chapter 4). In many cases, this connection is protected by public intimacy, which awakes and influences the behavior of the users through physical movements among others—for example, by moving the cell phone toward the body or by protecting the screen from being viewed by third persons. In other cases, these synchronous or asynchronous encounters are either shared or commented on physically or digitally.

Musical Geographies through Practice

Thirdly, I propose to make a reconceptualization of our field and a new approach[8] due to the multimedia reality of these musical practices. Since there is no preexisting space to step inside these practices, and it is only possible to construct our field and interact in it through the continuous multimedia interaction of physical and digital actors or personae, we need to increasingly focus on (1) interactions continuously created and experienced by the actors of this musicking; (2) the interrelations built, discussed, and experienced by the actors of this musicking throughout time; (3) the processes that enable the creation, discussion, and experience of personal and public multimedia locations.

Although multimedia music practices take place through complex distribution processes in completely different spaces scattered over the world, the creation and exchange of certain auditory knowledge, as well as several interactions between actors, occur in virtual and physical "local" situations (see Hepp 2020). Additionally, as Christine Hine points out, "[Internet] is embedded in various contextualizing frameworks, institutions, and devices, that the experience of using it is embodied and hence highly personal and that it is everyday" (Hine 2015: 32), for which its practices find themselves influenced by these contexts and infrastructures. For that, it is important to keep in mind

7 I use the concept of "empathic co-presence" as the affective and highly embodied association created after the conscious re-embedding in a synchronous and physical space, of a participation and interaction previously experienced as multimedia and asynchronous by the actors in the context of a musicking (see Bermúdez 2023a; see Chapter 4).

8 The need for theoretical-methodological thinking reflecting multimedia realities of cultural practices in ethnographic work has been long discussed in different scientific disciplines. To learn more about these different perspectives, see among others, Marcus (1995); Boellstorff et al. (2012); Hine (2015); Kozinets ([2009] 2015); Pink et al. (2016); Frömming et al. (2017); Pertierra (2018); Bermúdez (2020); Horst and Miller ([2012] 2020); Przybylski (2021).

that the articulation, negotiation, and maintenance of musical (and nonmusical) practices developed through the internet find themselves embedded not just on devices but also in local contexts and infrastructures, including national regulations and laws.[9] Furthermore, we also need to keep in mind that actors experience these practices in an embodied location, which is connected to other locations scattered all over the world. The exploration of the perception and experience of these localities make it possible to understand the dialectical interplay between macro (global) and micro (local) processes of knowledge construction (see Bermúdez et al. 2018).

In musical practices, such as TikTok, where the interaction between actors does not take place in a purely physically, closed geographical space, it is even more important to observe the interactions and interrelations between actors in these musical practices under a dynamic flow, between interlacement of the physical and digital worlds. Since no space exists until it is first constructed and discussed through the interaction and interrelation of the actors, it is very important to understand this "'local interaction' [as] the assemblage of all the *other* local interactions distributed elsewhere in time and space, which have been brought to bear on the scene through the relays of various non-human actors" (Latour 2005: 194) in order to theoretically (re)construct this "missing" physical-closed geography by focusing on the activity of the actors under different circumstances and contexts and in digital media. This implies that the field creates an (in)tangible and limitable territory when the (re)production and the immersion in the musicking takes place. In this case, we can speak about a kind of musical geography through practice[10] (see Chapter 4). Similar to usual interpersonal interactions, the interrelation of the actors involved in multimedia music practices is influenced and determined by the forms of interactions between the participants and also by the discourses, times, objectives, and so on.

9 Whether the platforms are allowed in the territory or not, whether they are permitted to present certain features or not, or whether the users are bound to specific norms, among others, are some aspects that influence such regulations. Multimedia musical practices, such as TikTok, are not only global and deterritorialized phenomena. These practices are strongly connected to local realities. The increasing use of TikTok and the thematization of the COVID-19 pandemic are clear examples, but also the imminent partial or total banning of TikTok in the United States and other countries, including Austria.

10 The idea of "Geography through practice" is analogously based not only in several aspects of Ruth Finnegan's ([1989] 2007) and Sara Cohen's (1991) work on music traditions in urban paces, but also on concepts such as place and space (de Certeau [1984] 1988), pathways (Finnegan [1989] 2007), dwelling (Ingold 2000), as well as the work of many theorists, who favor "the primacy of movement" (Ingold 2011: 12) in relation to the conceptualization of place (see Moores 2018).

The kind of interactions between the actors depends on circumstances, contexts, and positions of their analog/digital interrelation. In the case of my exploration in the musicking of TikTok, these multimedia observations resulted in encounters and interactions as expected, but surprisingly also in other interrelations and interactions that would have been difficult or maybe impossible to observe with a media-centered approach.

Conclusion

With the rise and expansion of the internet and with all the new developments, new devices, communication forms, and platforms that resulted from this, numerous interrelations between physical and virtual multilocal and multimedia spaces experienced a considerable transformation, letting new generations (digital natives) perceive many of these multimedia interrelations and spaces as an expansion to their reality. Several of our contemporary musical practices do not possess a precise physical location or only exist as abstract imaginary constructs, while others simultaneously create an understanding of other forms of making music by creating, processing, and experiencing sounds in different times and spaces and independently from each other. Multimedia musical practices like TikTok challenge our assumptions, methods, and theories. However, ethnographic thinking provides an excellent ground for exploring and researching any music culture of the world from a culture-relativistic perspective.

In the preceding pages, I have proposed a research paradigm that does not see digital media as a passive representation channel or an economical product but as a practice. This model, what I call E^3thnography, provides the possibility to observe and experience how the actors of a certain musicking historically construct concepts, behaviors, and sounds in different contexts, how they are socially maintained, and how they are individually created and experienced in everyday life in synchronous or asynchronous multimedia situations. This approach provides a new path to an interdisciplinary musical-ethnographic model for studying multimedia and multilocal music practices. Having introduced the theoretical and methodological basis on which this research is based, in the next chapter, I examine and discuss the elements that make up the interface of TikTok, the technical and performative possibilities provided, and some of the types of performances that exist in this application.

2

Performing TikTok

TikTok … TikTok … By the time I was writing these lines it had become less usual to meet someone who did not know about this application. TikTok, as you may know, is a smartphone application aimed at creating and sharing short videos, with a global presence and approximately one billion users worldwide, offering an interaction space for different music and video practices. Today, there is no denying that TikTok has become a part of the global popular culture imaginary. However, as I began doing my research at the beginning of 2018, things were very different, starting with the fact that the app in which I began my ethnographic research back then was called Musical.ly. I still remember how colleagues, friends, and family would be bewildered when I mentioned that name. Musical.ly? What is that? What is it for? By the fall of the same year, Musical.ly was acquired by TikTok, and although that meant that I had to change the topic of my research, people around me still did not know much about this app. TikTok? What's that?

Suddenly, as the COVID-19 pandemic broke out at the beginning of 2020, and millions of people around the globe were confined, TikTok took off to become a global phenomenon. Without a doubt, TikTok has gained visibility, and even though initiatives like TikTok Cultures Research Network and works by Crystal Abidin (among others: 2021, forthcoming), Trevor Boffone (2021, 2022, 2023), and Bondy Kaye et al. (2022) provided access for approaching this phenomenon, there is still much to learn from the performative world of TikTok. The fact is that the performative world of TikTok is still unknown to many colleagues, friends, and family, who keep on asking me the same questions: what is TikTok? What do you use it for?

This chapter is about the different ways in which participation is possible in the musicking of TikTok and the types of performances carried out through this application. In the first part of this chapter, I aim to understand the ways of interaction and interrelation present in this kind of musicking by discussing the elements that integrate the interface of TikTok, as well as the technical-performative possibilities provided by the application. After that, in the second part of this chapter, I examine the types of TikTok performances and develop a general categorization of these performances.

Getting to Know TikTok

I remember the first time I launched TikTok on my phone. I waited for the environment of TikTok to upload. I began moving in a digital environment that was new to me. Without being an active user, I already started a performance: a short self-playing video, a so-called "TikTok." It only took me a couple of minutes to get acquainted with the architecture of the application. As I scrolled, the performances continued appearing in an endless feed with small interaction buttons (such as like, comment, share) on the main interface of TikTok. The rest of the application is quite simple: there is a search engine, another page for recording TikToks, an inbox, and a TikToker profile. But how could I use all of these features? How were they used by other fellow TikTokers? It seemed a long way to learn all of this. In the following section, I discuss the elements of the interface of TikTok and the technical-performative possibilities it provides with the purpose of understanding the ways of interaction and interrelation existing in this musicking.

Main Elements of the Platform

Like any other application, TikTok is designed to encouraging interaction with the platform and among users in an intuitive and straightforward manner. The main elements that build the architecture of the application include (depending on the app version) some or all of the following sections: an Inbox and a Profile, For You, Following, Discover, Live, and Create pages.

The Profile Page

All adventures must begin somewhere. In the case of TikTok, the journey begins with the creation of a user profile. After downloading and installing the application, the first steps a newcomer must take in the interface of TikTok are intended for generating a profile page, the first digital "self" in TikTok so to speak. The Profile Page is the point of neuralgic representation in TikTok. Important public information about every TikToker is provided here, becoming the "face" or "cover letter" of TikTokers. This is the place in which TikTokers present themselves publicly and their musical persona in a centralized manner.

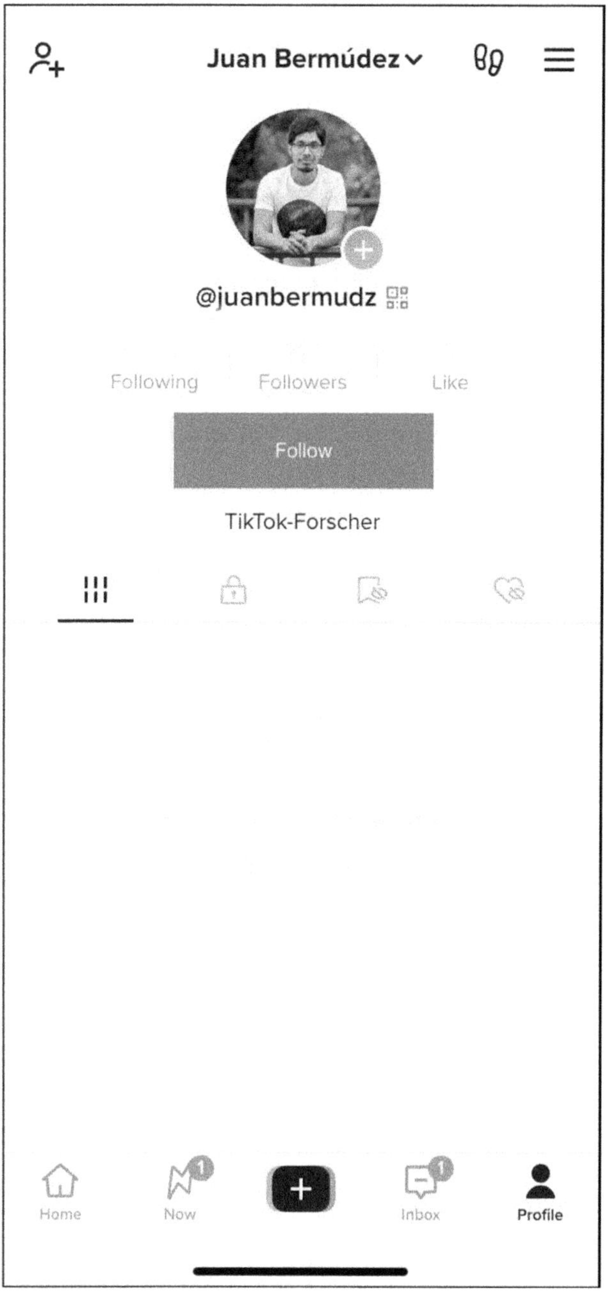

Figure 4 Profile Page, screenshot by author.

The Profile Page (Figure 4) consists of the following elements: at the top of the page the public name of the TikToker is displayed (e.g., Juan Bermúdez), together with the profile picture and the username (e.g., @juanbermudz). Then we see some statistical data specific to this user: the number of followers the user has, the number of TikTokers followed by this user, and the number of *likes* this user has received. Underneath this information, there is a "follow" button, but if you are already following this TikToker, then a "message" button will appear instead (see inbox). On this page there are also different icons that link the profile of the TikToker to other social media platforms like YouTube and Instagram, as well as a small tab displaying profile vignettes of other TikTokers suggested for following. Beneath that we can see a small text where TikTokers describe their position in the performative context of TikTok, and then the exhibition of a TikTok catalog published by the TikToker.

The Profile Page is designed from a production/representation perspective with the purpose of having a slower reception compared with the existing reception speed of the For-You-Page (FYP). Compared with the FYP, the function of the Profile Page is not centered on the presentation of performances to be discovered, but rather on the process of catching followers and therefore creating engagement with the users that have already liked their performance. For this reason, the Profile Page is a neuralgic point of representation for TikTokers: this page does not play a fundamental role in consuming TikToks because it is not necessary to access it to watch a TikTok. The main way of accessing the Profile Page of a TikToker is through the profile symbol in a TikTok on the FYP.

The For-You and Following Page

One of the most peculiar aspects in the architecture of the application lies in the FYP. The first thing that we encounter when we open the TikTok application is the FYP. Compared to other applications and/or digital platforms where the first thing that appears when opening/accessing the application/platform are the performances or posts of the people we follow (e.g., Instagram) or who are our friends (e.g., Facebook), TikTok presents a feed of random performances curated by its own algorithms. There is no need to be proactive to discover new creators because the architecture and algorithms of the application do this automatically, a paradigm change that is quite effective for TikTok (Figure 5).

Figure 5 For-You and Following Page, screenshot by author.

When you open TikTok you automatically find a "home" section, which is divided into two sections: the FYP, which is the one you see when opening the application, and the Following-Page, which shows videos of users you follow. Both pages are built with the following elements: in the upper section, there are four icons, one for accessing the Live Page, two for choosing between the FYP and the Following-Page respectively, and another for using the search engine of TikTok. In the right frame of the screen, there are a series of icons that are specifically linked to the TikTok that is playing. The icon on top shows the profile picture of the TikToker who uploaded that video. If you tap on it, the profile page of that TikToker appears. This same icon has a small plus sign that when tapped allows you to automatically follow this TikToker without opening their profile page. Below this icon, there is a small heart that works as a "like" button with a number underneath indicating how many "likes" the video has received. For liking a video, the heart icon must be tapped once.

Next, there is an image of a speech bubble for accessing the video's comment section. The number below this icon indicates how many comments have been posted for this TikTok. Like other platforms, each comment posted on this application can receive an individual like. After that, there is an arrow symbol that can lead to different options when tapped: send the video to other users, share it on other platforms, copy the link, save the video, report it, or react to it in different ways depending on the region and version of the app version being used. Similar to the previously described icons, the number displayed below this icon indicates how many times this video has been shared. The last icon on the right frame row is a small photo slowly spinning clockwise with small musical notes bubbling around it. This icon links to the page of the song that is being reproduced, and from this page, it is possible to listen to the original audio, immediately use it for performing a TikTok, seeing a collection of TikToks using this sound, and sharing and/or saving it to your favorite sounds. The name of the sound used is displayed on the lower left side of the screen. Finally, right above the sound name, the name of the TikToker is displayed together with the video description and hashtags.

The Discover Page

Similar to the FYP, the Discover Page is a place for discovering content. Most existing versions of this page provide the possibility of using a search engine for finding users and other featured content on TikTok, like events, *challenges*, and other material launched and/or sponsored by TikTok, including hashtags, filters, and sounds considered as trending by the application. Compared with the FYP, the Discover Page invites users to be more proactive in gaining access, as well as in searching and/or discovering content in it. Therefore, this page functions as a secondary point in which TikTok users encounter new content. This secondary role can also be observed in the little architectural stability of this section, which has been continuously modified.

The Discover Page (Figure 6) has not always been a fixed or stable element in the interface of TikTok. As I started my research—still on Musical.ly—the Discover Page possessed many more elements for discovering new content, which were presented by country, author, and category, among others. When the app became TikTok, these functions began to disappear and/or merge into other functions or sections. In some updates, this page would completely disappear from the interface of TikTok, as it happened at the beginning of 2022 when the Discover Page was removed from the interface of TikTok for a couple of weeks. Subsequently, this page reappeared as a Friends Page, a page constructed analogously to the FYP, providing the possibility of watching TikToks by contacts/friends from accounts/applications (like Facebook or the contacts saved on our smartphone) that have been linked to TikTok, as well as the TikToks uploaded by followers followed by the users. However, in September 2022, the Friends Page was replaced by *now*, TikTok's new function, to be replaced again by the Friends Page sometime later. Without a doubt, the Discover Page is the section in which I have observed most aesthetic and functional changes throughout my research.

The Live Page

The Live Page is the access point to one of the performative worlds in TikTok. This page is accessed by tapping the "LIVE" symbol on the upper left side of the FYP screen or on the profile photo of any TikToker who is streaming *live*. Compared to the FYP, which is filled with previously recorded TikToks uploaded in advance, the Live Page presents videos that are being transmitted (streamed) at the moment of occurrence. This page presents a similar architecture and way of working to the FYP. When accessing this page, a feed consisting exclusively of live transmissions appears. The order in which these videos are shown is determined by the algorithms of TikTok. The Live Page has its own "explore" section where users can navigate and search live videos.

The Live Page (Figure 7) consists of the following elements: on the top, we find a group of four icons, one for accessing the profile page of the TikToker who

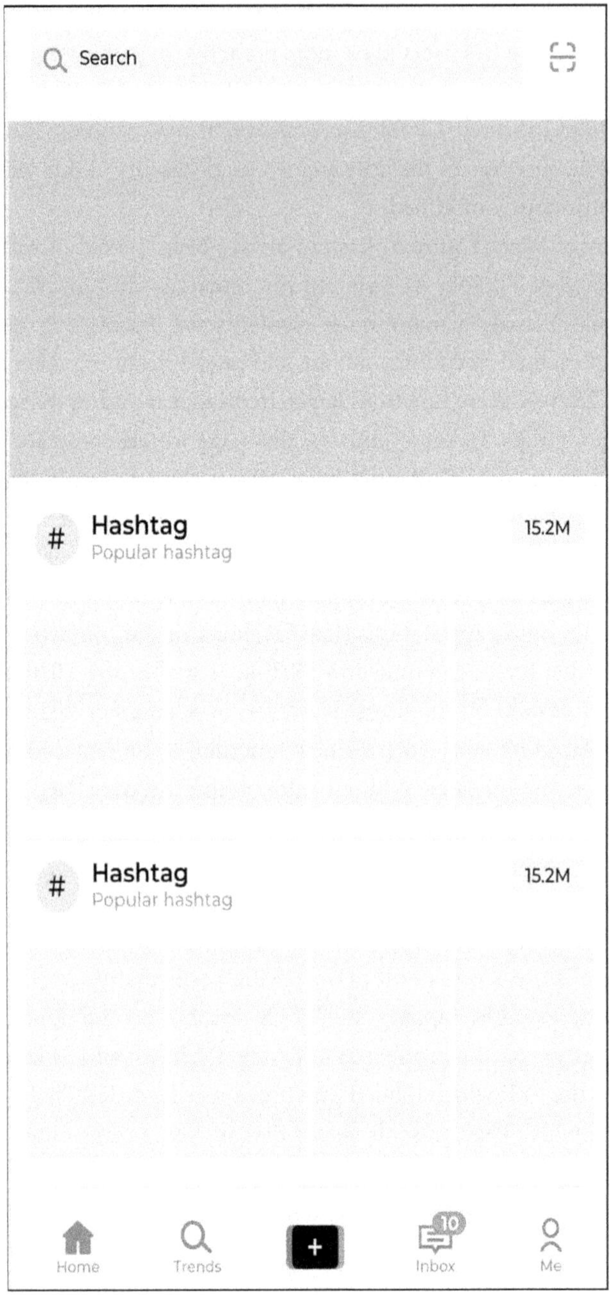

Figure 6 Discover Page, illustration by Belén Vera.

Figure 7 Live Page, screenshot by author.

is streaming live, another for seeing the number of top viewers and accessing their profiles, a third for seeing how the TikToker is positioned in different rankings, and the fourth for accessing the "explore" section of the Live Page. The bottom part of the screen shows live comments posted during the streaming, as well as a small box for writing your own comments. A speech bubble on the side takes users to a question-and-answer (Q&A) section. There is also a group of symbols—a rose, a gift box—with which users can buy "coins" and digital gifts for the TikToker who is streaming live, and an arrow symbol for sharing the video with other TikTok users or to other platforms directly or by copying the link in the phone's clipboard. The arrow icon also shows the options for saving the video, reporting it, or sending a reaction depending on the TikTok version and the region from which the device is connected.

The Inbox

The architecture of TikTok allows communication among users both in a public and private way. For public communication, users are provided with a comment section on each TikTok video. They can also communicate in an audiovisual way through the performative tools in the app, like duets or stitches. Additionally, private communication among users can take place in the Inbox section. However, for sending a private message, users must follow each other; otherwise, there is no way to establish private communication in the app. That is why a greater part of first contacts and (first) conversations among TikTokers begins in the comment sections and/or other digital platforms like Instagram or Snapchat.

The Create Page

The Create Page, as indicated by its name, is the neuralgic point of creation in TikTok. Through this interface, TikTokers can choose different sounds/songs for their performance, as well as use the different performative tools provided by the application. This is a place designed for recording and editing TikTok performances, and it is accessed in two ways. One way is by tapping a plus sign symbol in the central bottom part of the main interface, and the other is through the sound and/or filter archives of the application by tapping symbols like "use the sound" and "try effect," among others. Although the elements of the Create Page can change, some of them prevail throughout different versions of TikTok. First, there is an "X" on the top left side of the page for closing the create mode and going back to the last visited page. Then, there is a symbol with two quaver notes with the label "add sound" that takes us to the music library of TikTok to choose the sound/song for the performance. On the upper right side, there is a lateral bar with different symbols for different performative tools. On the very top, there are some small arrows with the label "flip" for switching between using the front and the back camera of the cellphone followed by a lightning symbol for activating and deactivating the flash of the camera. Then there is a stopwatch symbol with a label that says "timer." This function provides a countdown before starting to record the video, as well as the option for users to select what fragment they wish to record. With this tool, TikTokers can record their performances in different takes. Underneath this icon, there is an image with three circles indicating the "filters," which works similarly to the music symbol by taking us to the filter library of the application. After that, there is a small speedometer icon for choosing the recording speed of the video (0.3×; 0.5×; 1×; 2×; and 3×). Finally, at the very bottom of this lateral bar, there is a magic wand icon labeled "enhance" for adding different visual filters that automatically embellish the physical appearance of the performer by changing the color of their lips, adding eye shadow, softening skin texture, whitening teeth, and so on (Figure 8).

In the bottom part of the screen, other elements are presented. On the bottom left side, there is an "effect" icon for accessing the effect library of TikTok and choosing one for the performance. In this section, effects are arranged in different collections according to popularity or themes. Then, there is a red "record" button, which is not just to start recording the video but for choosing the duration as well (15s, 60s, or 3m). On the bottom right side, there is an "upload" button that takes us to the photo gallery of our smartphone. This enables the option for uploading videos that were not recorded through the application. Finally, in the bottom part of this section, there is a bar for choosing between using the camera to record a TikTok, making a Story, or using a template based on our TikTok.

Performative Possibilities of the Platform

Now that we have become acquainted with the main elements in the architecture of the application, I will proceed to introduce the technical-performative possibilities provided by the application. As suggested by Christine Hine, multimedia practices like the ones produced in TikTok are "embedded in various contextualizing frameworks, institutions, and devices" (Hine 2015: 32), which "in addition to 'determining' and serving as a 'backdrop for human action',

Figure 8 Create Page, screenshot by author.

might authorize, allow, afford, encourage, permit, suggest, influence, block, render possible, forbid, and so on" (Latour 2005: 72).

Recording Mode, Time, and Speed

One of the first kinds of affordances provided by the application is the recording mode, which frames the performative possibilities in TikTok. The architecture of the application allows choosing three recording modes for creating a performance: (1) "camera," for recording TikToks; (2) "Story," as its name says, for creating Stories; and (3) "Template," for using preestablished templates for creating TikToks or Stories. Each of these recording modes provides different performative possibilities in the application.

Stories are short videos that disappear twenty-four hours after being published. This function was introduced to TikTok in 2022 as a clear reaction to the success of Instagram Stories. With this recording mode, it is possible to use some of the performative tools from the Create Page, as well as other tools like "text," "stickers," "captions," and "voice effects," among others. Templates, on the other hand, are preestablished formats for creating short videos using photos saved on our cellphones and publishing them either as TikToks or Stories. Although Stories and Templates allow us to create videos and participate as creators in the musicking of TikTok, the main recording mode in TikTok is the "camera" mode (Figure 9).

"Camera" mode, as indicated by its name, is a mode with which creators can record their performances (from scratch) using the front and back cameras and the microphone in their smartphones combined with the creation tools provided by the Create Page. In this recording mode, creators are not restricted to adjustments or preestablished contents, as it is in "template" mode, but they are encouraged to experiment freely with their performances. Besides the 9:16 format, recording time (leaving aside the creators' abilities) becomes the main performative restriction, defining and framing the performative context of TikTok to be recorded. TikTok videos are restricted to fifteen-second, thirty-second, three-minute, and, since 2022, ten-minute durations. However, the shortest formats (15s and 30s) are still the most popular in the application. Besides recording time, TikTok provides one standard and four additional recording speed options: one-third standard speed, half standard speed, twice standard speed, and three times standard speed. With this, the performative possibilities provided for creators increase during their performance.

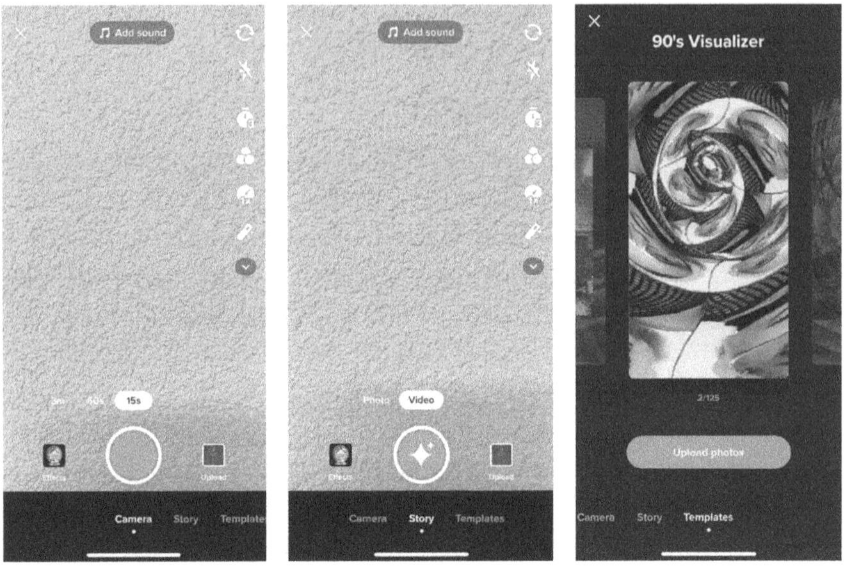

Figure 9 Camera, Story, and Template Mode, screenshot by author.

Effects, Tags, and Filters

Once the recording mode for the performance is defined, TikTokers can choose from different existing performative tools in the application. These tools can help TikTokers complement their performance, by highlighting a performative element, helping them develop a more complex dramaturgical frame, or completing some performative or aesthetic element in any given trend. Although each of these recording modes grants access to different editing tools, these can be put together in at least three different groups: effects, tags, and filters. Filters give TikTokers the possibility of changing the tone and/or color of the image they are recording. With this, they can create diverse visual environments in their performance, as well as generate and reproduce visual aesthetic models distinctive of TikTok. These types of filters present a strong influence in negotiating aesthetic preferences among TikTokers, clearly (re)creating and strengthening hegemonic aesthetic mandates of gender, class, and race. These filters can be found in both "camera" and "story" recording modes.

Besides the already mentioned, one of the most used performative tools in TikTok performances is the effect tool (Figure 10). Compared with filters, which allow changing tone and/or color in the image being recorded, effects can make

Figure 10 Filter and Effects, screenshot by author.

more radical changes in the recorded image, both in "camera" and "story" mode. On the one hand, effects can change the appearance of the TikToker in many ways, like altering their hair or skin color, adding accessories like hats and glasses, or turning them into one of the numerous digital avatars available. Besides that, effects can also change the appearance of the surroundings where the TikToker is, either by placing them on frames or predesigned environments, like in front of the LGBTQ+ flag or photos selected by the user. Yet, effects can also change according to the recording mode and interaction with the screen. In this case, some of these effects allow, for example, users to divide the screen into different recording sections, or to record as if the camera lens was moving or placed underwater. Other effects have a more interactive function. These kinds of effects need the participation/interaction of TikTokers to run, either by doing certain actions or activating and/or deactivating them in a performative manner. There are also other effects that simulate or work as if they were games and/or challenges.

Finally, there are text tools and tags. These tools allow TikTokers to add phrases or small images to their TikToks, usually to provide certain context or reinforce some message to the video. While captions are automatically visualized with spoken text on the TikTok video, tags and texts are typed and placed manually by TikTokers, attaching an additional semantic layer to TikTok videos. The use of tags and text is available in all recording modes of TikTok.

Duets

Besides the different recording modes and the previously mentioned tools, there are three functions in TikTok that frame and enable the development of different kinds of performances. The first of them is the "duet" function. As indicated by its name, the duet function allows TikTokers to create a video side by side with another already existing TikTok video. The performative characteristics of both TikToks are kept, allowing a performative conjunction of both performances. Besides, this function is not limited to two videos, but already existing duets can be used to create a new duet, creating an asynchronous web of shared creativity through the overlapping of individual performances. This function is accessed through the option "duet" in the "share" icon on the lateral bar of the TikTok we wish to make a duet with.

One aspect that stands out of the duet function is that it not only encourages interaction among TikTokers but also widens the performance possibilities of TikTokers by letting them make duets with themselves (Figure 11). For example, a TikToker alone can complete a performance by playing and recording separately each character or role in a sketch or the different voices or sections of a musical performance. Moreover, the duet function is a popular function among musicians for collaborating on musical performances on TikTok (see Kaye 2022). Here, musicians perform a voice and/or instrumental section of a musical work that can be completed by the performance of other musicians. One example of the use of this function in musical performances can be appreciated in the duets by bassist @caseybassy and the singer and pianist @annamaurer_music. Both musicians have done several duets with musicians around the world, as well as many collaborations with each other, resulting in collaborations outside the platform, like the duet[1] performed physically in May 2022. Similarly,

[1] @annamaurer_music, "When a tik tok duet becomes a real one!" May 25, 2022, TikTok video, https://www.tiktok.com/@annamaurer_music/video/7101561494394998022?is_from_webapp=1&sender_device=pc&web_id=7062339902340007429.

Figure 11 Duet, screenshot by Belén Vera.

the duet function has enabled the development of a shared creativity network on TikTok. On one side, the individual reactions to a particular TikTok have facilitated the creation and performativity of musical memes. Examples of meme duets are found in those created from the TikTok "Just trying to show my fit out but the good lord had other plans"[2] by @kateylorrell. In the original TikTok @kateylorrell tries to show off her outfit, as the name says, before she accidentally hits her back on the edge of a bedpost and shouts a short "ahhh." Duets created from this TikTok use this short "ahhh" and relate it and/or use it performatively with songs like "Happy" by Pharrell Williams or "Stayin' Alive" by the Bee Gees. On the other hand, meta-performances have developed thanks to the possibility of overlapping individual performances, like the case of "The Wellerman"[3] started by @nathanevanss on TikTok. This has come out as different meta-performances created by placing together different duets on TikTok, as well as new versions using YouTube aesthetics.

Stitch

Another function for developing different performance forms is the "stitch" function. Similar to the "duet" function, the "stitch" function is accessed through the "share" icon in the lateral bar of the TikTok we wish to create a stitch with. As indicated by its name, the stitch function lets TikTokers "sew" a TikTok video with a fragment of another existing TikTok. Compared to the duet function, where the performative qualities of both TikToks remain intact and both videos are reproduced simultaneously, stitched videos are presented one after the other, and only show a five-second segment from the original TikTok chosen by the TikToker.

The stitch function provides TikTokers with the tools for creating videos using a format of call and response. While the initial TikTok functions as a summoning call, the new performance responds to the original message and develops a new outcome by changing or complementing the semantic meaning of the initial video. An example of this can be seen through the series of comedy TikToks piled together with the hashtag *#nerfwars*. In these stitches,

[2] @kateylorrell, "Just trying to show my fit out but the good lord had other plans," April 14, 2022, TikTok video, https://www.tiktok.com/@kateylorrell/video/7086546104245882155?is_from_webapp=1&sender_device=pc&web_id=7062339902340007429.

[3] @nathanevanss, "The Wellerman," December 27, 2020, TikTok video, https://www.tiktok.com/@nathanevanss/video/6910995345421962498?is_from_webapp=1&sender_device=pc&web_id=7062339902340007429.

the initial TikTok shows a person aiming a Nerf gun toward the camera, which is then answered (stitched) with a new TikTok in which the TikToker laughs at the threat and takes out a bigger Nerf weapon. Many individual versions have been made following this idea, expanding to collaborative versions in which an already made stitch is taken and a new layer is added on top of it, creating a loop that turns the idea of having the biggest Nerf gun into something completely absurd. The stitch function is very popular in comedy and challenge TikToks, since it provides a simple and straightforward way for creating/performing challenges that can be enacted and "sewn" directly to the source TikTok. However, this call and response format has also been used for developing educational and activist practices on TikTok. The stitch function gives TikTokers the possibility of dialoguing with other TikTokers either in an affirmative or opposing way on topics like discrimination, gender, politics, civil rights, and so on. Through this function, TikTokers can support and/or add their thoughts to messages and ideas they agree with or respond directly to TikTokers that promote divergent thoughts. Although this situation can enhance a favorable environment for fructiferous dialogue by expanding the terrain for political discussion among certain social groups, this has also incited cyberbullying practices in the platform (see Hutchinson 2020).

Live

Apart from duets and stitches, the architecture of TikTok allows the development of other forms of performance thanks to the "live" function. In contrast to the previously mentioned performative possibilities in which the creation of performances is asynchronous, the live function offers TikTokers the possibility of creating synchronous performances online. As indicated by its name, the live function is for making live video transmission directly through TikTok. In contrast with the already mentioned functions, the live function is enabled just for TikTokers over the age of eighteen and with more than one thousand followers. The live function provides TikTok musicians a digital stage in which they can leave the digital database of TikTok on the side and directly perform their own music instead. Young musicians like @daniliamusik and many others use this opportunity to promote their music to diverse audiences in "living room concerts" or by transmitting presentations they make in public spaces, for example, a subway station in Vienna. Furthermore, TikTok also uses this function for broadcasting exclusive live concerts on their platform, as was the case of Ed Sheeran's "TikTok UEFA EURO 2020" on June 25, 2021; the presentation of Camila Cabello's album "Familia" in April 7, 2022; and the premiere of the TikTok Musical "For You, Paige" on April 14, 2022.

Types of Performances

In the spring of 2021, I was teaching a seminar at the University of Vienna about the conceptualization of the ethnographic field in multimedia practices like the ones on TikTok. In one of the sessions, I asked my students the following question as part of a reflection exercise on the observations they made about using the application: what types of performances can we find in TikTok? I had the feeling that this class had quite homogeneous experiences and knowledge on TikTok. Everyone but one student had just started using the application at the beginning of the seminar, and all of them were about the same age, living on the same city, and displaying a similar political sentiment. However, after listening to their answers, I realized that the way they experienced TikTok and the kind of performances they encountered were very different from each other. None of us seemed to have the same experience on TikTok. At the same time, this plurality of performative worlds differed with my own experience with the application. From the start of my research in 2018 until today, my own experience showed me that the performative universe of TikTok was immense and very diverse. The contrast of my experience with those of my students, who belong to a different generation and have a different sociocultural background to mine, made me confirm that the case of TikTok resonated with what Patricia Lange stated about YouTube being "a massive and ever-changing entity. Since videos come and go every minute, no two instantiations of YouTube are ever the same" (Lange 2019: 5).

This performative plurality engenders the possibility of including many communities to the musicking of TikTok, which was highlighted during the TikTok campaign "we are more than you think" launched in German-speaking countries in March and April 2021. As pointed out by Orlina Miller, TikTok country marketing manager DACH, the context of this campaign is: "The immeasurable wealth and depth of topics coupled with our diverse community is what makes TikTok so interactive. Everyone can find connection and togetherness here"[4] (TikTok 2021b). This message of performative plurality would

[4] "Die unermessliche Fülle und Tiefe an Themen in Verbindung mit unserer vielfältigen Community macht TikTok so interaktiv. Jede*r kann hier Anschluss und Zusammengehörigkeit finden" (Orlina Miller in TikTok 2021b). Translated from German to English by Natalia Neira Nieto.

be highlighted in the text of one of the main videos[5] of this campaign: "swipe for inspiration / find role models / swipe for challenges / find challengers / swipe for a good mood / find good deeds / swipe for dance steps / find moves [6] / swipe to discover / how much there is to discover / **we are more** than you think [highlighted in the original]."[7]

The message was clear: TikTok is **not just** a place for lip-syncing—a direct reference to its predecessor Musical.ly used for differentiating itself—but a profound and serious "adult"[8] application that can contain a wide array of musical-videographic practices and topics, both in their characteristics and aesthetic qualities. With this, TikTok as a platform positioned itself closer to YouTube (but with a reduced time in its performative format),[9] while seeking to attract a more diverse audience in age and gender by being less prompt for sexual abuse.[10] But, if TikTok does not aim to be a place for lip-syncing anymore as Musical.ly was, what kind of performances were to be developed in this application?

In the following section, I examine some existing TikTok performance types and propose a general categorization for these performances. It is important to point out that this categorization does not intend to represent existing TikTok practices in their totality, nor to have universal validity, but this is rather made with the purpose of creating a starting point for visualizing the performative universe of TikTok altogether. To achieve this, I have decided to classify the existing TikTok performances into four basic categories that represent in a

5 TikTok Deutschland, "Wir sind mehr als du denkst | TikTok," March 15, 2021, YouTube video, https://www.youtube.com/watch?v=alHwmBcfrL4.

6 Here is the image of the video that references the Black Lives Matter movement.

7 "swipe nach inspiration / finde vorbilder / swipe nach challenges / finde challenger / swipe nach guter laune / finde gute taten / swipe nach tanzschritten / finde bewegungen / swipe um zu entdecken / wie viel es zu entdecken gibt / wir sind mehr als du denkst." Translated from German to English by Natalia Neira Nieto.

8 Here I reference the efforts of TikTok in the last years for positioning the application as a wider, more adult audience than the one of Musical.ly, not to the level of software development, which can also be considered as mature.

9 Since 2021, TikTok began experimenting with the three-minute format for videos, widening a more direct competition with YouTube. We can also observe that YouTube is doing something similar: in summer 2021 YouTube Shorts were introduced to German-speaking countries, which is a clone of the function, format, and aesthetic of TikTok. Together with Instagram Reels, they enter the short (>60s) market.

10 This is to be understood within the context of pedophilia problems Musical.ly had to deal with. Linked to this problem, TikTok introduced diverse "design tools and policies that promote a safe and age-appropriate experience for teens 13–17" (Elizabeth 2021), besides taking part on networks for the protection of minors (Evans 2020).

general way the main variations of the TikTok performative universe I have observed in the last few years. These categories are *lip-sync performances*, *non-lip-sync performances*, *challenges*, and *trends*.

Lip-Sync Performances

As previously mentioned, the TikTok performative universe is very wide and diverse, which makes it impossible to understand in its totality. Therefore, a categorization based on a list of aesthetic and performative qualities seems to be inefficient because it would not consider the quickly changing characteristics of the application. As a result, it would either exclude many performances or lead to a categorization system that is overly complex and impractical to use. That said, I decided to base this categorization on general performative (and not aesthetic) characteristics. The videos gathered for the first category are centered on the presence of lip-syncing. Although topics and features in these TikTok videos can vary significantly, lip-syncing always plays a central role during the performance. These lip-sync performances were the ones that caught my attention at first in Musical.ly (and then TikTok). At the beginning of my research, still on Musical.ly, most performances I noticed in the application were of the lip-syncing kind. The actors performed many songs, most of them pop music, lending their bodies to an alien voice. Although the performative and recording quality and musical selections in this kind of performance were very different, they presented similar performative and aesthetic elements with each other. We can mainly observe that performers are positioned in the center of the screen in a medium shot or medium close-up shot. Also, these performances are recorded in self-portrait mode (selfie), reinforcing the center of the performance in the performer, who tries to move their lips as synchronized as possible.

Later I would find out new variants of these performances that used many other technical possibilities of the application, such as filters and effects for "enhancing" and/or making their performances more attractive, instead of exclusively using wider cinematographic shots (e.g. full shot). Besides, a growing tendency to record these performances at different times and locations can be observed. This creates a more complex dramaturgical aspect to lip-syncing compared to earlier performances, which often occurred in private, closed environments (like bedrooms or living rooms). This growing trend of recording in different times and spaces created a new kind of lip-syncing-based performance: *transitions*.[11] As indicated by its name, transitions are a kind of performance in which TikTokers use camera cuts to create transitions between performative scenes. These transitions can take place in different locations, times, objects, performative acts, and so on, and are used for accentuating different musical and/or textual aspects of a song/sound. The use of this kind of transition fluctuates in intensity (sometimes subtle or more intense) depending on the TikToker and/or trend in which the transition appears. These are entwined with a wide array of performative and dramaturgical possibilities for creating a kind of performance that, compared to "normal" lip-syncing, not only is considered TikTok native but also is only possible within a multimedia context.[12]

After the merging of Musical.ly and TikTok in the fall of 2018, the visibility in this kind of performances diminished, while other forms of lip-syncing performances became more visible in the application. Together with the appearance of an older audience in the application, I was able to observe a growing proliferation of performances focused on acting. In this context there were, on the one hand, performances centered on satire and comedy acts, and on the other, performances centered on theatrical and/or cinematographic scenes and/or sketches with different themes. In both cases, TikTokers performed already existing plots through their bodies—not their voices—with the purpose of (re) interpreting their own corporality through them, similar to the phenomenon identified as "schizophonic performance" observed by Kiri Miller (2012: 85–124) in her research about performative acts in video games like Guitar Hero and Just Dance (see Miller 2012, 2017).

Besides that, I was able to observe that it was not just acting but dancing that began to play a more prominent role in lip-syncing TikTok performances. The form and aesthetic qualities of dance moves became the focus of performances, leaving lip-syncing on a second visual level. Although lip-syncing was the base of these performances, this practice became more and more subordinate to the

11 Although transitions began in the context of lip-syncing, this phenomenon is not exclusive of this kind of performance. Today we can find transitions in performances with and without lip-syncing.

12 Lip-syncing practices like the ones developed on TikTok can be appreciated and have been developed in a similar way in physical contexts for many years: karaoke and other playback practices are clear examples of this kind of performances (see Brown 2015; Miller 2012, 2017). However, practices like *transitions* require the use of digital tools and/or the possibility of mixing asynchronous performances, and therefore cannot be done in a synchronous manner. Similar cases for this kind of "post-editing" phenomenon can be seen in playback singing in South India (see Weidman 2021) and audio edition processes analyzed and identified by Turino as High-Fidelity Music (see 2008: 67–78).

aesthetic and dance needs. This trend increased in the following years, moving performances away from lip-syncing practices. After a while, lip-syncing-based performative practices stopped being the predominating type of performance in TikTok, which was reflected in the increased visibility of non-lip-syncing performative practices throughout the application.

Non-Lip-Sync Performances

Especially after the merging of Musical.ly and TikTok, non-lip-sync performance forms became particularly popular in the application. Still today they are the most visible performative form in TikTok. Performances without lip-sync can cover a wide array of topics, from the very trivial and quotidian to educational and activist, with very different performative styles in their quality and aesthetic characteristics. One of the most common non-lip-sync videos is those that focus on topics from the daily life of TikTokers. Although these videos have a similar topic, the "daily life" scenes they show, as well as their performative styles, are very different among them. Some of these videos focus mainly on the presentation of the highlights of the day of the TikToker, using TikTok as a sort of journal and turning it into a space for expressing their feelings and worries, a place for raising their voice. In contrast, other videos show a clearer performative intention by focusing on showing skills and abilities in some activity, or by being part of the strategies for creating and negotiating a TikTok persona (see Chapter 3).

Like lip-syncing-based videos, comedy and/or acting performances are also a very common kind of video in non-lip-syncing TikToks. On the one hand, TikTokers act pre-established plots, reinterpreting these stories with their own voice and body, and using TikTok as another stage for developing their performances. On the other hand, TikTokers perform their own comedy and/or satire sequences and/or their own interpretations of already existing numbers, a common format in stand-up comedy practices. Besides this format, TikTokers also create parodies of daily situations by creating "spontaneous" jokes, which are reinforced by the music they choose. This way, they do not just create musical memes but also develop a particular form and aesthetic of TikTok comedy. These comedy and/or acting performances can have a wide variety of topics, from trivial everyday situations to political and activist matters. Examples of comedy/satire can be appreciated in the performances of @toxische_pommes, @wurstaufschnitt, and @onuaak, as well as the performances by Toni Titze published in the account of the periodical Der Standard. Beside these examples, @rachienoe, @themexicantenor, and @troysheperds show examples of comedy/satire performances centered on musical topics: about classical composers, the life of an opera singer, and the performance "If Orchestra Conductors Were TikTok Dancers"[13] respectively.

Although plenty of comedy formats are found throughout the application, in the last couple of years, videos with educational content have become one of the most common non-lip-synced videos in TikTok (see *#edutok*). Whether for learning/teaching how to perform a challenge or a trend or for learning/teaching the most diverse topics, today TikTok has become an alternative portal for knowledge transmission among young people. The topics transmitted through these performances are wide-ranging, including topics like civil rights and law (like the case of @herranwalt), gender and diversity (like @avalino.diversity), and even teaching languages, from the most visible like Italian and German, to less visible, like Quechua (as it is the case of @tikitawaea). This thematic plurality has contributed to making TikTok a space for exchanging ideas, which together with the wide presence of gender and diversity topics, as well as the use of TikTok by less visible sociocultural groups of people, has led to an increase of activist practices in and through the application. It is important to highlight the use of Stitches as a strategy for public confrontation, used for direct duels against publications containing discrimination, racism, homophobia, and/or xenophobia. Nevertheless, TikTok has also been used as a weapon for political sabotage, like the highly scandalized case of the 2020 electoral campaign by Donald Trump in the United States.

Besides this and in continuation with practices that emerged in Musical.ly, there is no doubt that TikTok is still a space for music and dance performance that can be and are developed without the need for lip-sync. On the one hand, the development and performance of choreographies are one of the practices developed in TikTok since its beginnings, without a doubt becoming a part of multimedia dance culture developed in and through different digital platforms (see Bermúdez 2023b), like Dubmash (see Boffone 2021), and in physical spaces of interaction. Young people create, appropriate, and/or perform different

[13] @troysheperds, "POV: You the orchestra playing this song and your conductor is addicted to tiktok dance trends," TikTok-Video, November 23, 2019, https://www.tiktok.com/@troysheperds/video/6762599101554117894?is_from_webapp=1&sender_device=pc&web_id=7062339902340007429.

moves—like floss, razorblade, and renegade—for showing their technical abilities and negotiating and performing their identities as artists, looking to integrate their work into current multimedia cultural practices. On the other hand, TikTok has become a platform for developing musical performances, turning it into a digital stage for presenting the work of young and/or amateur musicians (see Chapter 5). Here young musicians put aside the music database provided by TikTok and perform their own music during their performance, either in a synchronous way by using live or duet functions, or by uploading their own production to the application like @zoeweesofficial, @theartistfred, @binabianca89, @daniliamusik, and @annamaurer_music, among many others, using TikTok as a digital extension or stage for presenting and distributing their music.

Challenges

One of the most common TikTok performances is the *challenge*. This kind of performance is characterized by a preestablished plot of a defiant character in which TikTokers are invited to perform in a specific way. As indicated by its name, in this kind of performance there is a challenge to be completed. These challenges can or cannot be based on lip-syncing; nevertheless, all of them share an existing request commanded by TikTokers that should be reintroduced by them during their performance by following the preestablished instructions. The topic or topics upon which challenges are supported are as wide as the performative world of TikTok itself. During my research, however, I observed three main types of challenges, which I name amateur challenges, professional challenges, and challenge trends.

Amateur challenges are characterized by being launched by the community. Here a TikToker creates a performance, usually with a specific sound, through which they challenge/invite other TikTokers to perform a specific action/performance. An example of this type of challenge can be found in the challenge started by @ameerseyed with the sound "Some things about ameer version."[14] In this challenge, @ameerseyed invites TikTokers to share their name, age, favorite color, height, zodiac sign, marital status, nationality, and something/someone

[14] @ameerseyd, "Some things about me ameer version," TikTok sound, https://www.tiktok.com/music/Some-things-about-me-ameer-version-6792014326417935109?is_from_webapp=1&sender_device=pc.

that inspires them using this sound in the background of the performance. A challenge with a similar thematic was launched in German by @simonwill with the hashtag *#steckbrief*.[15] Just like the case of @ameerseyd, @simonwill invited TikTokers to share with the community their name, age, city of residence, favorite color, height, and languages they spoke. At the end of the video, he requested nominating another TikToker for this challenge.

Another example of this type of challenge—which is very widespread on TikTok—is those that invite TikTokers to show their knowledge about a specific topic in a performative way. An example of this kind of challenge can be observed in the series of challenges launched by @songversionen[16] with the hashtag *#WelcheSongsKennstDu?*, inviting TikTokers to demonstrate their knowledge about the repertoire of different musical genres. Here TikTokers are invited to listen to a series of songs and indicate through a performance if they recognize these songs with their fingers, annotations, or stickers. At the same time, we can find challenges with a similar logic inviting TikTokers to demonstrate their knowledge about different TikTok dances and/or trends. The challenge initiated by @elsarca with the name "TikTok Dance challenge by Elsarca"[17] is one example of many of this kind. These performances show different sociocultural levels through which TikTokers act their knowledge about TikTok dances or trends they possess and how different auditive information is negotiated and/or reinforced through the application.

On the other hand, what I call *professional challenges* are distinguished by (1) being created by TikTok or (2) being created as part of a bigger marketing campaign of a company and/or an artist, usually launched/promoted in conjunction with TikTok. In the first scenario, TikTok uses challenges as part of its strategy for keeping TikTokers hooked to the platform by continuously creating and launching challenges through the application, their website, or other platforms. These challenges are very diverse regarding topics, but one of the most typical characteristics is that they invite TikTokers to use certain

15 @simonwill, "Nutz den Sound & gi wiiild Leute," June 25, 2020, TikTok video, https://www.tiktok.com/@simonwill/video/6842300837235100933?is_from_webapp=1&sender_device=pc&web_id=7062339902340007429.

16 @songversionen, TikTok profil, https://www.tiktok.com/@songversionen?is_from_webapp=1&sender_device=pc.

17 @elsarca, "New TikTok dance challenge," February 17, 2022, TikTok video, https://www.tiktok.com/@elsarca/video/7065691716673703169?is_from_webapp=1&sender_device=pc&web_id=7062339902340007429.

effects or filters created for performing the challenge/activity. One example can be found in the *#10s-Challenge* launched by TikTok to promote the use of a homonymous effect, in which a chronometer is displayed on the screen and can be stopped when TikTokers blink. In this challenge, TikTokers are incited to blink exactly at ten seconds to stop the chronometer. These kinds of challenges aim to advertise new functions and/or technical possibilities featured on the application, as well as increasing engagement with TikTokers.

Secondly, many companies and/or artists use challenges for advertising and/or increasing interaction between artists and their audience. Challenges have become a tool used by advertisement companies and artists for promoting artistic contents and other products. With the chance of becoming viral, these challenges (and their respective message) can take artists and/or products to reach a wider audience, as well as to increase engagement between the company and/or artist with older followers. One example can be observed in the challenge *#duavideo* by Dua Lipa (@dualipaofficial) financed by Warner Music Group. This challenge incentivized TikTokers to upload their videos by stating they could be part of the official music video of the song "Levitating." This challenge invited TikTokers to upload videos dancing, making animations, or showing their makeup skills with the hashtag *#duavideo*. After that, Dua Lipa chose some of these videos for the official music video of "Levitating."

The third type of challenge is what I call *challenge-trend*, a type of amateur challenge that, although possessing a strong defiant character, does not explicitly incite the performance of an action. Here, the defiant aspect is performed in the original video and imitated in the performances of those joining the challenge. These kinds of challenges tend to appeal to courage and bravery ideals and its resulting social pressure under the statement "are you the only one who doesn't dare to accept the challenge?" For this reason, this kind of challenge can become a thread to the physical integrity of TikTokers. The *#kulikitaka-challenge* presents a clear example of this: using an extract of the song "Kiliki Taka Ti" by Toño Rosario as a starting point, this challenge encouraged TikTokers to perform a determined choreography before chasing a herd of cows with the purpose of scaring them off. Although this choreography and the occasional cows running away may seem funny, this act is quite dangerous, since animals can activate their defense instinct, attack the TikTokers, and lead to serious injuries or even death. This challenge was prohibited by TikTok Austria after a public call to the Austrian Federal Minister Elisabeth Köstinger in July 2020.

Trends

The final kind of performance in this categorization is the one I call *trend*. Trends, as understood here, are performances that have a clear sound-choreography relation. In other words, trends are performances that relate a specific sound to a specific choreography within a determined (usually short) duration. Although these performances are often called "challenges" by TikTokers, I approach trend performances differently because instead of identifying them by their defiant character, it's their sound-choreography relation that makes them stand out. This kind of performance is very visible inside and outside the application, considered as the "typical" performance of TikTok, at the same time exhibiting the continuity of performative practices from Musical.ly in TikTok.[18]

An example of this kind of performance is the trend generated from the sound "Laxed"[19] by @jawsh_685 in 2020. "Laxed" consists of two sections: a three-and-a-half-measure pre-chorus and a six-measure chorus. In the first section there is no clear sound-choreography relation. Here TikTokers perform freely, although it is possible to observe a preference for using this pre-chorus as a kind of "preamble" or "introduction" for walking into scene and/or briefly interacting with the camera and/or a virtual audience. Meanwhile, the second part has a clear sound-choreography relation. In this section, TikTokers perform to the beat of the music following the choreography: in the first measure, the right hand briefly touches the left shoulder, then the right shoulder, and then this hand is raised in the air for a longer time. This movement is done following the rhythm of the sound: short, short, long. In the next measure, with the hand still raised, TikTokers make a hip movement by bending their knees a little from right to left and continue with this same movement in the second part of this measure, this time from left to right. In the following two measures, TikTokers repeat this sequence of steps, this time beginning with the other hand: the left hand touches the right shoulder, then the left shoulder, and then this hand is raised in the air, moving on to the hip movement from left to right and from right to left. In the last two measures, TikTokers perform both sequences at the same time for ending the choreography.

18 For more on the continuity of these practices beyond Musical.ly and TikTok, particularly Dubmash, see Boffone (2021).

19 @jawsh_685, "Laxed," TikTok sound, https://www.tiktok.com/music/Laxed-6804093117843770118?is_from_webapp=1&sender_device=pc.

"Laxed" became viral in TikTok during the first two-thirds of 2020. TikTokers performed this choreography in countless settings and with different themes. However, the sound-choreography relation persisted during all performances. Although some TikTokers used the sound "Laxed" for very different performances, most of them follow the same performative plot previously explained, turning it into a trend. This relation can be clearly observed when this choreography was included in the videos of "Savage Love (Laxed—Siren Beat)"[20] by Jason Derulo and Jawsh 685, showing the clear sound-choreography relation present in trends. Besides, still today this sound-choreography relation prevails in different challenges, where it is expected that the sound of "Laxed" (or "Savage Love (Laxed—Siren Beat)") is performed with this choreography.

Although trends have a clear sound-choreography relation, like any other cultural practice, they can change with time, turning into new trends and/or other kinds of performances. One example of this can be observed in the performances linked to the sound "Mega Francesita (Remix)"[21] by DJ Dmonio, especially during 2018. Associated with the change of Musical.ly into TikTok, this sound was the source of the trend *#dibididance*. In this trend TikTokers perform the following choreography: during the first two bars of the song, TikTokers position their hands in front of their bodies at the level of the abdomen while staring at the camera. Then, the performer positions their hands in a way in which the little finger and thumb are extended while the other fingers remain closed in a sort of "call me" sign. Keeping this position, TikTokers move their hands up and down with a slight hip movement. These two bars can also be switched for a kind of "preamble" by walking into the scene and/or briefly interacting with the camera and/or virtual audience. During the next four bars, TikTokers extend their hands and place them parallel to their bodies at the level of their heads while rotating their hips from left to right, ending on the right side with the accentuated beat of the bar. In the next two bars, TikTokers perform a series of movements with their arms, placing them in front of them and pulling them to the sides with their elbows, preparing for the next two bars in which they begin to clap their hands in the level of their abdomen as if they were cleaning their hands from dust while moving their body sensually in an "s"-form. With

[20] Jason Deruloand Jawsh 685, "Savage Love," June 9, 2020, YouTube video, https://www.youtube.com/watch?v=gUci-tsiU4I.

[21] DJ Dmonio, "Mega Francesita (Remix)," TikTok sound, https://www.tiktok.com/music/Mega-Francesita-Remix-6586528252498545409?is_from_webapp=1&sender_device=pc.

this movement the last section of the performance takes place, where TikTokers perform a hip movement for two bars while they open and close their arms, crossing their hands in front of their abdomen.

As time passed, new variants for this trend emerged, each time more influenced by a racialized imaginary and hearing (see Stoever 2016; Eidsheim 2019; Müller 2022), leading TikTokers to relate this sound with "Arab culture." In 2019 and 2020, a while after the *#dibididance* trend lost visibility, the more visible performances associated with the sound "Mega Francesita (Remix)" would revolve around demonstrating TikTokers' abilities in belly dance. The fact that the name of the sound (=Mega Francesita) and the song used as the basis for the Remix (=Ieva's Polka) did not have any relation to belly dance did not seem to be relevant for TikTokers. By 2021, performances associated with this sound entered the challenge category, leaving aside its sound-choreography relation to focus on a confrontation theme.

Having introduced the elements that build the interface of TikTok and the technical-performative possibilities it provides, as well as some of the types of performances present in this application, in the next chapter I examine and discuss the process by which TikTokers become acquainted with TikTok and learn to use the application. After that, I analyze how performers go from being "common users" to becoming TikTokers, developing and performing an identity I call TikTok persona.

3

Becoming a TikToker

After my project had already been rejected many times by different institutions for not being ethnomusicological enough, in the summer of 2018, my journey eventually led me to the University of Vienna, where Julio Mendívil received me and my project with open arms. Everything seemed to be going wonderfully, but destiny had a surprise for me. On many occasions, I had already been warned that researching in and/or about a smartphone application had no future. On many occasions, I was told things like "Completing your doctoral studies takes a couple of years. What would you do if, in the middle of your research, the application disappears? Do you really think that in three years' time, there will still be Musical.ly?" I remember that train ride taking me back home after my project was officially accepted by the University of Vienna in the fall of 2018. I was ecstatic, thinking that I could finally dedicate myself to research Musical.ly. This was my moment, or so I thought. I remember reaching for my laptop, opening the internet browser, and downloading the newest issue of the newspaper *Der Standard*. I recall the feeling of paralysis that suddenly invaded me, and I couldn't believe my eyes: ByteDance had just bought Musical.ly, changing the course of this new app, meaning that Musical.ly would indeed no longer exist.[1] The automatic updates of my smartphone had finished the job. A new icon was placed on my screen.

That was my first encounter with TikTok. Like many Musers, I was suddenly facing a brand-new application. The performances and interactions that build this musicking were now carried out from a new interface. Some practices would disappear, while others began to emerge in this new environment. But how did other users get to know about the application? And how did they learn to use it? In this chapter, I focus on the performers of TikTok musicking. In

[1] For a more detailed vision of the merging of Musical.ly and TikTok see Kaye et al. (2021); Savic (2021); and Kaye et al. (2022).

the first part of this chapter, I discuss how TikTokers became acquainted with and began using the application. After that, I go through some of the different strategies used by TikTokers to learn how to use the application and develop their performances successfully. The second part of this chapter is dedicated to building on the concept of musical personae coined by Philip Auslander (2006, 2021). In this section I analyze how performers go from being "common users" to TikTokers by developing and performing an identity I call TikTok persona.

Becoming a Performer

As mentioned in the story at the beginning of the introduction, my first encounter with Musical.ly was by watching the videos my colleague showed me of his daughters performing. I became so fascinated by those videos that I downloaded the application soon after and made Musical.ly my research topic. A couple of months later, Musical.ly unexpectedly merged with TikTok, and well, without being able to do anything about it, that became my first encounter with TikTok. Was my experience very different from the experience of other TikTokers?

Encountering TikTok

The merging of Musical.ly and TikTok did not happen overnight but rather took a couple of weeks until it was completed. Like me, many users found out about TikTok for a simple reason: the application with which they performed their dances and lip-syncs transformed from one moment to the next. This situation produced a process of adaptation and renegotiation of practices and discourses that originated in Musical.ly that were now being transferred into TikTok. Although Musical.ly ceased to exist—as predicted by some colleagues—practices developed in this application continued being held on TikTok. Musical.ly changed its appearance, it turned into TikTok, but many of its users and their practices kept being the same.

This process of transformation was perceived by Musers in different ways. On one side, a group of Musers neither wanted nor agreed with this change. There were two main aspects I observed that irritated most Musers during this period of transition. The first aspect was having to take new identities as TikTokers. In many conversations I had back then, I repeatedly heard that Musers did not feel comfortable with this new identity, often arguing: "I'm not a TikToker, I'm not a clock. I'm a Muser!" Although they did not have any trouble carrying out the activities they enjoyed, their identity as performers had been damaged and/or put into negotiation. Many performers had strong loyalty bonds with Musical.ly, and for that reason, it was difficult to leave their identity and sense of belonging on the side to negotiate a new identity as TikToker. Besides this, TikTok began to prioritize promoting video-musical practices different from choreographies (trends) and lip-syncing with the purpose of appealing to an older—and less prone to sexual abuse[2]—audience. In consequence, numerous Musers did not feel welcome in this application anymore, and as a result, stopped using it. A prominent case was that of twins @lisaandlena. @lisaandlena began their activities on Musical.ly in 2015, becoming famous for their dance and lip-sync videos. The transformation of Musical.ly to TikTok in 2018, as communicated in many of their videos, stopped making them feel part of that community. In March 2019, a couple of months after the merger of Musical.ly and TikTok, the twins decided to delete their TikTok account, which had over 30 million followers.

Nevertheless, there is also a wide majority of Musical.ly users, who happily embraced the fusion of Musical.ly and TikTok. For them, this change represented a new phase in the creative development of the application. Even though Musical.ly had just existed for a couple of years, there had already been different performative phases marked by the development of different video-musical practices, aesthetics, and performative styles, which continued developing and growing with the users. @ar3miss shares her perspective on this process:

> It was Musical.ly in the past, and at that time it was actually these videos where you move your mobile phone and somehow lipsynced to it … Since then, I've always had the app and also participated in the change from Musical.ly to TikTok … Yes, it was simply Musical.ly and then it always grew, so when people posted other videos, it went more in the direction of Vine, which I also really liked and I liked that … I simply went along with the developments. I didn't

[2] Understand this in the context of the criticism and legal problems Musical.ly was facing.

> choose TikTok, it was just; I was always there. It has changed, I have changed with it.[3] (@ar3miss 2021)[4]

Like @ar3miss, many Musers accepted this transition without trouble and continued developing their musicking in TikTok, thus becoming part of the userbase that kept diverse practices and TikTok as an application in use. Old and new practices were created, developed, and combined, and the performative world of TikTok would soon be crystalized. This performative plurality attracted old users back, like @lisaandlena in the beginning of 2020, who shortly after their return to TikTok gained the status of the most successful TikTokers in the German-speaking area. Nonetheless, this would also attract new users for the application, which in the second half of 2019 was pointing to become one of the most downloaded apps in the world.

The success the application was having by the end of 2019 was reinforced by an event that would change the world. The sudden outbreak of the COVID-19 pandemic and the lockdowns that followed, while almost bringing the world to total stillness, would also become the detonator for the exponential growth of TikTok. TikTok was turning into one of the spaces in which social life took place. Boredom and lack of physical contact encouraged people to try new applications and/or activities, but also the influence of friends who were already using the application would become a common motivation for many to try TikTok. This can be appreciated in the way @annamaurer_music got to know TikTok:

> So I [started] with TikTok in all the lockdowns and thought I'd just have a look at it. A friend of mine uses it very cleverly, she is very successful with TikTok and I think every platform that you can use as a musician is somehow cool. Yes, and for me, on the one hand, it was a bit of a check-out to see what it was all about. On the other hand, I also saw, okay, there are these duets and things like that where you can interact with people and that's what I [needed] right now in this

[3] Es war ja früher Musical.ly, und das war damals eigentlich diese; ja halt, diese Videos, wo man das Handy halt bewegt und dazu irgendwie lipsynced. … Ich hab seit dem auch die App immer gehabt und auch die Entwicklung mitgemacht, von Musical.ly auf TikTok. … Ja, es war einfach Musical.ly und das hat sich dann immer entwickelt, also wenn dann Leute eben andere Videos gepostet haben, ist es dann mehr so in Richtung Vine gegangen, was mir auch total getaugt hat und das hat mir gefallen …. Ich hab einfach die Entwicklung mitgemacht. Ich hab mich nicht entschieden für TikTok, es war einfach; Ich war immer schon da. Es hat sich verändert, ich hab mich mitverändert. (@ar3miss 2021). Translated from German to English by Natalia Neira Nieto.

[4] With the purpose of facilitating their understanding, some of the quotes of the transcripts from interviews and/or comments by TikTokers have been slightly modified. However, the original structure, form, and grammar of the language used are maintained.

> weird time where you don't see people anyway and don't have the opportunity to play live with each other anyway. I found the whole thing interesting to jam with these short duets and yes. I also saw it as an opportunity to get to know people, for example Chasey Abrams from Postmodern Jukebox, with whom I did all the duets and was in contact a bit. It's just really cool to connect with people.[5] (@annamaurer_music 2021)

Although friends and family were highly influential in introducing new users to the application with the purpose of spending time and socializing (especially during lockdowns), many young musicians like @annamaurer_music began using TikTok because of the diverse performative and/or representative possibilities provided by the app. Some of the most appealing aspects mentioned by young musicians that motivated them to start using TikTok during the pandemic are the possibility of experimenting with new formats and of creating new collaborations, as well as that of performing *live* concerts. Other important aspects include the possibility of representing themselves, connecting with other artists, and increasing their visibility and/or reaching new audiences, as mentioned by @ian.draven:

> I started, quite honestly because of my girlfriend … I'm on social media because I know I have to have it to do some communication as an artist and for the label and stuff … On YouTube it's hard to get people to watch your stuff. It takes a long time. Instagram and the algorithm that's behind Instagram so you get to meet people new; there's so many people, great artists, but they have maybe two likes! Insanely hard! … She just told me: "Yeah, come on, try [TikTok]! It's only 60 seconds, there's not much to do! Why don't you try it, because there are good, but relatively few people who do modular things on TikTok as opposed to Instagram and YouTube!" So I said, "It's free, just give it a try," and I immediately got [views and likes] … Most people you'll never meet, they don't care about your life at all. But it's natural, everyone has an ego and somewhere you say to

[5] Also ich habe jetzt mit TikTok in den ganzen Lockdowns [angefangen] und habe mir gedacht ich schaue es mir einfach mal an. Eine Freundin von mir nutzt das sehr geschickt, die ist da sehr erfolgreich mit TikTok und ich denke mir jede Plattform, die man irgendwie als Musiker*in nutzen kann, ist ja irgendwie cool. Ja und für mich war es auch einerseits ein bisschen irgendwie um auszuchecken was ist das eigentlich. Andererseits, habe ich dann auch gesehen, okay da gibt es diese Duette und solche Sachen wo man interagieren kann mit Leuten und das habe ich gerade jetzt in dieser komischen Zeit [gebraucht], wo man eh keine Leute sieht und eh nicht die Möglichkeit hat live miteinander zu spielen. Ich habe das Ganze interessant gefunden zu Jammen mit diesen kurzen Duetten und ja. Ich habe das auch als Möglichkeit gesehen, Leute kennen zu lernen also da jetzt z. B. Chasey Abrams von Postmodern Jukebox, mit dem ich die ganzen Duette gemacht habe und ein bisschen in Kontakt war. Das ist einfach ganz cool, um mit Leuten zu connecten. (@annamaurer_music 2021). Translated from German to English by Natalia Neira Nieto.

> yourself: Oh nice! People react to what I did! Completely normal reaction—and there [in TikTok] it just went much faster.[6] (@ian.draven 2021)

The possibility of increasing their visibility and reaching new audiences became an important motivation for musicians to start participating in TikTok. Users appreciated the relatively low competition and performative plurality promoted by the algorithm of TikTok. Compared to other platforms, it did not take as much of an effort to reach a wider audience. Besides, the possibility of becoming viral and "being discovered" was always present. Before the pandemic, TikTok had already proved to be a good platform for gaining notoriety as an artist. Combined with the growing visibility TikTok was experiencing in many areas of public life and its integration with the popular global imaginary, young artists began taking their chances with this application. One example is the case brought by @hisham.tv:

> Like many others, I simply noticed that TikTok—that was in October 2019—was an app that was being hyped and where you can build up followers quite well and generate a reach. I then simply tried it and started with comedy videos and then just kept going.[7] (@hisham.tv 2021)

The experience of @hisham.tv is not an isolated case. Many musicians and other artists saw this possibility and began using TikTok to create and/or promote their music. But other creators had made this information part of their content. Creators like @garywvee invited other people to use TikTok as a tool for promoting their music through other digital platforms, as in the

[6] Ich hab angefangen, ganz ehrlich gesagt wegen meiner Freundin. … Ich bin auf sozialen Medien, weil ich weiß, dass ich es haben muss, um ein bisschen Kommunikation zu machen als Künstler und fürs Label und so weiter …. Auf YouTube ist es schwer, dass du Leute bekommst, die sich dein Zeug anschauen. Das dauert lange. Instagram und der Algorithmus, der hinter Instagram ist, damit man Leute neu kennenlernt; es gibt so viele Leute, tolle Künstler, aber die haben vielleicht zwei Likes! Wahnsinnig schwer! … Sie hat mir dann eben gesagt: "Ja komm, versuch [TikTok] doch mal! Sind nur 60 Sekunden, ist ja nicht viel zu machen! Probier es doch mal, denn es gibt gute, aber relativ wenige Leute die modulare Sachen machen auf TikTok im Gegensatz zu Instagram und YouTube!" Habe ich gesagt: Ist ja gratis, einfach mal probieren und hatte sofort [views und likes]. … Die meisten Leute wirst du niemals kennenlernen, denen ist dein Leben komplett egal. Aber es ist natürlich, jeder hat ein Ego und irgendwo sagst du dir: Oh schön! Leute reagieren darauf, was ich gemacht habe! Komplett normale Reaktion—und da [in TikTok] ging es halt viel Schneller (@ian.draven 2021). Translated from German to English by Natalia Neira Nieto.

[7] "Ich habe, wie viele andere, einfach mitbekommen, dass TikTok—das war 2019 im Oktober—gerade eine App ist, die halt gehyped wird und wo man ganz gut, Follower aufbauen kann und eine Reichweite generieren kann. Ich habe es dann auch einfach versucht und habe dann mit Comedy-Videos angefangen und dann halt immer weiter gemacht" (@hisham.tv 2021). Translated from German to English by Natalia Neira Nieto.

case of @liamkillenmusic, who got to know about TikTok through @garyvee's recommendation:

> I started with TikTok probably a year and a half ago, and the reason why I started is because I listen to this guy named @garyvee [(Gary Vaynerchuck)]. He's one of these marketing entrepreneur type guys almost like motivational speaker but he gives very valuable information for people like me. People who are trying to use social media to leverage themselves. So he's the one that kept saying: "Get on TikTok, you have to get on TikTok guys. This was like two years ago he said: 'post everyday on TikTok, post every day!' And he was right he predicted it and now it's exploded since then so he predicted that. That's the reason why I got onto it" cause I was already doing like the Instagram thing right? So it was kind of related. People were sort of getting bored of Instagram in a way and now because of TikTok Instagram has completely changed. It just shows how much of an impact it's had on everything. Even YouTube has been directly impacted by TikTok, the vertical reel videos, YouTube shorts—it's literally a copy of TikTok. That's the reason why I got onto it and it's worked. (@liamkillenmusic 2021)

The ways in which people learned about and began to use TikTok are infinite, as well as their reasons for doing so. Although the aforementioned cases do no justice to the countless possibilities for this to occur, they exemplify very well the explanations I heard throughout my research years. Because of permanence since the times of Musical.ly, a suggestion by friends and family members, mentally escaping lockdowns, or marketing matters, a lot of people became acquainted with TikTok and decided to develop their musical practices in this application. Starting this moment, their relationship with the platform took them through different paths. However, there was a path they all had to go through in their own way if they wanted success in the platform: they had to learn to perform, to learn TikToking.

The Path to TikToking

After downloading the application and beginning to explore it, I realized that performing TikToks was a much more complex activity than I thought. My first attempts were a total failure. I had a lot of trouble finding an adequate posture for recording myself and keeping the camera focused, and when I tried doing a choreography or a complex performance I just gave up. It was obvious that my body could not handle these movements and postures. Besides, my knowledge on the repertoire and my capacity to execute it were quite limited. My body had to get familiar with this new instrument—my smartphone—and all its performative tools. I also needed to learn how to read the repertoire and somehow execute it. But how could I do it? Where could I learn? Who could teach me? How did TikTokers manage to learn to perform?

After many conversations I had with TikTokers in the last years, I now understand that there is no TikToker school where one can go and learn. The best way to learn TikToking is learning through trial and error, learning by doing. Here, @MissBunPun comments about this in a clear way:

> I think it's also a lot to just look at things and learn by doing. So you really try things out a bit … There are different effects or something. But that's also really cool, because by scrolling through you [come] up with new things; how you can film something new, how you can make transitions or something, are actually quite cool ideas in part.[8] (@MissBunPun 2021)

However, this does not mean that TikTokers exclusively learn by themselves without any help. Sometimes, they interact with other TikTokers to learn and/or teach things to each other. On the other hand, TikTokers get together to learn and/or try different functions, choreographies, and/or practices in TikTok. Nevertheless, there are TikTokers who share this kind of knowledge through tutorials in TikTok or other digital platforms, as explained by @agnesmilewski:

> Somehow, everything you do on your mobile phone is so intuitive these days. You don't have to learn it. … I don't know. But I've also had younger people show me how to do it. Yes, and there are tutorials anyway. Everywhere, on YouTube and whatever. There are TikTok tutorials on TikTok![9] (@agnesmilewski 2021)

As we have seen, this learning process by trial and error is very common in TikTok. However, although at the beginning TikTokers continuously imitate other TikTokers, the search for their own voice and for the creation of their

[8] Ich glaub es ist auch sehr viel, wenn man sich einfach Sachen anschaut und learning by doing. Also wirklich herumprobieren bisschen. … Es gibt halt dann verschiedene Effekte oder so. Aber das ist auch ganz cool, weil man einfach durchs Durchscrollen auch wieder auf Neues [kommt]; wie man was Neues filmen kann, wie man Übergänge machen kann oder so, sind eigentlich ganz coole Ideen teilweise (@MissBunPun 2021). Translated from German to English by Natalia Neira Nieto.

[9] "Irgendwie, das ist so alles intuitiv, was man am Handy macht heutzutage. Das muss man ja nicht lernen. … Keine Ahnung. Aber ich habe mir auch von jüngeren Leuten zeigen lassen, wie es geht. Ja, und es gibt eh Tutorials auch. Überall, auf YouTube und was auch immer. Es gibt TikTok-Tutorials auf TikTok!" (@agnesmilewski 2021). Translated from German to English by Natalia Neira Nieto.

own contents is not bypassed. TikTokers continuously look to create their own styles and contents and/or adapt the performative contents of other performers to their own performative style. The experience of @hisham.tv gives us a closer look at this process:

> I just learned it on the platform by watching other videos and imitating things. There are always trends on TikTok and you imitate them and then the first video somehow blows up. You don't know for what reason, but you just follow a trend and your video just happens to get into the algorithm, where it suddenly gets a lot of attention. Then you find your own thing, you just start to get creative. You know, from the music itself and just thinking up something yourself, and those are the things that usually go down best, when you just create a video idea from your own head. Because TikTok is such a recycling thing, so you take a lot of things that you see and make your own thing out of it and out of that you develop your own [style], or in my case it was like that; your own [style], your own formats.[10] (@hisham.tv 2021)

Here it is possible to observe that, even if TikTokers use the performance of other TikTokers as a starting point to learn or develop their own TikToks, these performances are not the same. TikToks become a kind of score for the development of their own performative versions for each TikToker. While TikTokers search for developing their content, these videos become support material for creating the language and knowledge of TikTok and become the foundations from which TikTokers start and develop the search and negotiation of their own TikToker identity. @sarahnakya mentions:

> I don't necessarily copy it, but I usually try to do the videos differently. But if it's a trend or a challenge, I do join in and at the end you have to give the credits of the creator in the caption. But otherwise it's very often the case with TikTok that people "recycle" the videos or audio files, so to speak, and create their own

[10] Ich habe es einfach auf der Plattform gelernt so, indem das ich andere Videos geschaut habe und Sachen nachgemacht habe. Es gibt ja immer so Trends auf TikTok und die macht man dann erstmal nach und dann kommt das erste Video was irgendwie aufblowed. Man weiß gar nicht aus welchem Grund, aber du machst einfach mal irgendeinen Trend nach und genau dein Video kommt einfach zufällig, irgendwie in den Algorithmus, wo das dann plötzlich viel Aufmerksamkeit gibt. Dann findest du so dein eigenes Ding, dass du einfach anfängst kreativ zu werden. Du kennst ja von der Musik selber und einfach dir selber was ausdenkst und das sind dann die Sachen, die meistens am allerbesten ankommen, wenn du einfach aus deinem eigenen Kopf irgendeine Videoidee kreierst. Weil eben TikTok ist ja so ein Recycling- Ding schon, also du nimmst ja schon viele Sachen, die du siehst und machst dein eigenes Ding draus und aus dem heraus entwickelt sich dann dein eigener [Styl] oder bei mir war so; dein eigenes [Stil], deine eigenen Formate (@hisham.tv 2021). Translated from German to English by Natalia Neira Nieto.

> TikToks with their own interpretation. It is done differently compared to the original video but the plot is usually the same. Just like the memes, that there are different memes about the same joke. Of course I tried to do new things, but it wasn't that easy. That's also the reason why I make notes about different ideas. I also like to watch dance covers and singing covers on TikTok and I plan to make some myself.[11] (@sarahnakya 2021)

An important and interesting aspect mentioned by @sarahnakya is that, during the process of learning the language and practices of TikTok, some TikTokers take notes on the performative aspects that make them interesting and then use them for developing their content. This shows the existence of a more complex process in the moment of planning and creating performances. However, not all performances are exhaustively planned. Spontaneity in the moment of creating and/or deciding what to do is an aspect that is very emphasized by TikTokers. The experience of @MissBunPun shows us an example of spontaneity:

> So it's really then very spontaneous inspiration, with these duets for example. When I hear something where I think to myself—Oh, that's pretty cool. Or I see some dance that I like extremely [and] they are easily learned because they are so short. So, it's either duets, so inspirations that come spontaneously, because I see someone ... I don't know playing something cool on the guitar and I like singing to it or something. Or it's some dance that I think is pretty cool and just want to learn spontaneously now and have time for it and so on and want to record it quickly and post it.[12] (@MissBunPun 2021)

11 Ich mach's nicht unbedingt nach, sondern versuche ich meistens anders die Videos zu gestalten. Wenn's aber ein Trend oder eine Challenge ist, mach ich da schon mit und am Ende muss man die Credits von dem Urheber bei der Caption angeben. Aber sonst ist bei TikTok sehr häufig der Fall, dass die Leute, die Videos bzw. Audiodateien sozusagen ‚recyceln' und mit einer Eigeninterpretation ihre eigene TikToks kreieren. Es wird im Vergleich zu dem Originalvideo anders gemacht aber der Plot ist meistens derselbe. So wie die Memes, dass da verschiedene Memes über denselben Joke gibt. Ich habe natürlich auch versucht neue Sachen zu machen, ist aber nicht so einfach gewesen. Das ist auch der Grund, warum ich mir Notizen über verschiedenste Ideen mache. Ich schaue auch sehr gerne Dance-Covers und singing covers auf TikTok und habe auch vor, selbst welche zu machen. (@sarahnakya 2021). Translated from German to English by Natalia Neira Nieto.

12 Also es ist wirklich dann sehr spontane Inspiration, bei diesen Duetts zum Beispiel. Wenn ich irgendwas höre, wo ich mir denk—Oh, das ist ziemlich cool. Oder ich sehe irgendeinen Tanz der mir extrem [gefällt] und die sind dann leicht gelernt, weil sie eben so kurz sind. Also, es sind entweder Duetts also so Inspirationen, die spontan kommen, weil ich eben irgendjemanden sehe, ... weiß ich nicht auf der Gitarre was Cooles spielt und ich mag dazu singen oder so. Oder es ist irgendein Tanz, den ich recht cool finde und einfach spontan jetzt lernen will und Zeit habe dazu und so und den schnell aufnehmen will und posten (@MissBunPun 2021). Translated from German to English by Natalia Neira Nieto.

Being spontaneous in the moment of performing and/or deciding what to perform is an important aspect TikTokers stressed on many occasions during my research. For many of them, spontaneity is considered a necessary attribute when creating content for becoming a good TikToker. When compared to other digital platforms, this was mentioned as one of the most attractive aspects of TikTok. However, this does not mean that TikTokers do not make some planning for their performances. As already mentioned by @MissBunPun, taking notes and ideas from other TikToks is a common practice for developing your own content. In the case of @hisham.tv, we can observe how spontaneity is mixed with more planned performances, going from taking notes to writing complete sketches:

> Yes, sometimes I write something down, [but] sometimes it's just there, something just comes and I just record it. In the beginning, I almost never wrote anything down. In the beginning I just took the mobile phone and thought about something and did it right away on the mobile phone in the app and then at some point I really started to write scripts because I really started to do real sketches. Or when I was just in the metro and a video idea came to me and I just wrote it down, and yes, that has already developed more into scripts a little bit.[13] (@hisham.tv 2021)

Learning TikToking is a process of trial and error that takes TikTokers not just to learn new practices but also to reinvent themselves as performers, as TikTokers. The imitation and appropriation of contents let TikTokers internalize intellectually and physically the practices and knowledges that conform TikTok musicking. This knowledge helps them promote the development of ideas and their own styles, giving TikTokers the tools to perform with a certain quality, which is simultaneously spontaneous and premeditated. However, this learning process is not limited to learning how to use the performative tools provided by the application: TikTokers must also learn to read and use the aesthetics and ways of positioning themselves on TikTok. As in many other musical traditions,

[13] Ja, manchmal schreib ich mir was auf, [aber] manchmal ist es einfach da, da kommt einfach irgendwas und ich nehme es einfach auf. Also gerade am Anfang habe ich eigentlich fast nie was aufgeschrieben. Am Anfang habe ich einfach das Handy genommen und mir irgendetwas überlegt und es gleich am Handy in der App gemacht und dann irgendwann habe ich auch wirklich angefangen Skripte zu schreiben, weil ich wirklich angefangen habe richtige Sketches zu machen. Oder wenn ich einfach in der U-Bahn war und mir eine Videoidee kam und ich das einfach aufgeschrieben hab, und ja, also das hat sich schon mehr zu Skripten ein bisschen entwickelt" (@hisham.tv 2021). Translated from German to English by Natalia Neira Nieto.

TikTok has its own aesthetics in which performers are expected to meet and/or negotiate to satisfy their audience.

> The thing is also quite exciting that you can actually get quite a lot out of it just with your mobile phone camera and in the nine-to-sixteen format and it just consciously uses [certain aesthetics;] … if something looks too professional on TikTok, it loses its shame for me. And we try to find this balance of it being real, that is, authentic and not produced in a high-end way, but still appealing in terms of quality.[14] (@floundwisch 2021)

What @floundwisch mentions brings out a fundamental aspect in performing and negotiating the aesthetics that TikTokers are expected to consider. The idea of authenticity in TikTok is bound in a certain way to the idea of spontaneity. Authenticity seeks to be simple and spontaneous, without neglecting the performative quality. Therefore, performances must follow specific quality rules for each style without turning into overblown cinematographic productions. In that sense, a good performance would be visually simple, with a touch of spontaneity, and performatively concise. During their learning process and search for their audience and identity as users of the application, TikTokers must learn to identify what is allowed within the aesthetic limits of their performative niche through a long process of trial and error.

For this, it is very important for TikTokers to find their performative niche and quickly learn to effectively connect with it from the start of their adventure in TikTok. This allows them to adapt and develop their performance, as well as their musical persona, to meet its aesthetic demands more easily. Once TikTokers broadly identify the niche in which they wish to perform, they must learn how to place their performance effectively in the wide performative universe of TikTok so they can reach "their audience" successfully. It is easy to conclude that the more effectively TikTokers reach their audience, the bigger their visibility, and therefore their chances of success. A very common way of placing a performance is by using hashtags. The experience of @ian.draven provides a good insight into this:

[14] Das Ding ist ja auch ganz spannend, dass du halt nur mit deiner Handykamera und im Neun zu Sechzehn Format eigentlich auch ziemlich viel rausholen kannst und es halt bewusst [bestimmte Ästhetik nutzt;] … wenn was zu professionell aussieht auf TikTok, verliert es für mich seinen Scham. Und wir versuchen da diese Balance zu finden aus, es ist echt, also authentisch und nicht High-End produziert und trotzdem qualitativ ansprechend (@floundwisch 2021). Translated from German to English by Natalia Neira Nieto.

> I looked up what was on the other videos. You have to do your own research, I think. Depending on the hashtag, you have a lot of differences in how many people actually watch it and of course I try to be relatively precise. Of course I have the #foryou and then in French #pourtoi, which means the same thing, so that you have more chances [to land in the for-you page]. But otherwise super precise: #techno, #modularsynth, #synthtok, #eurorack etc., so that it's already classified. Because I know that of course you can meet people who maybe don't know that at all and think it's cool what you're doing, but it remains very little in the percentage. Most people, if you now somehow only enter #foryou as a hashtag, ok, I think you have more views, but fewer likes, and the goal is that the whole thing remains relatively at the same level.[15] (@ian.draven 2021)

TikTokers learn strategies like this one to position their performance effectively throughout their performative career and create a performative niche from which they become part of a community. At first, imitation and appropriation of contents allow TikTokers to internalize both intellectually and physically, the practices and knowledge that build TikTok musicking. After that, along with a process of trial and error, they learn new practices and aesthetics, as well as how to negotiate and reinvent their identity as performers. In some cases, this effort is paid with more visibility in the application, which may in turn allow TikTokers to access new functions to widen their performative possibilities. The case of @ian.draven is an example of the expectation generated by this possibility:

> I also want to do [a live], I promised, if I got the 1000 followers, I would love to play live on TikTok. Definitely! And at the same time with another camera on YouTube, so then you have the alternative of either watching it on your phone in portrait format, or in normal format on YouTube. It'll just be: Let's go! Just like I play live—so live I had to say: I'll turn this thing on, okay—then quickly play a

[15] Ich habe nachgeguckt, was auf den anderen Videos draufsteht. Da muss man sich selber schlau machen, denke ich. Je nach Hashtag hast du ja wahnsinnig viele Unterschiede, wie viele Leute das wirklich anschauen und natürlich versuche ich doch relativ präzise zu sein. Natürlich habe ich den #foryou und dann auf Französisch #pourtoi, das heißt das gleiche, damit du halt da mehr Chancen hast [in der for-you-page zu landen]. Aber ansonsten super präzise: #techno, # modularsynth, #synthtok, #eurorack usw., damit das schon eingeordnet ist. Denn ich weiß, dass natürlich kannst du Leute treffen, die das vielleicht gar nicht kennen und es cool finden, was du machst, aber es bleibt sehr wenig in der Prozentzahl. Die meisten Leute, wenn du jetzt irgendwie nur #foryou eingibst als Hashtag, ok ich glaub du hast mehr Views halt, aber weniger Likes, und das Ziel ist ja, dass das Ganze relativ auf einem gleichen Niveau bleibt (@ian.draven 2021). Translated from German to English by Natalia Neira Nieto.

> 4/4 kick in yes four on the floor—that's the most important thing if people want to dance, and then the rest is built up.[16] (@ian.draven 2021)

Moreover, visibility, growth, and access to new performative possibilities allow performers to begin the process of creating their TikTok persona, a process in which they will put to practice everything they have learned to establish their identity as TikToker and develop their musicking in a more professional way.

Becoming a TikToker

I still remember those conversations during the merger of Musical.ly with TikTok, in which performers used their voices to show discontent toward this change: "I'm not a TikToker, I'm not a clock. I'm a Muser!" This was evidence of how the development of musical practices in the platform had encouraged performers to create loyalty bonds strong enough to develop an intense sense of community and belonging. At the same time, these words made me realize that these performers had created or were creating an identity as a Muser—and then as a TikToker—an identity that was being damaged and/or put into negotiation during the merge process. I found this phenomenon very interesting, as the idea of musical persona by Philip Auslander (see 2006, 2021) popped into my mind. But could this concept be appliable here? Are TikTokers indeed a kind of musical persona?

Musical Personae 2.0—TikTok Personae

Based on the ideas by Erving Goffman (1959), Philip Auslander states that "what musicians perform first and foremost is not music, but their own identities as musicians. ... Seen this way, the object of musical performance is the successful presentation of an identity, a musical persona, in a defined social context, rather

[16] Ich möchte auch [ein Live] machen, habe ich versprochen, wenn ich die 1000 Followers bekommen würde, würde ich sehr gerne live auf TikTok spielen. Auf jeden Fall! Und gleichzeitig mit einer anderen Kamera auf YouTube, das heißt dann hast du die Alternative entweder schaust es dir auf deinem Handy an im Hochformat, oder im normalen Format auf YouTube. Das wird dann einfach: Let's go! Genauso wie ich Live spiele—also live musste sagen: Ich mach das Ding an, okay—spiel dann schnell ein 4/4 Kick rein ja four on the floor—das ist Wichtigste wenn die Leute tanzen wollen, und der Rest wird dann aufgebaut (@ian.draven 2021). Translated from German to English by Natalia Neira Nieto.

than the execution of a text" (Auslander 2006: 102–4, 118). It is worth pointing out that this musical identity or musical persona, which represents a partial selection of habits and attributes used to represent oneself as a musician, is merely one of the multiple—existing or possible—identities that constitute the self (see Turino 2008: 95–108), and that can be performed in digital as well as physical contexts. The way in which we present ourselves in many of the activities we take part in varies according to the contexts and cultural cohorts with which we interact (see Goffman 1959; Turino 2008). My behavior, the way I speak, and how I articulate my interpersonal relations, among many others, differ according to the situation in which I act: I'm not the same Juan at home with my children, than the ethnomusicologist Juan working at the university, the Juan on the many digital platforms, or the anonymized and racially marked Juan trying to avoid the effects of structural racism on the street. This everyday situation of the performativity of a certain identity is likewise applicable to musicians. As very clearly put by Auslander: "There is no reason to suppose that musicians perform the same identity when playing music as in their other life routines. The version of self that a musician performs qua musician is what [Auslander calls] the musical persona" (2021: 95). Following this logic, we could then say that just like musicians (in the traditional sense), TikTokers perform their TikToker identity when conducting their musicking in the app, and therefore, they are also performing or developing a performer identity which we could call TikTok persona.

However, this act of performing a TikToker identity—the TikToker persona—must be understood as a process of "becoming." A person is not a TikToker just by using the application, but it is necessary to actively create, negotiate, and perform this identity as a TikTok persona. This process of becoming can be seen reflected in the two existing modes of TikTok personae I have been able to observe through my research. First, (1) we can observe a kind of TikTok personae in performers, who even though they perform their identity as performers have not been recognized by any community as such, nor have been recognized as possessing a particular kind of "TikTok identity." These are characterized by taking place in the process of searching for or consolidating the "own voice" as a TikToker. Their performative identity, their TikTok persona, is much more generic and has little visibility. On the other hand, (2) there is another TikTok persona we can observe in performers who perform an established, individual, and recognizable performer identity. Their TikTok persona already holds wide visibility and has already gained recognition by an audience. Additionally, due to its wide visibility, this kind of TikTok persona has the possibility of being performed (and recognized) beyond the platform. Most TikTokers mentioned in this book refer to this kind of TikTok persona. Both modes of TikTok personae can be understood as part of a continuum during the development process of a TikToker identity.

In the first place, for performing their TikTok persona, similar to the case of musical persona, the performer must execute their musicking according to the conventions and expectations of a given social performative context. To satisfactorily achieve this, performers must then develop a series of habits and attributes that will allow them to acquire knowledge of the conventions and expectations of this musicking and learn to TikTok. In this sense, they would not just have to learn to make satisfactory TikToks but also to "behave correctly" in each of the contexts of the musicking they participate in. On the one hand, performers must know the conventions and expectations of the performative genre(s) or subgenre(s) upon which their performance is built, since it is through the perspective of this particular genre and performative context that the appliable conventions and expectations will be determined for performing, perceiving, and/or judging the performance. Moreover, this will be the perspective from which the performance will be read and contextualized. These conventions and expectations allude to all aspects of the performance, including the setting, the physical appearance of the performer, the selected music, the performative aesthetics, and the way of behaving, among many others. All of these aspects must be coherent with the identity the TikTok persona ascribes to themselves and the performative context in which the performance is developed.

On the other hand, performers need to keep in mind the goals that each performative context (musical field) pursues. Thomas Turino defines four musical fields guided by the kind of participation among musicking actors: participatory, presentational, high fidelity, and studio audio art (see Turino 2008: 23–92).

> Briefly defined, *participatory performance* is a special type of artistic practice in which there are no artist-audience distinctions, only participants and potential participants performing different roles, and the primary goal is to involve the maximum number of people in some performance role. *Presentational performance,* in contrast, refers to situations where one group of people, the artists, prepare and provide music for another group, the audience, who do not participate in making the music or dancing. *High fidelity* refers to the making of recordings that are intended to index or be iconic of live performance ... *Studio audio art* involves the creation and manipulation of sound in a studio or

> on a computer to create a recorded art object (a "sound sculpture") that is not intended to represent real-time performance. (Turino 2008: 26–7)

Although these "musical fields" were not conceptualized to represent a kind of musicking like the one in TikTok, the idea behind them is very applicable to this musicking. In TikTok there are also performances that do not have a clear "artist-audience distinction" and whose primary aim is that of "involv[ing] the maximum number of people in some performance role," as it is in the case of some challenges and trends, as well as some performances in TikTok that stand close to what Turino calls "presentational performances" (see Turino 2008: 23–92). In these performances, the most important part is to present certain abilities, rather than the degree of participation of other actors. Whatever the case, each of these performative contexts has different aims to accomplish through performance, and therefore the conventions and expectations of a given social context would also be different for each case. Understanding these aims is the priority for accomplishing a satisfactory performance development.

However, the presence of conventions and expectations, as well as the performative aims in a performance do not mean that performers do not have agency in the moment of developing their musicking. Following Richard Bauman, we could say that "conventions may provide precedents and guidelines for the range of alternatives possible, but the possibility of alternatives, the competencies and goals of the participants, and the emergent unfolding of the event make for variability" (Bauman 1986: 4). Performers find themselves in a constant negotiation process with other actors of TikTok musicking to assert or counteract existing conventions, expectations, and aims in a given performative context. Entering the dialectical process reflected in the extended model of Alan P. Merriam (1964): concepts about music create behavior in relation to music and music sound itself, which are perceived by an audience and negotiated among musicking actors to produce new concepts, which in turn create new behaviors and music sounds, which are perceived by an audience and negotiated among musicking actors to produce new concepts and so on (see Chapter 1).

The aforementioned dialectical process is equally valid for the negotiation process of an own identity as TikToker. As indicated by Auslander, "the production of musical identities takes place within social frames that provide musicians and audiences alike with sets of conventions and expectations that govern, but do not determine, their definitions of the situation and corresponding behavior" (Auslander 2021: 127). It is important to emphasize that, just as conventions and expectations linked to a certain performance, this set of conventions and expectations could be (re)negotiated at the moment of performing. What is important here are aspects like "setting, appearance, and manner, the music performed and the style of performance must cohere with the identity claim the musician [—or TikTokers in our case—] stakes" (128), since a radical rupture in the coherence between one or many of these aspects and the identity claimed by the TikToker could result in the audience rejecting her. Therefore, performers try to create and consolidate their TikTok persona through a long negotiation process between the actors in TikTok musicking. Through this process, the performer learns to create, (re)negotiate, and actively perform without radical contradictions and within these contexts their identity as TikToker—their TikTok persona.

One aspect of this that is often pointed out by TikTokers is the search of their own voice as TikToker. This search process is linked to concepts of individuality and authenticity, perhaps the most important for TikTokers. @annamaurer_music comments about this search:

> I just want to present myself and still try to do what makes me me, my themes that occupy me, be it music or something that occupies me, or even a bit of make-up art, because that's what I do now. I want to do something that represents me, I don't want to do something funny that just doesn't fit me or something, just so that I get calls. Of course, you also think about which songs could be well received, but I've also done things, jazz things, where I thought "okay, nobody's interested in that anyway," but it still gets clicks, so it's very difficult to judge … I think the quality of the image and so on is quite important … I also have a ring light so that the light is just halfway OK. Such considerations, where you place yourself or I don't know. Yes, these duets, too, you think about what people think, what could be relevant somehow. Yes, and of course there are also these TikTok trends that you come across automatically and then get an idea for a video by following these trends.[17] (@annamaurer_music 2021)

[17] Ich möchte einfach mich präsentieren und versuchen einfach trotzdem das was mich ausmacht, meine Themen, die mich beschäftigen, also sei es jetzt eben die Musik oder halt irgendwas, was mich beschäftigt, oder auch ein bisschen Visagistik, weil ich das jetzt auch mache. Ich möchte jetzt schon das machen, das mich repräsentiert, ich möchte jetzt nicht irgendwas Lustiges machen, dass einfach nicht zu mir passt oder so nur damit ich Aufrufe kriegt. Voll, ja natürlich überlegt man auch, welche Songs ankommen könnten, aber ich habe auch Sachen gemacht, Jazz-Sachen, wo ich mir gedacht habe "okay, das interessiert sowieso keinen," kriegt trotzdem auch Klicks, also das ist ganz schwer einzuschätzen. … Ich glaube, also die Qualität von wegen Bild und so ist recht wichtig. … Ich habe auch so ein Ringlicht, das einfach das Licht halt halbwegs in Ordnung ist. Solche

Here @annamaurer_music clearly illustrates the importance of representing "herself" through her performances. We can observe how the first performative experimentation phase in the platform approaches its end: although the search for being recognized by an audience is important for her, she is not willing to achieve this by performing a TikTok persona with which she does not feel comfortable or represented. Now @annamaurer_music is concentrated on her own voice as a TikToker, a TikTok persona that is congruent with the other identities of her *self*. With this, we could say that @annamaurer_muisc finds herself in a consolidation phase of her TikTok persona. Moreover, an interesting aspect in this passage can be found in the topics @annamaurer_music has chosen to build her identity as TikToker: music (Jazz) and visagist (Make-up artist). These topics can be understood as genres and/or performative worlds in TikTok, which mark the context from which @annamaurer_music will negotiate her identity as a TikToker. Both performative contexts in which she participates have their distinct sets of conventions and expectations related to how the performance is executed and the identity portrayed by the TikToker. These are conventions and expectations she needs to be mindful of and adeptly fulfill. Therefore, the performance of her TikTok persona will be situated between two different performative contexts. This means that she has to move between conventions, expectations, and different aims in each context. Her task here will be to negotiate how this identity can be established and satisfactorily performed between these two contexts, negotiating with the audience a middle ground in which her TikTok persona is accepted in both contexts as it is: a particular TikTok identity for @annamaurer_music.

However, the process of finding "their voice" is for many TikTokers much more related to the idea of being "authentic." This is about being "authentic" in what they do, of having that *gewisses Etwas* (certain something), of making any performance their own, even if it wasn't the case originally. According to these TikTokers, what matters most is being authentic, because if you are authentic, performative and/or aesthetic qualities go to second place. @ar3miss mentions about this:

> A person simply has to be authentic … TikToks can also be shot with totally bad lighting or no good editing and so on, but if the person is authentic or

Überlegungen, wo man sich platziert oder keine Ahnung. Ja diese Duette, eben auch, da überlegt man, was denken die Leute, was könnte irgendwie relevant sein. Ja und ja natürlich dann gibt's halt auch diese TikTok-Trends, auf die man dann halt irgendwie automatisch kommt und dann eine Idee für ein Video bekommt, durch des, dass man diese Trends verfolgt (@annamaurer_music 2021). Translated from German to English by Natalia Neira Nieto.

> has something, so if a person makes a TikTok, [it will probably be successful.] Many videos have [a certain something,] authenticity or just something you can identify with.[18] (@ar3miss 2021)

Although the focus on authenticity is very common among TikTokers, being authentic is not a quality that TikTokers may or not have, as we might wrongly conclude. On the contrary, just like other aspects of the TikTok persona, authenticity is a performative act that can also be learned and is tied to the conventions and expectation of the social context where interaction is taking place. As mentioned by Kevin Brown, "the implication of framing 'authenticity' as a performance points out that notions of the authentic and inauthentic are merely constructions. Although authenticity does not 'exist' in the real world, performances of authenticity do" (Brown 2015: 78). These "performances of authenticity" are created and constituted through a long dialectic process of negotiation between the actors of TikTok musicking and are framed by conventions and expectations within a given social context. Just like authenticity ideals in jazz, baroque music, mariachi, or rock performances are not the same, neither are they between the different TikTok performative worlds. The work of TikTokers lies in getting acquainted with them and performing them. Therefore, being authentic is an act that TikTokers perform as part of their TikTok persona.

As previously discussed, performers seek to create and consolidate their TikTok persona through a long process of negotiation among the actors participating in TikTok's musicking. Either by betting on their performative individuality or creating certain authenticity conceptualization, TikTokers seek to learn to create, (re)negotiate, and actively perform—without radical contradictions—their identity as TikTokers in these contexts. For this reason, we can talk about musical performances and the performance of a TikTok persona as a double-performative act: on one side, this act is performed and (re)negotiates the identities of the musicking actors, both the TikTok persona and the audience. However, knowledge related to the developed musical practice is also performed and (re)negotiated. The development and negotiation

[18] Ein Mensch muss einfach authentisch sein. … Da können TikToks dann auch gedreht werden mit total schlechter Belichtung oder kein guter Schnitt und so, aber wenn die Person authentisch ist oder irgendwas hat, also wenn dann eine Person ein TikTok macht, [wird wahrscheinlich dieses erfolgreich.] Viele Videos haben [ein gewisses Etwas,] Authentizität oder halt irgendwas mit was man sich identifizieren kann (@ar3miss 2021). Translated from German to English by Natalia Neira Nieto.

process of a TikToker identity is a complex process. To continue approaching this phenomenon, I proceed to analyze some of the aspects Auslander calls the musical front.

Musical Front: Digital Intersectionalities

As previously discussed, the development and negotiation process of a TikTok identity is a process framed by conventions, expectations, and aims, as well as by aesthetic and authenticity conceptualizations according to the performative contexts in which the TikToker develops their musicking. However, negotiating and performing a TikTok persona is not exclusively framed by context and type of performance in which musical practices are carried out. A fundamental part of negotiating a TikTok persona is found in what Philip Auslander calls "the musical front" (see 2021: 97–109). Following Goffman (1959), Auslander suggests analyzing two levels in which "performances intersect with larger social contexts" (2021: 101), on one side, the "setting" that regards the physical context in which the performance takes place, but on the other, the "personal front" in which reference is made to the physical appearance and behavior of the performer during the performance. Thus, the appearance of the performer, as well as the physical context of the performance will equally frame and influence the development of musical practices, as well as the development and (re) negotiation of the TikTok persona.

Setting

According to Philip Auslander, the setting "contribute[s] to the impressions created by musical performances by drawing upon existing cultural connotations" (2021: 101). Although the performance is already framed by conventions, expectations, and aims, as well as by aesthetic and authenticity conceptualizations according to the performative genres developed by the TikToker in their musicking, the setting converges these ideals, thoughts, conventions, and so on about the established performance beyond a specific performance by a determined cultural cohort. This physical context, which could be a street, a bar, or a concert hall, will then determine the performance in a similar way. As observed by Christopher Small:

> Every building, from tiniest hut to the biggest airport terminal, is designed and built to house some aspect of human behavior and relationships, and is design

> reflects is builders' assumptions about that behavior and those relationships. Once built, it then has the power to impose those assumptions on what goes on within it. A conventional school building, for example … is built in accordance with certain assumptions about what young people in our society ought to learn and how they ought to learn it. But it also enforces those assumptions, making difficulties for those who might have different ideas. Even so everyday a structure as a family house or apartment makes, and enforces certain assumptions about family life and its relationships, about childhood, privacy, cleanliness and sex. (Small 1998: 20)

The performer positions their performance through the setting, either intentionally or coincidentally, in a specific cultural cohort. In this sense, the performer is forced to negotiate with the existing conventions and expectations of that cultural cohort, either to reaffirm or contest them just by performing in this setting. An example could be executing a performance of "contemporary classical music culture" in a concert hall that was exclusively designed for this purpose. This is not a basic need for this kind of musicking, but rather a reflection of certain ideals and thoughts, as well as distinction mechanisms (see Bourdieu [1984] 2010) of the cultural cohort in which this practice is developed.

> [Modern concert halls] are highly specialized buildings … The architects who design them, and the committees of civic authorities who commission and approve the designs, are for the most part members of the social group that tends to take part in such events. They know how people are supposed to behave there and will shape the building in ways that will encourage that behavior, at the same time closing off the possibility of behaviors of different kind … The grandeur of this building … tell us loudly and clearly [too] that the performances that take place here are an important social activity in their own right, not just as part of another ceremony or event. It tell us also that those who consider them important have the confidence and possess, or at least control, the wealth and the power to actualize that belief in architectural form. (Small 1998: 20–1)

Following this argument, we could then say that if a concert hall or any other setting is just a part of musicking "contemporary classical music culture" or any other musicking, these "do establish some general limits, or parameters, for [the] relationships [between actors] which can be, and are, brought into existence every time a musical performance takes place there" (Small 1998: 27). That said, settings frame and influence the development of musical practices, as well as the development and (re)negotiation of a musical persona, a situation that is equally valid when we reference TikTok musicking. Like any other musicking, TikTok musicking is also influenced by the ideals, thoughts, conventions, and so on related to the setting where performances are taking place. However, what is the performance setting of TikTok? How could this be understood in musical performances developed in multimedia environments?

There is no doubt that the idea of a setting can be applied to the musicking of TikTok. However, this idea is limited in its original conceptualization, since the original focuses on the physical characteristics of buildings and/or stages, which have marked "classical" performance contexts in many musical traditions. Therefore, digital and/or multimedia performative contexts in current musical practices were not considered in depth. For this reason, it is necessary to adapt this idea to the performative reality of multimedia musicking, which can be developed asynchronously and framed by a context that goes beyond a specific physical space. Consequently, when we talk about the setting of TikTok performances, we must consider and analyze at least three aspects that are complementary to each other: (1) the context of devices and infrastructure; (2) the performative possibilities of the platform that, though they are not exactly physical, influence the development of musical practices in a similar way; and (3) the physical context from which the performance is developed. The confluence of these three aspects creates the setting in which TikTok performances are developed.

Device and infrastructure context: The first aspect that constitutes the setting in TikTok musicking is the physicality of the devices and the connection infrastructure behind them. Whether a smartphone, a video camera, a computer, or other device, the physical properties of the devices frame the way in which performances are developed and how they relate with existing social factors. Similar to the stage of a concert hall, devices used for accessing the platform and/or recording a TikTok determine the action possibilities during the performance, as well as the relations between the main actors. The performative form and its possibilities will not be the same, for example, if we use a smartphone with reduced memory space and poor battery to record a video while holding it with our hands compared to using professional equipment to make the same recording. This would not just influence the form and context of the performance, but this would also shed light—and put into negotiation—certain class aspects, as well as notions of authenticity. Therefore, it is important to keep in mind that devices are not a neutral territory.

In the same way as with other buildings and/or stages, devices are "designed and built to house some aspect of human behavior and relationships," and just like them, their "design reflects builders' assumptions about that behavior and those relationships" (Small 1998: 20). Therefore, devices and connection infrastructure behind them are likely to converge the performance with ideals, thoughts, conventions, and so on that are linked to certain cultural cohorts and/or certain lifestyle particularly linked with the Global North. For example, an internet connection is required to access TikTok. Although this might seem trivial, access to the necessary infrastructure and the cost for that influence greatly on the way a performance will be articulated and negotiated. For instance, although theoretically anyone can partake in the musicking of TikTok, observing this from an Austrian context may differ greatly from a Cuban one. This situation presents one of the existing technological disparities in the contemporary world, which can be contemplated in correspondence to what Nick Couldry and Ulises Mejías call *data colonialism* (see 2019: 83–112).

Performative possibilities of the platform: The second aspect in the setting of TikTok musicking is found in the performative possibilities of the platform (see Chapter 2). Although these affordances are not exactly physical, their influence on the development of the performance is equally present. A clear example of this kind of influence is observed in the 9:16 video format, which clearly frames the way in which TikToks are recorded. In addition, they converge performances with ideals, thoughts, conventions, and so on established beyond a specific performance, similar to the device context and infrastructure. In the first place, and related to the previous point, though it is possible to assume that any person can download and use TikTok, not all musicking actors have access to all existing functions of the application. One reason for these differences is that, on the one hand, TikTok—as a company—is framed under the conditioning of national laws and regulations. These laws and regulations condition the action frame in which TikTok can develop its platform. Whether the platform is permitted or not, whether it has certain features or not, provides a clear example of this influence. That said, the possibility of using certain performative functions of the platform depends in some cases on where the TikToker is physically located.

However, these variations on the performative possibilities of the platform can also be generated by internal decisions of the company. For starters, TikTok follows internal politics and goals, from which decisions about enabling or disabling certain functions of the application in different countries or regions are taken. But also, as part of these politics, it is possible to observe that the availability of these functions differs depending on the level of popularity of the TikToker. One example, as already mentioned in previous chapters, is the *live* function, which is only available for users with more than a thousand followers. Additionally, as part of their creator support program, TikTok provides some TikTokers with exclusive or early access to certain functions before they are available for other performers. That way, the platform's performative possibilities, influenced by geopolitics and business strategies, constitute another level in which performers converge with ideals, thoughts, conventions, and so on about established performances beyond a specific performance by a determined cultural cohort. Performers will find themselves converging with geopolitical aspects beyond their control simply by having access and using certain functions of the platform, which consciously or unconsciously positions performances on certain social context beyond the particular identity of the performer.

Physical context of the performance: Finally, the third aspect constituting the setting in TikTok musicking is found in the physical context of the performance. Without a doubt, this is the most visible aspect and easiest to relate to the original idea of setting. The physical context of a performance regards the physicality of the place where it is taking place, either a private space, like a bedroom, or a public space, like a park or building. By using this physicality, the performer positions their performance—intentionally or not—in a specific cultural cohort, which therefore frames the development of their performance, making it converge with other specific sociocultural aspects, especially class and gender. In this sense, the performer is forced to negotiate with the existing conventions and expectations of that cultural cohort, either with the purpose of reaffirming them or confronting them, by the simple fact of being performed in that location.

Both the context of the devices and infrastructure and the performative possibilities of the platform, as well as the physical context from which the performance is developed, constitute altogether the setting in which TikTok performances are played out. These three aspects converge and intertwine with each other at the moment a performance takes place, carrying with them existing cultural connotations. By positioning their performance in this setting, the TikToker frames their performance in such connotations, intentionally or not. Consequently, all settings must be "congruent" with the performative identity of the TikToker. Deviating from anticipated conventions and expectations in this setting could create a misunderstanding of the performative context among actors in this musicking, a circumstance reflected in situations of rejection and/or criticism of performances that show another social reality from the one expected within a certain setting.

Personal Front: Performing Intersectionality

The process of creation, negotiation, and establishment of a TikTok persona is a complex one. TikTokers must negotiate conventions, expectations, and aims, as well as aesthetic and authenticity conceptualizations about performative genres and the setting in which they develop their musicking. Besides the aforementioned, this process of becoming is also framed by the body and voice of the TikToker. If, as already discussed, musicians perform their identity as musicians during a performance, they also perform their gender identity, class, race, and so on, and in a similar way, their performances are also read under the already existing mandates of genre, class, race, and so on. That said, the personal front refers to the point where the body and voice of a performer meets the intersectional mandates of genre, sexuality, race, age, class, ability, and so on linked to a given performative context.

Following Erving Goffman (1959), Philip Auslander proposes two levels for observing the performance and (re)negotiation of the socially constructed intersectional mandates: the "relatively fixed signs" (like gender and race) and the "relatively mobile signs" (like the way they dress or behave) (2021: 102). First, mandates of gender, class, and race are related to the bodies/voices performed, challenged, and negotiated during performances. The way these determine how the actor performs musicking depends on the performative context. However, this factor is always present. This influence can be easily observed in the fact that, for example, musical instruments appear subject to certain gender and class connotations (see Doubleday 2008) but also in the acceptation and/or rejection of certain subjectivities under a certain performative context. As mentioned by Auslander, "It is also the case that, for better or worse, such signs are crucially important in music cultures, given the way so many musical genres are stratified in relation to social identities (e.g., the problematic status of white jazz musicians, Black classical musicians, female conductors, women in rock and jazz, among others)" (2021: 102). This can be observed in the age of the actors, as in the case in which TikTok occasionally takes for granted that actors of a more advanced age have less knowledge and performative abilities than younger actors, the opposite of other musical traditions.

These intersectional mandates determine a great part of the first impressions the audience will have of the TikTok persona being performed, and consequently how this performer should behave according to their context and if they should carry out certain practices. For example, the expectation generated by the body of a young Black woman read as feminine performing a determined choreography is not the same as the expectation generated by an adult white male read as masculine performing the same choreography. As commented by Kiri Miller on popular dance genres, "[performances] transmit and reinforce established norms for moving one's body in ways considered appropriate to one's identity. Dance practices often articulate a bodily habitus that 'matches' an individual's intersectional profile of gender, sexuality, race, age, class, and ability, while dance-floor interactions model possible social relations" (Miller 2017: 62; see too Foster 2009, 2011). But it does not stop in the body: these embodiments also create an expectation of the voice (see Eidsheim 2019; Müller 2018, 2022). Accepting and/or rejecting one performance or another depends greatly on how the expectation generated by the performing body and/or voice corresponds to the identity attributed to the TikToker.

The expectations generated by the intersectional mandates that a performer attributes or is attributed to her body/performing voice frame how the performance will be carried out or how the TikTok persona will be performed. Thus, they consciously or unconsciously reproduce existing intersectional mandates through the performance of their TikTok persona. Whether ideals of "femininity," "masculinity," or "queerness," "whiteness," "blackness" or "alienness," the intersectional mandates that these subjectivities perform are, as Judith Butler would put it, "the forcible citation of a norm, one whose complex historicity is indissociable from relations of discipline, regulation, punishment" (Butler [1993] 2011:176; additionally, see Butler [1990] 2006; Connell [1995] 2005), which reflect assumptions about behaviors and ways of relating considered "acceptable" for a given society. What I find particularly interesting is that, although TikTokers are the ones who perform these intersectional mandates, the citation of these "norms," these are reinforced by the algorithms of the application.

The algorithms of TikTok are made for "catching" TikTokers and keep them using the application for the longest time possible. One way in which they try to do this is by creating a user profile based on the interactions this person has with the application, which will then structure to a great extent the future content presented to the user. In other words, TikTok algorithms aim to get to know our tastes and preferences for showing as accurately as possible what we *want* to see. By presenting previously curated content according to the specific sociocultural preferences of the user, the algorithms reinforce the intersectional mandates consumed and/or created by TikTokers. After a while, the algorithm exposes the user to cultural cohorts, and with it to a particular group of intersectional mandates that is getting closer to the ones known and reproduced by the user. By doing this, the algorithms exclude performances that are different from what it perceives are the tastes of the user, consequently excluding possible divergent intersectional mandates, putting into practice "the normative force of performativity," which, as said by Butler, has the power "to establish what qualifies as 'being' … not only through reiteration, but through exclusion as well" (Butler [1993] 2011: 140). It is interesting to observe that these exclusion processes are more clearly reflected on race aspects than those of gender, class, age, and ability.

Inequality and mechanisms of exclusion resulting from historical colonialism are also reflected on the application. TikTok has shown to be a predominantly white territory. BIPOC performers have much more difficulties for establishing themselves as professional TikTokers, besides the fact that credit for their work has been (and continues being) taken mostly by white performers (see Boffone 2021). The following comment by @mintydkalu shows her perception of this phenomenon:

> We have many black creators who contribute to the app like dancing, which is one of the most important factors of the app. Everyone knows a dance from TikTok and most of the dances from TikTok are created by black creators. Often the problem was that a black creator created a dance and then the same dance was performed by a person with a different skin colour and that video ended up being pushed by the algorithm [more] than the original one.[19] (@ mintydkalu 2021)

This situation has been very well documented by Trevor Boffone (2021). One of the examples presented by Boffone is that of the "renegade" choreography by Jalaiah Harmon, which was appropriated by Charlie D'Amelio, who became one of the most followed TikTokers in the world by performing these dances and earning millions of dollars for doing so, while Harmon, like many other young black people, remained completely ignored for a very long time. After receiving

[19] Wir haben viele schwarze Creators, die der App beitragen wie das Tanzen, was einer der wichtigste Faktor der App ist. Jeder kennt einen Tanz von TikTok und die meisten Tänze von TikTok kreiert von schwarzen Creators. Oft war das Problem, dass ein schwarzer Creator einen Tanz erstellt hat und dann wurde der gleiche Tanz von einer Person mit einer anderen Hautfarbe aufgeführt und dass dieses Video im Endeffekt von dem Algorithmus [mehr] gepushed wurde, als das Originale (@ mintydkalu 2021). Translated from German to English by Natalia Neira Nieto.

a lot of criticism on these situations, TikTok has tried to change by increasing their support for BIPOC performers in the platform. This is reflected not only on support programs for BIPOC creators but also by introducing and promoting a "give credit" function for recognizing the original performance and its creator. However, there is still a long way to go. Many intersectional inequalities are still present in the application, reminding us that digital platforms are not neutral territories but rather reflect assumptions, ideals, and prejudices of a certain society, circumstances to which TikTokers are exposed.

As we have seen up to now, these intersectional mandates frame the acting of musicking actors and determine to a great extent how the TikTok persona of a performer will be perceived and read by an audience. However, since these intersectional mandates are a performative act, these can be put to negotiation by performers during their performances. We can observe an example of this in the negotiation of intersectional voice-body relationships. The technical possibilities of the application allow separating the voice from the performing body, which makes it easier to do transgression acts against these mandates. This way, an act of transgression toward these intersectional mandates used on TikTok can take place in the performance of a voice that does not "fit" to the visible body.

As observed by Johan Fornäs in the case of karaoke:

> Performers can opt to sing a song in a new and different way, but it is also possible to create a provocative contrast to the original only by one's choice of song, i.e., by virtue of one's social and subjective identity. For example, one might choose a song that "fits" an age group, sex, class, ethnicity, geography or taste that is far from one's own position. When men sing a song that is normally sung by women, the "first-person voice" of which is conventionally perceived as female, exciting tensions may arise. (Fornäs 1994: 98)

This ability to perform with a voice that does not "fit" with the performing body puts into negotiation a series of conventions and expectations during the performance, which are marked by existing genre mandates, creating a confrontation space, an in-between space in which new meanings are created, and maybe in the future new intersectional mandates too, giving TikTok a space for creating and negotiating the TikTok persona.

The prevailing intersectional mandates do not only influence musicians and audiences in the contexts in which they perform, but they also reproduce and negotiate these and other intersectional mandates, both using their persona (i.e., using their corporality and multivocality [Meizel 2020]), as well as in the visual and sound worlds that they create through their musical performances (see Buttler [1993] 2011; Eidsheim 2019; Auslander 2021). Musical and vocal practices and their corporality are also a fundamental social space for the construction of gender, class, and race (see Cusick 1994; Eidsheim 2019; Müller 2018, 2022). The audience, as we will discuss in the following section, will play an exceptional role in the construction and negotiation of these meanings.

The Audience

Up to this point, we have been discussing the process of becoming a TikToker as a dynamic and multilevel process framed by conventions, expectations, and goals, as well as aesthetic and authenticity conceptualizations in the performance, the performative contexts, and the corporality and vocality of the performer. Although this process seems to already be very complex, there is still one more factor to consider, which determines if a performer will be able to perform their TikTok persona satisfactorily. I refer to the audience accepting and acknowledging the identity as a TikTok persona claimed by the performer. After all, it depends on the audience if a performer is able or not to perform a certain TikTok persona. As stated by Philip Auslander:

> The presentation of a front is not an end in itself, of course: it is the first step in the execution of a routine, a step that constitutes an implicit claim to be taken seriously in a particular social role … Following the performer's staking of [an implicit or explicit claim to be a person of a particular kind], the actual performance of the routine either bolsters the audience's willingness to accept the performer's claim to a certain identity, or provides the audience with reasons to discredit it. In relation to musical performance, this means that performers use their fronts to claim musical identities that are ultimately either secured or problematized by the relationship of their actual playing of music to the initial definition of the situation they projected. (Auslander 2021: 117–18)

The first step for achieving this legitimization lies on being recognized—to be taken seriously—as a performer inside and outside the application by other musicking actors. Being acknowledged as a performer is essential for constructing a TikTok persona. Without it, a performance may not be considered as such and even perceived as a failure, a situation that would not permit the performer to consolidate an identity as a TikToker and put at risk the development of their musicking. This is the reason why, before anything else, a TikToker must seek the acceptance of their identity as a performer. This is not a difficult task inside the application. Learning to read the stipulated musicking roles does not take much time when using the application and taking part in the musicking of TikTok. For example, when I watch a TikTok, I interpret the role of the audience whereas when I record a video, I interpret my role as a performer. Consequently, the person who watches the TikTok that I previously performed will recognize me as a performer and react to my persona as such. This is an act of make-believe continuously performed. However, outside the application, there is a very different reality.

Certainly, the quest for acknowledgment also takes place outside the platform with the family and friends of the TikToker. Although these groups of people are not automatically TikTok users and therefore do not need to actively participate to support the performances, these friends and/or family will nonetheless be part of the support network in the career of the TikToker. For this reason, their acknowledgment of the performer identity of the TikToker is key. In this sense, the following anecdote by @mintydkalu allows us to approach this phenomenon:

> In the beginning I know exactly. I've always shot my videos in my room and I share the room with my big brother. In the beginning, my setup was really weird. I had a music stand that I always had to push down to shoot TikToks, and my brother had to listen to the sound I used over and over again because I had to record more often and he didn't understand what I was doing. "Michi, you've been listening to this sound for five minutes, please stop." That was his reaction and I had to explain to him what I was doing and what TikTok actually is. So for him it was really funny and above all my parents were worried about me because I was partly recording TikToks in the room for an hour while the others had already finished eating and my mother asked "Michi, what are you doing" and I was halfway through changing and had to explain that I was filming TikTok. So they didn't really understand and were of the opinion that since I have Instagram and Snapchat anyway, TikTok wasn't really necessary. But then I showed them a funny video, which they could understand. I also made videos for a short time where the topic was family and the topic was often the African family and there were also scenarios that only the Congolese from my culture could understand and they understood that and also found it funny. And after a while, I also told them that my follower count is constantly growing and that I am getting more likes and views and then through these short conversations have become long conversations and we even had a conversation with the whole family about what

> TikTok is doing and I explained to them that there are a lot of people on TikTok who are making money and who have also got business offers like from Nike to school offers, acting career etc. and the current point of view is that TikTok is not just a place for people to go to. and the current point of view is that my little brother also started with TikTok because he saw how I also benefit from it, like money but also that I get a lot of followers, likes and comments. My mum is also impressed with what I have been able to create on the app, my older brother also talks about me to his friends and he tells me that they found me on the app.[20] (@mintydkalu 2021)

The anecdote of @mintydkalu clearly exemplifies how he got his performer identity to be taken seriously by his family. Their support made it easier for him to carry out his musicking, easing the process of creating, negotiating, and performing his TikTok persona. However, the situation experienced by other TikTokers without this kind of acknowledgment is not so optimistic. The lack of encouragement and/or recognition—either by their families or friends—not only deprives them of a support network during their careers, but they might also have to confront many other obstacles (disapproval, discussions, prohibitions, etc.), making it hard for them to develop their musicking. Here lies the importance of TikTokers having their performer identities acknowledged by their families and friends, especially if they are hoping to professionally perform a TikTok persona.

Being accepted as a performer by participants in TikTok musicking and/or by family and friends is not just the first step to acquiring legitimacy for their TikTok persona. Once the TikToker is recognized as a performer, they must continue creating and negotiating their specific TikTok persona identity with the audience. As we have discussed in this chapter, the performer will keep on sculpting their TikToker identity with their performances, creating a dialogue with their audience to build a niche in which they can consolidate their TikTok

[20] Am Anfang habe ich noch ein bisschen reagiert auf die negativen Kommentaren und irgendwann hab ich mir gedacht okay das bringt nix, das macht keinen Sinn da irgendwie Diskussionen online zu führen mit random Leuten, aber es hat mich schon schockiert, also diese negativen Kommentare, die haben schon sehr heftig gewirkt auf mich. Ich habe [mich] dann schon ein bisschen befassen müssen damit. Aber ja es war weird, weil ich noch nie so stark mit Sexismus konfrontiert war und eben auch aus meinem Umfeld nicht kenn, deshalb hat es mich besonders schockiert. Ja und ich glaube das muss man ein bisschen ausblenden und man muss zu seinen Kommentaren und seine Videos dann stehen und was dann diese Leute, denen das vorgeschlagen wird und mit dem Thema nix zu tun haben, was die dann darüber denken, muss man dann ein bisschen ausblenden aber vielleicht triffts den einen oder anderen, der dann ein bisschen umdenkt, die Hoffnung stirbt zuletzt (@mintydkalu 2021). Translated from German to English by Natalia Neira Nieto.

persona. This way, the TikToker will not only learn to position their performance and use positive aspects for consolidating their identity as TikToker but also learn to endure, negotiate, and/or counteract possible rejection against their persona. As mentioned by @annamaurer_music:

> At the beginning I reacted a bit to the negative comments and at some point I thought to myself, okay, there's no point, there's no point in having any kind of discussion online with random people, but it shocked me, these negative comments, they had a very strong effect on me. I had to deal with it a little bit. But yes, it was weird, because I've never been confronted with sexism so strongly and I don't know it from my environment, so it shocked me particularly. Yes, and I think you have to fade out a bit and you have to stand by your comments and your videos, and what these people, to whom this is suggested and who have nothing to do with the topic, think about it, you have to fade out a bit, but maybe it will hit one or the other, who will then change their mind a bit, hope dies last.[21] (@annamaurer_music 2021)

As already mentioned, the process of developing and negotiating a TikToker identity is framed by conventions, expectations, and aims, as well as aesthetic and authenticity conceptualizations regarding the performative contexts in which the TikToker develops their musicking. These contexts frame the foundation from which the TikToker negotiates their identity as TikToker. This way, the role of these conventions, expectations, aims, and so on, as well as the audience, is essential for the process of establishing a TikToker identity. These roles not only frame the kind and direction in which this process of identity creation will be shaped, but they will also determine the chances of being solidified satisfactorily or not. As indicated by Auslander:

> There is a continuum from types of musical performance in which the musicians' personae are strongly mandated because they are built into the framing

[21] Am Anfang habe ich noch ein bisschen reagiert auf die negativen Kommentaren und irgendwann hab ich mir gedacht okay das bringt nix, das macht keinen Sinn da irgendwie Diskussionen online zu führen mit random Leuten, aber es hat mich schon schockiert, also diese negativen Kommentare, die haben schon sehr heftig gewirkt auf mich. Ich habe [mich] dann schon ein bisschen befassen müssen damit. Aber ja es war weird, weil ich noch nie so stark mit Sexismus konfrontiert war und eben auch aus meinem Umfeld nicht kenn, deshalb hat es mich besonders schockiert. Ja und ich glaube das muss man ein bisschen ausblenden und man muss zu seinen Kommentaren und seine Videos dann stehen und was dann diese Leute, denen das vorgeschlagen wird und mit dem Thema nix zu tun haben, was die dann darüber denken, muss man dann ein bisschen ausblenden aber vielleicht triffts den einen oder anderen, der dann ein bisschen umdenkt, die Hoffnung stirbt zuletzt. (@annamaurer_music 2021). Translated from German to English by Natalia Neira Nieto.

> conventions of a particular genre … to types in which musicians have a great deal of freedom to construct personae. In no case, however, is the musician in a position to construct a persona autonomously—personae are always negotiated between musicians and their audiences within the constraints of genre framing. (Auslander 2021: 122)

This way, the TikToker will depend on the acceptation and legitimization of the audience for being able to claim and perform their TikTok persona. It is here, in this legitimization, where we can observe the difference between the two types of TikTok persona I mentioned at the beginning of this subchapter. Although any performer may carry out a particular identity after being recognized, not all identities get acknowledged and legitimized as possessing a specific TikTok persona. Once a specific TikToker identity is consolidated, the performer persuades the audience—either intentionally or unintentionally—to begin a process of legitimization of their TikToker identity, a process through which the performer becomes a TikToker. Through my research I have been able to observe two kinds of legitimization with acts that could be considered rituals: the process of legitimization by the community and the process of legitimization by TikTok as a company.

In the first case, the audience decides whether to legitimize a TikToker identity or not. This legitimization process can be seen through mutually related factors. One factor is the number of followers and likes, which function as indicators of the acceptance certain TikTok persona has in the community, in turn becoming a sample of legitimization granted by the community. Although it is difficult and almost useless to quantify and/or set an exact number to indicate the border of legitimization, it is possible to observe that once a TikToker reaches one hundred thousand followers, they are given a special status and prestige. Additionally, having a high number of followers reflects the acceptance and legitimization the audience gives a TikTok persona.

This status and the consequent legitimization of their TikTok identity represents a milestone in the career of TikTokers, while additionally bringing certain pressures and expectations linked to their status as TikToker. @savage.hersi mentions that:

> Once I've cracked my 100 K, I think I would develop a pressure, because there's also this "shadow banned"[22] at TikTok, that your videos are simply not shown

[22] For an example of a "shadow banned" process, see Rauchberg (2022a).

> if you don't upload regularly, I think that's where the pressure comes in, but fortunately I haven't had that yet. Most of the time, when I have uploaded them, I still see that my community is well reached and that they really interact, but with very many, with a friend for example, I think she has 200,000 or so or a bit more. With her, I really see that if she hasn't uploaded anything for a month or two weeks, she really only has 2,000 views, which doesn't match up with the amount of followers she has.[23] (@savage.hersi 2021)

Moreover, acceptation and legitimization of a certain performative identity is reflected by the sense of community and the reciprocity bonds created between the TikTok persona and their audience. When the audience decides to accept and legitimize a TikTok persona, they also accept and legitimize their identity as follower, generating emotional and reciprocity bonds with the TikToker as well. Thus, the existence/performance of a sense of "belonging" between a TikToker and their audience shows us another aspect of legitimization. One example of this sense of community and reciprocity can be observed in the comment by @ar3miss:

> There are those who have been with TikTok for, I don't know how long, and they've been with me since the beginning, and they write me "I just love you" and "I've been with you since the beginning," "I've been through every phase of you," where I know exactly, ok, they've seen every [video.] They've also seen sad videos now; it's not like "I only want the dance videos from you, I'm not interested in the rest of you," but they really like me as a person, so from that point of view I would say that this is a community. I don't know … People have often written to me on Instagram and talked about their problems and that they can identify with me here, and it has also given me support, not just them, and that is already community-like.[24] (@ar3miss 2021)

[23] Wenn ich mal meine 100 K geknackt habe, ich glaub, dann würde Ich schon einen Druck entwickeln, weil da sind ja auch, bei TikTok ist halt dieses "shadow banned," dass deine Videos einfach nicht angezeigt werden, wenn du nicht regelmäßig hochlädst, ich glaub, da kommt der Druck dann auch, aber das hatte ich bis jetzt zum Glück noch nicht. Meistens, wenn ich die dann hochgeladen habe, dass ich dann immer noch sehe, dass meine Community gut erreicht wird und die dann auch wirklich interagieren, aber bei sehr vielen, bei einer Freundin beispielsweise, ich glaub die hat 200.000 oder so oder ein bisschen mehr. Bei der ihr sehe ich das wirklich, wenn die ein Monat oder zwei Wochen nichts hochgeladen hat, dass sie dann wirklich nur 2000 Aufrufe hat, was ja bei der Menge an Followern, die sie hat, nicht zusammenpasst (@savage.hersi 2021). Translated from German to English by Natalia Neira Nieto.

[24] Es gibt halt welche, die seit, ich weiß nicht wie lange es TikTok gibt, und die sind schon seit Anfang an dabei, und schreiben mir dann halt "ich liebe dich einfach" und "ich bin schon von Anfang an dabei," "habe jede Phase von dir durchgemacht," wo ich genau weiß, ok die haben jedes [Video gesehen.] Die haben auch traurige Videos jetzt gesehen; es ist jetzt nicht so "ich möchte nur die

A substantial peculiarity of this phenomenon lies in the fact that the presence and development of a sense of community and reciprocity lead to creating a performative act in TikTok musicking, which allows to set a point of inflection in the relationship between the audience and the TikTok persona: the Meetup. These events in which TikTokers meet their followers are organized by TikTokers who have reached certain recognition of their TikTok persona and wish to legitimize themselves as such. The transformative power of these Meetups lies in the power they have for converting a virtual reality into an actual embodied reality, generating a bodily sense of community, and thus, enabling the negotiation of much more intense and lasting relationships of friendship and reciprocity between the TikToker and their audience. In this sense, a Meetup works as a kind of ritual process (see Turner [1969] 2017) that consents and legitimizes the status of TikTokers as such, additionally creating and/or renewing reciprocity and community bonds between the TikToker and their followers.

Although the TikToker depends on the acceptance and legitimization of the audience for claiming and performing their TikTok persona, this can also receive legitimization directly from TikTok. In the course of time, TikTok has created many programs to support creators. Being a certified creator or participating in any of these programs serves as a visible indicator of the status and prestige a TikToker holds, comparable to the number of followers (see Figure 12). This status is a form of capital that legitimizes the TikToker as a TikTok persona and enables them to develop their performances from this position.

Additionally, an interesting aspect of this validation strategy of TikTok is found in the fact that besides acknowledging a certain TikTok persona, this validation leads the TikToker to develop reciprocity bonds with TikTok. One example of this is clearly noted by @mintydkalu:

> I think so [that I watch a lot of TikTok] and one reason is because the videos are fun and sometimes you can't stop watching TikToks. But the second reason is because the programme invests in me and I believe that I also need to show so that the algorithm recognises that I am a friendly user and I show that by

Tanzvideos von dir, der Rest von dir interessiert mich nicht," sondern die mögen mich wirklich als Mensch, so von daher würde ich schon sagen, das ist eine Community. Ich weiß nicht. … Es haben mir oft welche geschrieben über Instagram und geredet über ihre Probleme und, dass sie sich hier identifizieren können mit mir und es hat halt mir auch Halt gegeben, nicht nur ihnen, und das ist schon Community-mäßig (@ar3miss 2021). Translated from German to English by Natalia Neira Nieto.

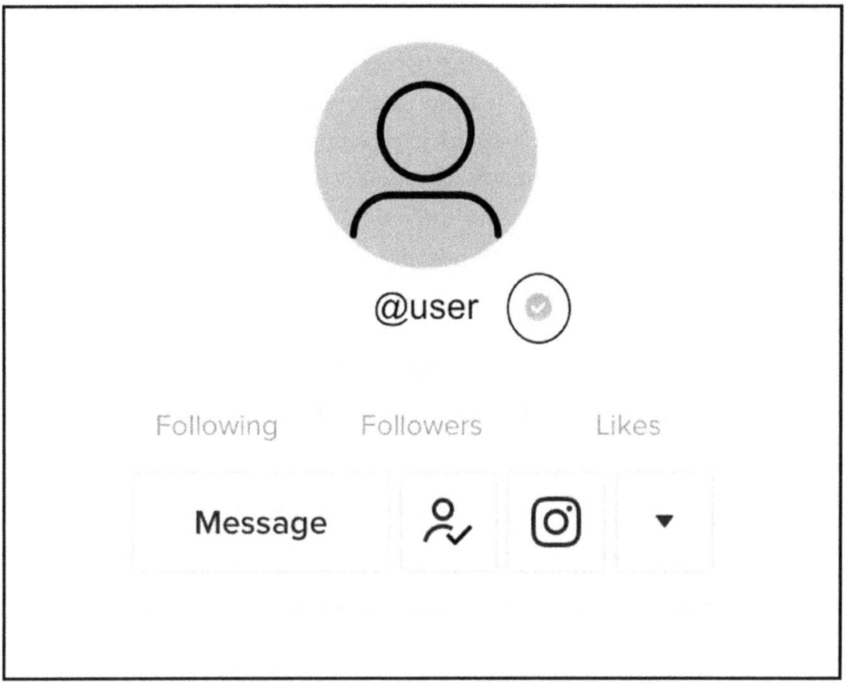

Figure 12 Certified creator, illustration by Belén Vera.

> commenting on other TikToks, liking, following other people and interacting with the programme.[25] (@mintydkalu 2021)

Creators feel grateful with the recognition and support given by TikTok and seek to demonstrate this in some way. It is not just the identity of the TikToker being recognized, but through this legitimization, TikTok encourages the TikToker to continue with their practices on the application, reinforcing a sense of belonging and ensuring musicking continuity.

[25] Ich glaube schon[, dass ich viel TikTok schaue] und ein Grund dafür ist, weil die Videos Spaß machen und manchmal kannst du nicht aufhören TikToks anzuschauen. Aber der zweite Grund ist, weil das Programm investiert in mich und ich glaube, dass ich auch zeigen muss, so dass der Algorithmus erkennt, dass Ich ein freundlicher User bin, und das zeige ich indem ich bei anderen TikToks kommentiere, like, Andere Leuten folge und mit dem Programm interagiere (@mintydkalu 2021). Translated from German to English by Natalia Neira Nieto.

TikToking a Musical Persona

Up to this point we have been able to observe that the creation, negotiation, and performance of a TikTok persona is a dynamic and multilevel process. This process is framed by conventions, expectations, and aims, as well as by the aesthetic and authenticity conceptualization regarding the performance and the performative contexts, and the corporality and vocality of the performer. Performers find themselves in a constant process of negotiation with other actors in TikTok musicking for reaffirming or counteracting the existing conventions, expectations, and aims in a given performative context, stepping into a dialectic process for generating knowledge, which is reflected in the amplified model of Alan P. Merriam (1964; see too Chapter 1). But beyond the performance negotiation, TikTokers seek to learn to create, (re)negotiate, and actively perform their TikTok identity in these contexts without radical contradictions. Likewise, they seek recognition and validation of their identity as a particular TikTok persona, either directly from TikTok or from the audience. This allows us to view musical performance and the performance of a TikTok persona as a dual act of performance. The TikTok persona and the audience perform and (re) negotiate their identities as musicking actors, as well as the associated knowledge related to the musical practice in which it is developed.

4

Localizing TikTok

My first encounter with TikTok and its musical practices took place in digital form. I started to move in a digital environment that was new to me. Without really being an active participant, I had already played a short video, a so-called "TikTok." After a couple of minutes of watching these videos, my interaction with the screen became more profound. Little by little I would start to feel a strange sense of proximity with the performing TikTokers on my phone. A peculiar feeling of closeness to the performing TikTokers surged; a sort of co-presence would grow between us. After a few minutes, my perception of the physical environment surrounding me gradually vanished. As I was scrolling, there was nothing else but the performance, the performer, her audience, and me, an intimate space created and lived just between us. Time passed and I got involved in two parallel conversations that revolved around fashion and coolness, which were flooded by a vehement discussion about the "I-follow-you-if-you-follow-me principle."[1] An abrupt movement pulled my perception back to the physical world: the train where my physical self was sitting was on its way again, as I realized that I had missed my station a while ago. In the meantime, I had become part of the musicking of TikTok, but at this moment, all I could perceive was a specific, reduced musical geography. It was easy for me to assume that behind most of those performances, an actual physical person was there. Yet, from my point of view, I was not able to observe the physical body and its resulting interactions.

On another occasion, after a long day at the university, I took the train home. The train was crowded with young people. In the middle of an orgiastic mix of sound, I recognized a striking melody that was briefly played over and over, which was currently being used for TikTok performances. Four youngsters were sitting around a table in the train, and a smartphone was laying on the

[1] A similar phenomenon was observed by Patricia Lange (2019) in her research on video sharing on YouTube.

table. They were all staring at the screen as the distinctive TikTok melody was playing. I observed a typical practice of TikTok musicking: just like in my own experience, these kids were watching an asynchronous performance and, unlike me, they were watching it as a group. What happened next took me by surprise. These young people started to analyze the performance, to imitate the sequences, and to criticize the aesthetic properties. They played the same TikTok over and over again and established a correlation to other versions of the same music piece. Then they started a discussion to explore different possibilities of making individual or group versions of the same TikTok, a discussion that would end thanks to a final message sent through WhatsApp by a certain Julia from school, saying that it would be better if they met the next day to do a duet after school.

Although the previous scene took place in a physical environment, this encounter was part of a network of multimedia interactions and interrelations that different actors constructed through asynchronous spaces of experience. What I saw was four teenagers using a smartphone, who were practicing choreographic movements and analyzing a video; four teenagers who were spending leisure time together. What I was not able to see were the other localities that were coming across each other through asynchronous mediatized connections. I did not see the performers, nor the other actors, much less the connections created. Julia was also invisible to me. Nevertheless, all of them were present there. In this ephemeral instant, all these asynchronously created and experimented locations connected with each other to create a unique multimedia locality. And well, here is where the real problem for us resides. As ethnomusicologists and ethnographers, we usually convey ourselves to the field to observe, analyze, and describe the practices that help us to understand the construction of knowledge in a musical tradition. But how does this work when our musical practice does not seem to have a discernible field?

This chapter is about the musical geography of TikTok from an Austrian context. To understand the way in which localities in the musicking of TikTok are articulated and negotiated, in the first part, I will discuss the concepts of presence, co-presence, empathic co-presence, and non-presence as ways of critically reflecting on the ideas of "being there" or "being present," which are very important for ethnographic work. Additionally, I will introduce and discuss the concept of *musical geography through practice*. Following these reflections, the second part of this chapter examines and discusses how some of the TikTok practices can and did take place across multiple, interconnected platforms. For the third part of the chapter, I will analyze the different strategies that the

TikTokers use for inhabiting, transforming, and making sense of the musical geography of TikTok from an Austrian context.

Toward a Musical Geography through Praxis[2]

Even if we supported the idea of multilocality in musical practices, assuming the existence of a predominant physical interaction in these practices could become a "problem" for researching musical traditions with multilocal physical and virtual spaces of interaction, such as the case of TikTok. The problem lies in that we often still lean into thinking about the ethnographic field the way that Malinowski experienced and conceived it (see Malinowski 1922). However, many of our contemporary musical practices show us a very different reality from this ideal. The locality of many of these practices does not have a clear physical location or exists almost exclusively as an abstract and *imaginary* construct. Also, many of these practices do not need face-to-face contact among their actors to maintain the mechanisms of production and experience of their auditive knowledge (see Mendívil 2008). In other cases, as Peter Wicke has pointed out, these practices barely experience a concrete location in the moment of their reception (2001: 25), processes that have made the synchronous experience of the physical performance unnecessary for the actors. This multimedia reality shown in many of our contemporary musical practices invites us to rethink how we understand the ethnographic field, taking our notion beyond the idea of a *field* as a delimited physical geography with synchronous practices, but instead inviting us to take our conceptualization of this field beyond the *tangible*.

Me and the Others

Like other ethnographers, ethnomusicologists often go to the field to observe, analyze, and describe practices that allow the construction of an auditory

[2] This subchapter was originally published in a slightly different form in: Juan Bermúdez. "It's All About 'Being There': Rethinking Presence and Co-presence in the Ethnographic Field During and After the Covid-19 Pandemic." In "Between Memory and Knowledge–Sounding the Pandemic," edited by Maurizio Agamennone, Antonella Dicuonzo, Daniele Palma, Ludovico Peroni, and Giulia Sarno. Special Issue, *Journal of World Popular Music* 10, no. 1 (2023): 19–35. © Equinox Publishing Ltd [2023]. https://doi.org/10.1558/jwpm.26375. Reprinted with the permission of Equinox Publishing Ltd.

knowledge in a musical tradition. Ethnomusicologist believe in fieldwork (see Nettl 2005: 12–15) and the virtue of "being there" still marks the discipline, or as put by Timothy Rice: "in [ethnomusicological] credo we have the privileging of ontology (being there) over epistemology (knowing that)" (2008: 46). However, to investigate a musicking like that of TikTok it is necessary to reflect about the meaning of this condition under the multimedia reality already presented and adapt its conceptualization based on a phenomenological perspective.

In a multimedia ethnographic research (E^3thnography), "being there" cannot be seen from the point of view of how our physical body is positioned anymore, but from our embodied consciousness that forms part of these practices. Therefore, this embodied consciousness is the one that inhabits our environments, virtual or physical. This also applies to all actors in the musicking of TikTok, not just to us researchers. The relationships between actors are also based on their embodied consciousness, and not on their physical bodies, for which it is important to rethink the concept of *presence* and understand it beyond the *tangible*.[3] In the idea of a geography through practice, our social relations and the practices within them are based in the imperative of "being there," of the encounter of actors through and for the development of practices, which enable making sense and meaning to the spaces in daily life. Understanding this, I assume four basic forms in which the relationships between actors in these encounters can be understood: *presence*, *co-presence*, *empathic co-presence*, and *non-presence*.

Firstly, I use the term *presence* to refer to the *conscious participation in physical and synchronous interaction* among actors in the context of a particular musicking. In other words, actors articulate and negotiate their practices at the same time and in the same physical space, in this case, the social space created occupies a concrete and delimitated physical place. Under this form, "being there" takes place in an ethnographic field that somehow obeys the ideal of Malinowski (1922) of concrete and delimitated physical place and time. In TikTok, we can find this kind of presence when observing some of the relations that the actors perform outside the application, like in the story at the beginning of this chapter about the four teenagers discussing a TikTok performance on their way home from school. This scene is not observable from the application by itself. Our ethnographic field here occupies—during the moment of the

[3] It is worth noting that while relationships are not based primarily on the physical body, it does not mean that the physical body is not a necessary and primary condition for any possible relationship.

discussion—a concrete and delimitated physical place, where the actants of our studied musicking and us (researchers) are interacting on a same space and time, we are *present*.

In contrast, I use the term *co-presence* to refer to the *conscious participation in multimedia and asynchronous interaction* of the actors in the context of a particular musicking. In this case, actors articulate and negotiate their practices through multimedia spaces, for example, the internet, and during different times and rhythms (see Couldry and Hepp 2017; Lange 2019). In this case, the social space created does not exclusively exist on a concrete place and time but is rather spread along diverse physical and digital spaces, and therefore evoking through the practices that make it up. Under this figure, "being there" happens in an articulated and negotiated ethnographical field through the practices of musicking itself. Our body "is not (physically) there," but our embodied consciousness makes part of this field through its practice.

In TikTok we can find this kind of *co-presence* in two ways. The first kind of co-presence can be observed in performances and practices developed outside the application and along digital media, that is, YouTube, Instagram, Snapchat, among others. Here our field is constructed along multimedia localities that are spread around the world. Our embodied consciousness is part of an articulated field and is negotiated through different times and spaces. Our smartphones—or any other device—play an important role, not as a portal of representation but as a corporal extension of our consciousness. The second way we can observe *co-presence* is through the practices of this musicking that are developed through multimedia spaces. Taking again the example of the story about the teenagers on the train, a state of *co-presence* can be experienced in the moment in which the actors see the video together in a physical location, become part of the performance, comment through the application, and discuss among themselves physically and with Julia through WhatsApp. The actors of the musicking we are studying and ourselves are interacting asynchronously in a multimedia space; we are *co-present*.

The third type of relation is what I refer to as *empathic co-presence*, a much more abstract and less visible phenomenon. *Empathic co-presence* refers to the *affective and highly embodied association created after the conscious re-embedding in a synchronous and physical space, of participation and interaction previously experienced as multimedia and asynchronous* by the actors in a particular musicking. In other words, this type of affective relationship manifests after experiencing a physical encounter with someone we only know through a multimedia environment. This relation is supported by the feeling resulting from the actualization of a virtual relation. When inhabiting our environment, we not only make sense and give meaning to the spaces in which we act, but we also make them our own through the highly embodied affective associations we create. Surely you know this feeling, it feels different to interact with someone we know physically as opposed to someone we know only through the internet: a kind of co-presence charged with a strong sense of proximity, confidence, and embodiment. In the same way as co-presence "being there" takes place in an ethnographic field that is articulated and negotiated by the embodied consciousness through its musicking practices, but the feeling of community and confidence is different.

Based on my ethnographic research, I can affirm that the creation and preservation of an empathic co-presence are of great importance for the actors of the musicking of TikTok. The TikTokers not only seek contact with their followers through the app but also seek to meet them physically. In this context, the many "spontaneous" or "organized" meetings that TikTokers set with their audience, such as those carried out by @anna_strigl or @lisaandlena in February 2020 in Vienna, stand out particularly. Through these meetings, TikTokers do not just seek economic incentives, but they also expect to create a more intensive embodied confidence between the actors, which allows them to create strong ties of reciprocity and maintain what Anthony Giddens calls *ontological security*[4] (1991: 92). This ontological security allows us to feel *at home*, and therefore it is necessary for inhabiting and appropriating the phantasmagorical realities of our modern world, placing here its importance.

The fourth type of relation encompasses a series of phenomena complementary to the previously mentioned, which I refer to as *non-presence*. On one side, this concept refers to the *unconscious presence* of the actors in the context of a particular musicking. For articulating and negotiating a practice with another actor, the participation with our embodied consciousness is necessary, and therefore "being there," unconsciously sharing a physical and/or digital space, does not automatically make us present, but takes us to a *non-present* condition instead. An example of this kind of non-presence can be observed during the Meetup of @lisamarie_schiffner at a Viennese mall. Around three hundred teenagers are in

[4] With *ontological security* Giddens "refers to the confidence that most humans beings have in the continuity of their self-identity and in the constancy of the surrounding social and material environments of action. … Ontological security has to do with 'being' or, in the terms of phenomenology, 'being-in-the-world'" (Giddens 1991: 92).

line to take a photo with her. @lisamarie_schiffner and the teenagers perform one of the many physical activities that make up TikTok musicking. Nonetheless, for those who were not acquainted with this musicking, for the other people in the mall, this crowd was not comprehended and was perceived as an impediment to their activities. The name of the TikToker, TikTok, or the reason for the practice that took place there were completely foreign for these people. I could see that the bodies of the other people in the mall were there, a few meters away from the TikToker and her followers, but their minds were elsewhere. They were not part of the musicking of TikTok; these people were non-present.

On the other hand, the concept of non-presence also refers to the phenomena of *digital death*. Our digital practices can leave digital objects and/or personae that still exist and have agency independently from us as individuals, even after our death. However, this posthuman existence is not infinite. Under the idea of musical geography through practice, these digital objects/personae can only *actually exist* as long as *conscious* participation and interaction by the actors of our musicking is there, be it physical or multimedia, synchronous or asynchronous. If these digital objects/personae stop being co-present for the actors, they lose their current existence, passing to a state of *non-presence*. Digitally they exist in some server—in "the cloud"—but they are no longer existent for us, for the actors of musicking; these digital objects/personae become alive and dead at the same time: a state of uncertainty that could remind us of Schrödinger's cat (Schrödinger 1935: 812).

Having already introduced the concepts of presence, co-presence, empathic co-presence, and non-presence, I will develop the idea of musical geography through practice. In the following pages, I will be questioning and reflecting on several of the existing problems in our conception of the ethnographic field through a multimedia practice such as TikTok to invite us to go beyond the idea of a field with a closed, physical geography and synchronic practices and inviting us to take our conceptualization of this field beyond the tangible. I argue that digital platforms are not closed spaces but interconnected spaces in which musical practices can and are developed across different platforms, thereby creating fluid networks of creativity.

Thinking Beyond the Tangible Body

In the deterritorialized and multimedia world we currently live in, it has become less sustainable to consider any kind of cultural configuration as a homogeneous object contained in a static physical geography. The idea of *the* culture (in singular) based on a sole physical geography—for example, "*the* Austrian culture exists *in* Austria" or "*the* Mexican culture *in* Mexico," implying that such cultures do not exist anywhere else[5]—quickly becomes contradictory when comparing the practices that these homogeneous cultures say they do with those performed by its actors on their day to day. This essentialist idea of *the* culture is also often extended when referring to the actors of these cultural phenomena. By saying, for example, that it is Austrians who enact the Austrian culture, the actors are turned into natural and inherent carriers of *that* culture, and therefore rejecting de facto the possibility that members considered foreign to *that* culture are capable of producing *agency* or *culture*.

In *The Location of Culture* (1994), Homi Bhabha reflects on the modern diasporic movements and points out the aforesaid tensions, inviting us "to think beyond narratives of originary and initial subjectivities and to focus on those moments or processes that are produced in the articulation of cultural differences." Since it is in these moments or processes where hegemonic cultures collide, "these 'in-between' spaces provide the space for elaborating strategies of selfhood—singular or communal—that initiate new signs of identity, and innovative sites of collaboration, and contestation, in the act of defending the idea of society itself" (Bhabha [1994] 2004: 2). When Bhabha speaks of the moments of "the articulation of cultural differences" he refers to *minorities* that are forced to negotiate *their* (hegemonic) culture with *the* (hegemonic) culture of a certain country—and society—in which these minorities do not belong to. Thus, Bhabha talks about the encounter of two hegemonic cultures contained in the physical bodies of the actors in a certain physical geography. However, the idea that new identities are created "in the articulation of cultural differences" is highly valuable, and when disassociated from a geographical concept and the physical bodies of the actors, it can be used for conceptualizing and understanding any kind of cultural configuration, either hegemonic or not, being physical, digital, or hybrid. This allows us to see cultural configurations not as static preestablished objects of a hegemonic culture but as dynamic processes of negotiation and articulation between people who interact in "in-between" spaces.

[5] Although these cultures may exist elsewhere, through this conception they are "exiled"; they are not in *their* "natural" place.

Following what Arjun Appadurai (1996) proposes about understanding "the configuration of cultural forms in today's world as fundamentally fractal, that is, as possessing no Euclidean boundaries, structures, or regularities," which are not only "fractal" but "are also overlapping" (1996: 46), I suggest to understand the configuration of these cultural forms, as well as what ethnographers conceive as *the ethnographic field* based on the practices that shape them, in other words, understanding the conceptualization of a musical geography through practice. To that end, I propose that these cultural configurations should rather be thought of as a set of multiple and dynamic identities, and not as physical bodies that are exclusively united by their physical proximity but are united through the articulation and negotiation of multilocal and multimedia practices together. What keeps these cultural configurations together are not the bodies and/or physical environments of the actors, but the practices that these actors do, which contribute to the negotiation and maintenance of a certain knowledge (see Bermúdez et al. 2018; Brabec and Winter 2018), which we could call *culture.*

For this, we need a model that allows us to conceptualize the musicking groups parting from the individuals that are contained in it, since, as Elliot pointed out, "music involves sonic products, but these are created, maintained, adapted, reinterpreted, and appropriated by people in and across musical communities" (Elliott 2007: 85). However, these communities not only share a relationship among its members, but they also share a common musical practice and interest, creating what Ailbhe Kenny names *communities of musical practice* (2016: 16).[6] These groups of people creating their sense of community through musical practice or interest also share certain knowledge and practices that make them "distinguishable not just by their differing musical styles but also by other social conventions: in the people who took part, their values, their shared understandings and practices, modes of production and distribution, and the social organization of their collective musical activities" (Finnegan [1989] 2007: 32), allowing them to be recognized and experienced as what Ruth Finnegan ([1989] 2007) calls *musical worlds.*

Following the logic from the words of Appadurai, that "the configuration of cultural forms in today's world [are] fundamentally fractal" (1996: 46), we could then say that the actors in these *musical worlds* (Finnegan [1989] 2007) should be also understood as "fractal." While our physical body is difficult to

[6] Kenny defines community of musical practice (CoMP) as: "a group of people who form a community of practice through shared music-making and/or musical interests" (Kenny 2016: 16).

understand—and practice—as a fractal, our *self* can be easily conceptualized and practiced this way. For this, I propose to take Bourdieu's term *habitus or habit*[7] and understand the concepts of *self* and *identity* as defined by Turino:

> [Turino] conceptualizes the *self* as comprising a body plus the *total* sets of habits specific to an individual that develop through the ongoing interchanges of the individual with her physical and social surroundings. *Identity* involves the *partial* selection of habits and attributes used to represent oneself to oneself and to others by oneself and by others; the emphasis on certain habits and traits is relative to specific situations. Finally, what is usually referred to as *culture* is defined here as the habits of thought and practice that are shared among individuals. (Turino 2008: 95)

Thinking of cultural practices as "habits of thought and practice" that are developed, experienced, negotiated, and shared between people allows us to understand that these cultural practices cannot be reduced to one sole homogeneous culture for a determined society. If we consider that "individuals develop habits from their personal experience," then a homogeneous culture would mean that all members of a certain society have "similar experiences and [are] in similar social positions and circumstances in relation to the environment" (Turino 2008: 110), unsustainable in our contemporary world. Beyond this, this way of conceptualizing the *self* and our *identity* allows us, on the one hand, to conceptualize the actors of our musicking as fractal actors, which lets us understand the physical body not just as unique and inseparable but as a containing space and a departure point of the intertwining of multiple virtual identities, dissociating it from its intrinsic geography. Understanding this, Thomas Turino proposes two ways of conceptualizing the diverse forms in which these multiple identities may intertwine. For this, Turino introduces the concepts of *cultural cohort* and *cultural formation*:

> Since people will identify with others because of shared habit trajectories, [Turino] suggest the terms *cultural cohort* or *identity cohort* to refer to social groupings that form along the lines of specific constellations of shared habit based in similarities of *parts* of the self … Because of the pluralistic nature of the self,

[7] Thomas Turino uses the term *habit* based on Charles S. Pierce as "a tendency toward the repetition of any particular behavior, thought or reaction in similar circumstances or in reaction to similar stimuli in the present and future based on such repetitions in the past" (Pierce after Turino 2008: 95). The concept *habitus*, introduced by Bourdieu ([1972] 1977), is equally important for understanding the cultural practices as practices.

> each person will belong to a variety of cultural/identity cohorts having a greater or lesser social salience and prominence in their lives … [In turn, Turino] use the term *cultural formation* to refer to a group of people who have in common a majority of habits that constitute most parts of each individual member's self. It is the *pervasiveness* and often the time-depth of habits influencing individual thought, practice, and decision making that distinguish *cultural formations* from *cultural cohorts*. (Turino 2008: 111–12)

These concepts allow us not just to think in much more dynamic cultural configurations but also to create configurations—musical geographies—in a much more fractal sense and which may overlap with or be overlapped by other cohorts through online, offline, and mixed spaces. Additionally, the idea of *habit* allows us to think in these cohorts and formations as configurations that are "grounded not in ideas, but in *everyday action*, that is, in *practice*: the reality in which we as human beings act and that we articulate by our interaction" (Couldry and Hepp 2017: 21), which allows us to easily focus on the dynamic processes of negotiation and articulation in the musical practices (see Bermúdez et al. 2018: 286–8).

Thinking Beyond the Tangible Space

The concepts of *cultural cohort* and *cultural formation* let us understand our musical practices as cultural configurations based on practice—and habit—, which are fractally intertwined in online, offline, and mixed spaces. These concepts help us as well to focus on the moments of encounter, where these practices are generated, experienced, and negotiated, and can exist in very different and independent times and spaces between each other. This conceptualization of musical practices allows a much more dynamic acting in the moment of thinking about the *ethnographic field*; however, it does not automatically free us from the dilemma triggered when thinking about the *locality* of these practices. If the practices of the actors, and not the bodies, are the ones that bring cultural phenomena together, then where do these practices take place, and where and in what way can we observe them?

When asking these questions, the need to critically reflect on our notion of *locality* and adapt this concept to the diverse realities experienced in our contemporary musical practices is evident. According to Anthony Giddens (1991), modernity brought with it a process of abstraction in the interpersonal and interobjective relations when creating systems and processes that allow us to relate with people and objects beyond an immediate and specific space and time, creating more and more *facework* and *faceless commitments* (1991: 80). The space in which our social practices happen became "phantasmagoric," since its negotiation and articulation structures ceased to develop exclusively in an immediate physical locality, leading the local and the global to become "inextricably intertwined" (1991: 108–9). Although our physical body inhabits a certain physical location, its relationship with other humans and nonhumans does not necessarily depend on sharing a certain locality and time; these articulations can exist in a myriad of *localities*, online, offline, and/or mixed, and in multiple times, synchronous and/or asynchronous.

These processes of time and space abstraction in our social relations invite us to think the *localities* articulated in habits of thought and practice as "primarily relational and contextual rather than as scalar or spatial … As a complex phenomenological quality, constituted by a series of links between the sense of social immediacy, the technologies of interactivity, and the relativity of contexts" (Appadurai 1996: 178). Following this logic, the localities in which our musical practices take place only exist beyond a punctual physical locality, existing then in a conceptual intertwining built across diverse physical localities and digital and analogous technologies, which are recombined "in forms which permit the precise time-space 'zoning' of social life" (1991: 16–17). The entwining of these localities experienced through highly embedded and embodied digital and virtual daily circumstances (see Hine 2015) builds what Henri Lefebvre ([1974] 1991) refers to as *social space* ([1974] 1991: 68–168), a space that cannot be compared with the physical space that exists in *nature*, which is experienced in a special, synchronous, and physically immediate—a space that usually pops into our minds when speaking of localities. In contrast, *social spaces* are relational; "they are not *things*, which have mutually limiting boundaries," but they can "be intercalated, combined, superimposed" with other *social spaces*, and due to their fractal constitution cannot be "absorbed by the regional, national or even worldwide level" but are "traversed by myriad currents" (Lefebvre [1974] 1991: 86–8). Similar to how the concepts of *cultural cohort* and *cultural formation* allow us to understand music traditions as cultural configurations based on practice that are entwined in a fractal manner in assorted spaces, the idea of *social space* by Lefebvre ([1974] 1991) allows us to conceptualize *space* as the practice of inhabiting our virtual or physical environments.

Conceptualizing our relationship with *space* as a practice has been widely discussed by many authors (see Heidegger 1971; Merleau-Ponty [1945] 2014; de

Certeau [1984] 1988), and the discussions by Tim Ingold are particularly relevant in this context (see 2000, 2011, 2015). In *The Perception of the Environment* (2000), Ingold invites us to think about our way of relating to our environment through a "dwelling perspective" (see 2000: 153–287), from which "the world continually comes into being around the inhabitant, and its manifold constituents take on significance through their incorporation into regular pattern of life activity" (153). It is through practice—inhabiting our environment—that space and its places of interaction begin to make sense to us. From this perspective, we do not relate to the world but inhabit and make sense of it through our practices. As a result, and from a similar phenomenological thought, in their reflections about the mediatized construction of reality Nick Couldry and Andreas Hepp point out that "we live *embedded* in places, moving from one to another through the day, and building our path through life out of more or less successful *appropriations* of space in the form of the places that we occupy" (Couldry and Hepp 2017: 85). Following the aforementioned, the "places do not have locations but histories" (Ingold 2000: 219); therefore, similar as cultural cohorts, these places are configured "by the itineraries of their inhabitants" existing as "nodes in a matrix of movement" (219), existing through practice.

Comprehending our relationship with *space* as a practice provides the possibility to have a better approach toward the study of musical traditions with digital and/or multimedia interaction spaces, such as those experienced in the musicking of TikTok. Despite the arrival of modernity and its globalizing tendencies, the abstraction of space and time has increased, while the invention and expansion of the internet has taken this process of abstraction to other dimensions. Our way of inhabiting the world today is not only based on physical and synchronous relations but on the digital and *imaginary* relations as well (see Anderson [1983] 2006). In our contemporary world, the places in which we move and interact daily, those in which we inhabit our space, are widely spread throughout multimedia spaces, bringing new challenges with it: is it possible that the articulations and negotiations of our musical practices made on multimedia spaces, like TikTok, are only representations of the *real*?

This phantasmagoric reality encourages us to critically think about our understanding of the real and the virtual in order to incorporate these multimedia realities to the argument of a *geography through practice* discussed in the previous pages. For this it is fundamental to think beyond the dichotomic separation between *real* and *virtual*. In line with this, Pierre Lévy (1998) invites us to think the virtual not as something inexistent or an illusion but as "a fecund and powerful mode of being that expands the process of creation" (Lévy 1998: 16).

> The virtual should, properly speaking, be compared not to the real but the actual. Unlike the possible, which is static and already constituted, the virtual is a kind of problematic complex, the knot of tendencies or forces that accompanies a situation, event, object, or entity, and which invokes a process of resolution: actualization … Actualization thus appears as the solution to a problem, a solution not previously contained in its formulation. It is the creation, the invention of a form on the basis of a dynamic configuration of forces and finalities. Actualization involves more than simply assigning reality to a possible or selecting from among a predetermined range of choices. It implies the production of new qualities, a transformation of ideas, a true becoming that feeds the virtual in turn. (Lévy 1998: 24–5)

The virtual does not lack actual reality, but instead it refers to a way of being that produces "a change of identity" (Lévy 1998: 44) through a practice of *actualization*. The space-time abstraction brought by modernity—imagined as a phantasmagorical reality—transformed "a specific and circumscribed activity into a delocalized, desynchronized, and collectivized functioning" (44), and therefore kept virtualizing the relationships between humans and nonhumans, turning them into phantasmagorical relations. Conversely, practices that allow the articulation, negotiation, and configuration of our cultural cohorts, as well as the processes of residing our social spaces (see Lefebvre [1974] 1991), are the ones that let us actualize this phantasmagorical reality into actual reality. By understanding the real and the virtual on these terms, we can observe that actual multimedia practices are experienced through a dialectic process of virtualization and actualization.

If we live in this intertwining of the virtual and the real, then so is our relationship with the world (being-in-the-world), and therefore our way of inhabiting and (re)creating it. "The virtualization of the body is therefore not a form of disembodiment but a re-creation, a reincarnation, a multiplication, vectorization, and heterogenesis of the human" (Lévy 1998: 44). Following this logic, Marie-Laure Ryan (2015) accurately illustrates that:

> The difference between "being in space," like things, and "inhabiting" or "haunting space," like the embodied consciousness, is a matter of both mobility and virtuality. Whereas inert object, entirely contained in their material bodies, are bound to a fixed location, consciousness can occupy multiple points and

> points of view, either through the actual movements of its corporeal support or by projecting itself into virtual bodies. The ultimate test of the material existence of things is our ability to perceive them under many angles, to manipulate them, and to feel their resistance. When my actual body cannot walk around an object or grab and lift it, it is the knowledge that my virtual body could do so that gives me a sense of the object's shape, volume, and materiality. Whether actual or virtual, objects are thus present to me because my actual or virtual body can interact with them. (Ryan 2015: 54)

Considering our body—either virtual or physical—in constant movement through space and time (instead of a static entity anchored in a physical location), we can better understand how we inhabit our space through constant multimedia interaction created by different physical and digital actors spread throughout different spaces around the world. We make sense of this world through the practices of our "embodied consciousness"; we model communities and social spaces. Just like walking, thinking, speaking, or playing an instrument, the use of digital media is a practice that allows us to make sense of the world in which we live. Musicking in TikTok is not just about representing a physical reality in a digital environment, but a practice that is experienced through our embodied consciousness in a phantasmagorical multimedia reality with the purpose of inhabiting and making sense of it. As mentioned by Ingold, "we do not have to think the world in order to live in it, but we do have to live in the world on order to think it" (Ingold [1996b] 2005: 115–18). To continue with the argument of a geography through practice from the perspective of "embodied consciousness," in the following pages I will explore different components of the multimediality present around musical performances.

Performing On and Beyond TikTok[8]

At present, it is not easy to imagine any mainstream musical practice without acknowledging the role that digital platforms—especially YouTube—play in its

[8] This subchapter was originally published in a slightly different form in: Juan Bermúdez. 2023. "Performing Beyond the Platform—Experiencing Musicking On and Through YouTube, TikTok, and Instagram." In *Remediating Sound: Repeatable Culture, YouTube and Music* (= New Approaches to Sound, Music, and Media), edited by Holly Rogers, Joana Freitas and João Francisco Porfírio, 187–202. Reprinted with the permission of Bloomsbury Academic US, an imprint of Bloomsbury Publishing Plc.

creation and articulation. Although the growing use of digital platforms, especially YouTube and TikTok, has led them to become musical and performative worlds by themselves, many of the musical practices on these platforms are developed beyond a single platform and/or specific medium. This transmedial flow has fostered the development of networked creativity and practice. In the following pages I reflect on how these practices can and did take place across multiple interconnected platforms.

Performing Beyond the Platform

The rise and expansion of the internet and the development of new devices, forms of communication, and platforms have developed and established a vast number of interrelations between physical and virtual multilocal and multimedia spaces as a fundamental part of our daily lives. As already seen with the introduction of (new) technologies in the past, the current appropriation of digital spaces in the globalized world, as well as the continual development of digital music platforms (YouTube, Spotify, and so on) and devices have not only shaped and augmented the interactive possibilities between users but also enabled and reinforced the adaptation and development of (new) forms of musical practices (see Smudits 2002). Musicians use social media and other digital technologies both as a tool to represent and promote themselves and as an active part of their artistic creation and exploration. They use digital platforms (like YouTube) for their broadcasting and participatory, process-driven qualities. In his work on Web 2.0, Axel Bruns notes that this double role has made the borders between digital production and reception fickle (2008: 9–36; 227–58). We can extend this to suggest that the dissolving borders between musical articulation and experience have forged new and radical relationships between digital environments and daily life.

Music creation, articulation, processing, and experience may occur autonomously at different times and in separate digital or physical spaces. Nowadays, we no longer have to be in front of musicians to listen and experience music, as we would just one hundred years ago. Now, in the contemporary globalized world, it is possible for us to listen to practically any recorded music from around the world—whether performed long ago or recently—simply by using a small device, perhaps no larger than a couple of centimeters. We can connect it to the internet, log into a platform of our choice (such as YouTube Music, Spotify, or Apple Music), and suddenly have access to a discography so vast that no one person could live long enough to listen to it all. Critics like Tia

DeNora (2000) and Anahid Kassabian (2013) have shown how such accessibility and portability have enabled the conscious and unconscious embedding of musical practices throughout our daily lives (see too García Quiñones et al. 2013; Bull 2007). We listen to music while we go from one place to another or perform various activities; we share music videos that we like with friends and family through YouTube, TikTok, and other platforms; and we make and share playlists that reflect our tastes and moods and become an essential part of our personalities. In short, we frame many of our daily activities with our own personal soundtrack(s).

Besides this, anyone can actively participate in one way or another in the generation of content around or about the musical performance itself. Thanks to the development and expansion of Web 2.0, the ways in which we can interact with various platforms changed from the consumption of online data to a more active and direct participation in its creation and circulation through likes, comments, shares, playlisting, and remediation. Growing technological development, as well as the increasing accessibility to it, has also enabled users to actively participate in content creation by producing original compositions or remixing, parodying, and mashing up preexistent work. Cheap and easy-to-use technology means that users no longer need a professional recording studio to generate a track or video: music and music videos can now be produced at home with outstanding quality and shared, as Patricia Lange has shown, through YouTube's vast amateur networks (see Lange 2019).

The creation and sharing of music and media through YouTube and TikTok accelerated with the development of portable devices, especially the smartphone, which allowed access to the internet—and therefore to digital music platforms—and provided the hardware and software necessary for the quick generation and dissemination of content.[9] Taking a photo, making a video, recording a sound or a song are all activities that can now be done using the same handheld device. It is no longer necessary to carry a computer, a camera, and a video recorder with us to create, frame, and share our daily lives or to generate our own personal soundtracks almost instantly. As a result, platforms like YouTube, and later TikTok, have become a fundamental part of everyday life, creating a musicking based on multimedia networks of creativity and practice.

[9] For a much more detailed and in-depth overview of these processes, see: Cook et al. (2019); Gopinath and Stanyek (2014).

Amateur short music videos that move through YouTube, TikTok, and Instagram show how this everyday multimedia musicking has produced new audiovisual forms based on multimedia networks of creativity and practice. An example of such a phenomenon can be found in the remediation and viralization of the choreography created around "Jerusalema"[10] (2020) by Master KG and Nomcebo. In this example it is interesting to note that the choreography and the piece of music used are constant; however, the creative ways of reproducing the trend and the way it was performed on each of the platforms, as well as on the street as part of everyday popular culture, were different. Whereas on YouTube we find especially collective videos, with much longer and more extensive visual shots, on TikTok and Instagram this trend was based much more on individual performances, with shots focused on the individual and of short duration. On the street in everyday life, this trend was performed by some people as a mimetic allusion, performing small fragments of the choreography as a joke during conversations or when listening to a song in the street. A similar phenomenon to that was generated by "Happy"[11] (2013) by Pharrell Williams a couple of years ago, although with different scopes, contexts, and aesthetics.

These short music videos made by young people as part of their daily lives show us an example of the vast performative world of these platforms and help us understand the interrelationship of these practices through different digital platforms and physical spaces. Through these videos, young people thematize their joys, sorrows, and concerns—in short, their day-to-day existence. They comment on other creators' videos and share them with friends and family. Videos are shown between friends while they eat, walk, or do some activity. Beyond that, young people get together to make TikToks, Shorts, and Reels. At the same time, they create bonds and friendships between creators.[12] This integration of video creation and experience in everyday life, as well as the experience of these practices through very diverse spaces and platforms, has generated the creation of cultural discourses and knowledge that go beyond local context into the glocal cultural imaginary. This allows musical styles and trends

[10] Openmic Productions, "Master KG—Jerusalema Remix [Feat. Burna Boy and Nomcebo] (Official Music Video)," October 23, 2020, YouTube video, https://www.youtube.com/watch?v=9-RhCvYpxqc.

[11] Pharrell Williams, "Pharrell Williams—Happy (Video)," January 8, 2014, YouTube video, https://www.youtube.com/watch?v=ZbZSe6N_BXs.

[12] The word *creator* is used here as an emic concept. The actors of the analyzed musicking can and should be understood under Axel Bruns's concept of *produsers* (see Bruns 2008).

to influence cultural practices and behaviors far beyond the original platform or geographical locale.

A sound/track made by a teenager in her house can become a world hit and later accompany the day to day of young people around the world, as in the case of Justin Bieber. The video of someone dancing in the street shared on YouTube can become the next viral trend on TikTok. Beyond this, dances and memes are also taken up by popular culture and taken to other contexts, being remediated, and reproduced in movies and other formats. However, videos of tragic events, like the videos of @valerisssh about her experiences when fleeing the Russian-Ukrainian War, or protest actions shared through these networks can also become the spark that ignites social movements, like the *#BlackLivesMatter* movement, leaving a mark on the memory of our generation. YouTube, as well as TikTok, has not only become a part of contemporary mainstream popular culture but also operates as a portal into the social, political, and cultural spectrums of everyday life. The interaction and networked creativity and practice have been developed and articulated on and through YouTube, and later on TikTok and Instagram; they have made it possible for amateur video practices to interrelate in a highly fluid way through different digital platforms, creating creative multimedia practices. But how do the interrelations of creative practices between platforms work, and how have they influenced and made possible the creation of a larger glocal cultural imaginary? In the following, I explore how the interaction and networked creativity and practice of these short videos have been articulated on and through TikTok, YouTube, and Instagram, to understand how these interrelationships lead us to conceptualize creative networks on digital platforms in different and more dynamic ways.

From One Platform to the World and Back Again

Just like YouTube has for many years, TikTok has become one of the most widely used video creation and viewing apps globally. People around the world make countless videos through this platform, sharing both joy and sadness with other people and sharing both serious and frivolous topics. People spend their time watching videos in the app while they go about their daily lives. They create new TikToks and appropriate and remediate existing ones. They participate in the discourse around these practices by commenting on other videos. However, as we had seen in the story at the beginning of the chapter, some modes of engagement are carried out outside TikTok, both in physical spaces and through other digital platforms. Many of the videos created and shared on TikTok are also shared through YouTube and Instagram, and many of the discourses about these platforms are broadcasted through both digital and physical magazines, as well as through websites.[13] However, there are also videos and other practices that were previously developed on YouTube and are now readapted to the aesthetic contexts and languages of digital video platforms like TikTok and Instagram, enabling the creation and renegotiation of multimedia practices that utilize the specific contexts of the original platforms, followed by their remediation, and the development of new multimedia creative practices and glocal aesthetics.

Transmedia movements reveal much about user behavior. Thanks to the fact that TikTok videos are shared on YouTube, Instagram, and other platforms, we can observe how interrelationships are created between accounts and/or creators across different digital environments. For instance, the video of some creator that we know from TikTok is shared with us and/or advertised through Instagram or YouTube, while in the profile of some TikTokers we find links that take us to their YouTube channel or their Instagram account, and vice versa. While TikTokers create profiles on YouTube and/or Instagram to represent and market themselves, YouTubers and Instagrammers expand their performance networks through TikTok and other platforms, as in the example of the twins Lisa and Lena (@lisaandlena) in Germany, who became famous on the Musical.ly application, and later developed successful careers on YouTube and Instagram, conquering TikTok in German-speaking countries after the merging of Musical.ly with TikTok. Or the case of Charli D'Amelio from the United States, who is not only one of the most followed TikTokers globally but is also widely successful on YouTube and Instagram, as well as outside of social networks.

In addition to this, we follow different people through different platforms, experiencing their performances and sharing a joint space with them. This takes us to create relationships of admiration and/or friendship, and these relationships may motivate individuals to meet in person. Beyond this, these interrelationships encourage the development of specific performative styles, which promotes the creation and recognition of a musical persona. In the same way as Auslander's musical persona (see 2021), these creators perform

[13] The German-language magazines *Bravo* and *Cool*, among others, are clear examples of physical magazines that dedicate great writing spaces to the performative and aesthetic practices of digital platforms like TikTok. In addition to this, these magazines and other various newspapers and television programs have chosen to make their own accounts on YouTube, Instagram, and TikTok.

their identity as YouTubers, TikTokers, and Instagrammers. Additionally, these performative or representation practices that go beyond a specific platform led creators to adapt their creations and/or persona to the practices and aesthetics developed in these new digital environments (see Chapter 3), making the creation of a recognizable meta-musical persona through different performance networks possible.

On the other hand, the growing existence of intertwined practices between different platforms is reflected through the stylistic transference and referencing of videos and sonic practices from one platform to another. During my ethnographic research I have observed the importance that TikTokers give to these cross-media convergences. TikTokers no longer only create and experience videos on TikTok but also use YouTube to search for new dances, performative forms, trends, and other related practices. A common practice related to this is searching, viewing, and creating tutorials on YouTube that teach particular dance routines that can then be remediated into new TikToks. For instance, it is possible to find countless tutorials on YouTube, showing relatively simple steps like "floss" or much more complicated ones like "renegade." However, one can also find countless compilations of these or other dances and trends. Dances like "renegade" help young people articulate their identities within a communal space as part of a larger conversation (see Boffone 2021): they can respond to an existing dance routine and, in turn, their version can be remediated by other creators to form a complex audiovisual landscape of adaptations and translations that are then subject to the negotiation of aesthetic and racial discourses by other users who compile the "best" and "worst" versions of these dance steps. These practices of creation, copying, sharing, and cataloging influence how new dance videos are created and experienced in TikTok afterward. In addition, the practice of commenting and rating various aspects of TikToks through videos on YouTube has become common, as in the case of the YouTubers TwoSetViolin. This musical duo, like many other creators, brings local performances, knowledge, and aesthetics to a more heterogeneous public, spreading particular cultural discourses and knowledge beyond their local context and allowing them to become part of a larger glocal cultural imaginary.

While some of the dances and sounds used in TikTok videos have been taken up by other creators and brought into new contexts and platforms, the cross-platform influence and interconnected practice may run deeper. An example of this type of influence and interconnected practice between platforms can be seen in the creation process of the music hit "Savage Love (Laxed—Siren

Beat)"[14] by Jawsh 685 and Jason Derulo. In July 2019, the young New Zealander Joshua Nanai (Jawsh 685) posted his new sample titled "Laxed (Siren Beat)"[15] on YouTube. It was after he uploaded a fifteen-second version of him dancing to this sample[16] to TikTok in March 2020 that "Laxed"[17]—as it was called on TikTok—went viral, initiating more than forty million TikTok versions (as of April 2022). This immense popularity drew the attention of various record labels, and Jawsh 685 signed with Columbia Records, releasing "Laxed (Siren Beat)" on various streaming platforms in April 2020. As a result, "Laxed" became the musical base for developing various trends on TikTok during the start of the COVID-19 pandemic, reaching various social groups around the world. One of these users was the singer Jason Derulo who uploaded his own TikTok,[18] in which he danced to the rhythm of "Laxed." On May 11, 2020, Jason Derulo published another TikTok[19] announcing his new song, which he had just composed: "Savage Love." However, "Savage Love" used the "Laxed" sample available on TikTok without crediting Jawsh 685. After much criticism and legal issues, Jason Derulo and Jawsh 685 reached an agreement and ended up releasing "Savage Love (Laxed—Siren Beat)" together in June 2020. Although this example can be seen as a sample of some unethical practices that we can find throughout the various digital platforms,[20] it is also an excellent example of the influence and interconnection between the users and practices of the various digital platforms and how a video or song can be taken to other contexts to generate new practices, performances, and meanings.

14 Jason Derulo and Jawsh 685, "Savage Love," June 9, 2020, YouTube video, https://www.youtube.com/watch?v=gUci-tsiU4I.

15 Jawsh 685 [L & S], "Laxed [SIREN BEAT]," July 25, 2019, YouTube video, https://www.youtube.com/watch?v=k7xOBle0D_g.

16 @jawsh_685, "Kefe your ass," March 29, 2020, TikTok video, https://www.tiktok.com/@jawsh_685/video/6809484002802666757?is_from_webapp=1&sender_device=pc&web_id=7062339902340007429.

17 @jawsh_685, "Laxed," TikTok sound, https://www.tiktok.com/music/Laxed-6804093117843770118?is_from_webapp=1&sender_device=pc.

18 @jasonderulo, "Is this a trend?," April 17, 2020, https://www.tiktok.com/@jasonderulo/video/6816519886328663302?is_from_webapp=1&sender_device=pc&web_id=7062339902340007429.

19 @jasonderulo, "Made this song last night," May 11, 2020, TikTok video, https://www.tiktok.com/@jasonderulo/video/6825494195659115781.

20 In his work on the renegade dance, Trevor Boffone (see Boffone 2021) extensively exposes the problems that black artists experience in being stripped of credit for the choreography they create. Although in the last year, TikTok has tried to change this situation by running information campaigns to create an awareness of authorship in the application, BIPOC artists continue to contribute choreography and performances to the TikTok community without being recognized for it.

"Laxed" shows how the sounds, dances, memes, and other variations performed on and through TikTok, YouTube, Instagram, and other platforms can be taken up by other creators and brought into new contexts and platforms to forge new cultural practices and aesthetics that drive popular internet culture into refreshed artistic realms. An example of this process and its influence on multimedia aesthetics can be found in the video "Don't Lie to Me"[21] by the German singer Lena released in March 2019 on YouTube. Unusually for videos on this platform, "Don't Lie to Me" is recorded in portrait mode with and from the perspective of an iPhone. The video demonstrates how many of our daily practices are developed and framed by using digital devices and platforms. The visual perspective constantly changes from that of an omnipresent observer to the perspective of the videographer, giving the sensation of being embedded in a smartphone and continually referencing the styles of Instagram, iMessage, YouTube, and other social media platforms. "Don't Lie to Me" thus exemplifies the multimediality that exists in the practices that we carry out in our day-to-day activities and of the influence that these practices generate in the production of new multimedia aesthetics, reminding us of processes similar to what Carol Vernallis calls "media swirl" (2013; see too Vernallis et al. 2020).

So far, we've seen how affect and style can transfer between platforms, how content can refer to the aesthetics and specificities of other forms of social media, and how everything can flow into the real world. But dances and memes have also bled into other audiovisual contexts like movies and television series. The dialogue between Jodi and her parents, Helaine and Richie Kreyman, in the Netflix movie *Tall Girl 2* (2022), for instance, addresses TikTok in such a way as to demonstrate the generational differences in the articulation of multimedia practices:

Helaine: —Dr. Seeger probably saw me on the Tok—
Richie: —Huh?—
Helaine: —The Tickety Tok. I was doin' all of that. I was plugging your show, though–
Jodi: —You're on TikTok?—
Helaine: —You don't follow me?—[22]

[21] Lena, "Don't lie to me," March 15, 2019, YouTube video, https://www.youtube.com/watch?v=B_BLi76JPqA.

[22] See Emily Ting, dir. *Tall Girl 2*. Netflix, 2022; minute 28.

While this movie embeds the platform within its cultural setting, other cinematic examples play on social media's constant recontextualization of sounds, memes, and routines. An example of this can be seen during the performance of the song "Surface Pressure"[23] by Luisa in the Disney movie *Encanto* (2021). Luisa's dance performance not only refers to the dance culture on TikTok but has also influenced the development of new trends on this platform. TikTokers make versions of Luisa's dance, imitating her steps or creating new versions of that choreography. They do duets with her and other TikTokers and share these performances and other compilations through YouTube and Instagram. By becoming part of popular culture, these moves, which could previously have been shared on TikTok itself, are recontextualized and performed (in a new way) on other platforms, only to be taken up on TikTok and readapted to this environment.

These are not just processes of reinterpretation and recontextualization, but also of appropriation, with the potential of going viral, and are used by various artists to promote their work. Due to the different audiences that each platform can reach, some artists include aesthetics from these platforms in their performances, as we saw happening in Lena's "Don't Lie to Me" video. On the other hand, however, some artists use the specific practices of a particular platform to help their music go viral. Austrian singer Andreas Gabalier's song "LIEBELEBEN"[24] is a good example of this. Before launching his song in June 2021, Gabalier published various Stories through his Instagram account. These Stories did not explicitly announce the release of his next single but invited his followers to learn a particular choreography, step by step, Story by Story. After the official launch of the song through YouTube in commemoration of Pride Month, it was clear that these dance steps would turn out to be the choreography for the song's chorus. The prelude to the video offers different Reels showing young girls performing the choreography, and, in the official video, Gabalier performs the moves with a group of dancers each time the chorus is heard. In the weeks following the release, Gabalier encouraged fellow users to join the *#LIEBELEBEN* Dance Challenge, inviting people to dance the choreography and share their Reels under that hashtag through Instagram. Although this request

23 Jessica Darrow, "Surface pressure," December 24, 2021, YouTube video, https://www.youtube.com/watch?v=tQwVKr8rCYw.

24 Andreas Gabalier, "LIEBELEBEN," June 4, 2021, YouTube video, https://www.youtube.com/watch?v=ECG72etNlsQ.

was not particularly successful, it was another platform responsible for making this choreography and its respective sound viral: TikTok. This demonstrates how TikTok was used to make a particular dance and its respective sound go viral.

Musicking through TikTok, YouTube, and Instagram

So far, we have seen how various musicking practices are performed and experienced on and through YouTube, TikTok, and Instagram and the ways in which sounds, dances, and memes can be brought into new contexts and platforms by fellow users through version, references, and refreshed forms of networked creativity and into the professional sphere via film and television. There are also many examples of the ways in which TikToks, Reels, and Shorts have extended beyond the smartphone landscape. For example, although "Happy" (2013) by Pharrell Williams and "Jerusalema" (2020) by Master KG and Nomcebo initially appeared on YouTube, they generated millions of reinterpretations on different platforms by users around the world, while their remediation through the flash mob movement demonstrates how viral songs and dances, like these, can be taken into real-world practices. In addition, various musical traditions, such as electronic dance music (Madrid 2008), Argentinian tango (Steputtat 2020), or German Schlager (Mendívil 2008), have merged and continue to merge these digital environments and platforms into their performance, representation, and/or communication practices.

For many, the experience and performance of music and dance on and through TikTok, YouTube, and Instagram have become necessary for the economic survival of young artists and cultural institutions in a hyperconnected world. An example of this type of phenomenon can be observed in the search for new formats and scenarios for the diffusion of music, as the streaming of live concerts through different platforms, as well as in the development of partnerships with institutions and objectives beyond those seen in traditional cultural institutions (see Chapter 5), like the so-called TikTopera—"Tiger King 2 The TikTopera"[25]—produced between Netflix and The English National Opera in 2021 and launched on TikTok and YouTube as a preamble and promotion to the launch of the second season of the Netflix Series *Tiger King 2*—a situation that has been reinforced by the COVID-19 pandemic.

[25] The English National Opera and Netflix, "Tiger King 2 the TikTopera," November 15, 2021, YouTube video, https://www.youtube.com/watch?v=lnh1UD8t_nA.

Beyond this, however, we can observe in turn the experimentation of new performance formats as shown by the example of the adaptation of Mozart's "Die Entführung aus dem Serai" (1782) as "#FREE_Constanze"[26] in 2021 and Bizet's "Carmen" (1875) as "Carmen by Carmen"[27] in 2022 made on TikTok by the Opernloft team from Hamburg. These were created as part of Opernloft's strategy to attract new audiences to its theater, taking advantage of the financial support provided through TikTok's #CreatorsForDiversity campaign in Germany (see Chapter 5). These TikToperas not only experimented with new formats and dramaturgical strategies but also used various practices and aesthetics widely spread on TikTok, YouTube, and Instagram, in addition to the use of various trends and challenges already existing on TikTok, as well as the attempt to create their own challenges such as *#TikTokDanceChallangeMozartEdition*. Likewise, the idea of intermediality has been already present and has been explored in different ways by different conceptual composers (see Voithofer 2024).[28]

Even though the growing popularity of digital platforms like TikTok and YouTube has generated radical new musical and performative worlds, many of the creative practices once unique to each platform now flow through the contemporary "media swirl" and beyond the digital world altogether. When I witnessed four youngsters viewing, analyzing, and copying a video on TikTok and YouTube on their smartphone, it was clear that they were deftly navigating between different online and physical spaces, combining and superimposing on the other to forge a new hyperreal mode of communication. From my seat on the train, I could not perceive these locations, which were accessed via asynchronous and mediatized paths. I did not see the other users or networks. "Julia," writing from school through WhatsApp, was invisible to me, yet all these people and locations were somehow present. These interrelationships, enabled by the interoperability of platforms, have fostered the development of exciting forms of networked creativity and practice, a multimedia network that emerges through the articulation of joint musical and dance practices experienced in an interlacing of physical everyday places (e.g., school, parks) and digital

[26] @opernloft, "That escalated quickly," October 8, 2021, TikTok video, https://www.tiktok.com/@opernloft/video/7016741268130696453?is_from_webapp=1&sender_device=pc&web_id=7062339902340007429.

[27] @opernloft, "Welcome to 'Carmen by Carmen'!," January 20, 2022, TikTok video, https://www.tiktok.com/@opernloft/video/7055349879744318725?is_from_webapp=1&sender_device=pc&web_id=7062339902340007429.

[28] A more current example of this type of exploration can be seen in the multimedia compositions of Belenish Moreno-Gil, Óscar Escudero, Karel Stulens, among others.

interaction spaces (such as TikTok, YouTube, Instagram): a multimedia network in which we live and experience our day to day. In the following, I will examine and discuss different strategies that TikTokers use to occupy, transform, and make sense of the musical geography of TikTok from an Austrian context.

Re-embedding TikTok

Although deterritorialized music practices take place through complex distribution processes in completely different spaces scattered over the world, the creation and exchange of certain knowledge, as well as several interactions between actors, occur in virtual and physical "local" situations (see Heep 2020). Besides, as noted by Christine Hine, "[Internet] is embedded in various contextualizing frameworks, institutions, and devices, that the experience of using it is embodied and hence highly personal and that it is everyday" (Hine 2015: 32), therefore its practices are influenced by these contexts and infrastructures. For this, it is important to first keep in mind that the articulation, negotiation, and sustaining of musical (and nonmusical) practices developed through the internet are not just *embedded* on devices but in their local contexts and infrastructures as well. Although the musical geography of TikTok can be inhabited through multimedia spaces scattered around the world, the practices actors develop are strongly framed and influenced by at least three aspects that cannot be separated from their physical location[29]: (1) the device embodiment, (2) the connection infrastructures, (3) national laws and regulations.

Device embodiment: Just like traditional musical practices, musical practices developed in multimedia environments need physical devices for their realization. In TikTok, these are predominantly smartphones. Although the use of computers, smart-TVs, and/or other portable devices is possible, these are used much less. In the same way as with musical instruments, these tools generate a new embodied relation that performers must acquire and maintain to effectively and satisfactorily perform their musicking. This embodied relation

[29] It should be clear that there are, without a doubt, many other aspects that are influenced by the physical location of the actors; among them are various aesthetic-cultural aspects of the own performances (sign system, aesthetics, etc.) and/or digital intersectionalities of the performers (gender, class, race, digital literacy, etc.). However, these aspects can only be treated in specific performative cases and moments. Therefore, they are not addressed in conjunction with the aspects discussed in this section.

directly influences the way in which the musicking of TikTok is developed (see Chapter 3). On the one hand, the embodiment generated by interacting with the device determines the way in which certain practices may or may not be developed. On the other hand, this interaction with the devices allows the creation of embodiment in the relationships between actors, thus helping the creation of an embodied sense of locality and community in this musical practice.

Connection infrastructure: Many of the practices developed in the musicking of TikTok require an internet connection. This might seem trivial, nonetheless access to the necessary infrastructure influences to a great extent the way in which musicking is articulated and negotiated between actors, as well as how important these practices are. For example, although theoretically anyone can partake on the musicking of TikTok, observing this from an Austrian context may differ greatly from a Cuban one. Such aspects must be further contemplated in correspondence to what Nick Couldry and Ulises Mejías call *data colonialism* (see 2019: 83–112). Another aspect related to this is the cost of the service itself. Similar as problems regarding access, service costs have a great influence in our musicking practices. The way we use different digital platforms that are connected to the internet would not be the same if they meant a lower or higher economical cost to us. This situation leads to giving different meanings and importance to these practices. One example would be the difference in use and importance that I have personally observed in the use of WhatsApp in Mexico and Austria. This idea of connection can also be extended to specific needs from each device regarding, for example, the battery performance and how specific behaviors arise from this.

National laws and regulations: A particularly influencing aspect that cannot be completely separated from the physical location of the actors is the fact that actors find themselves framed under the conditioning of national laws and regulations. Whether the platforms are permitted or not, and whether they have these certain features or not can be a clear example not only of this influence but also of how the users are bound, or not, to specific norms, such as the requirement of tagging a post as "publicity" when explicitly mentioning a brand. In other cases, we can observe direct interventions by authorities in the musicking development, such as the case of the "Kulikitaka-Challenge," where users frighten cows, which was removed from the Austrian TikTok after a public call made to the Austrian Federal Minister Elisabeth Köstinger on July 7, 2020.

Understanding that the musicking of TikTok is embedded on the previously mentioned embodiments, infrastructures, laws, and regulations allows us to see some of the mechanisms and processes that set up a local frame of action for the practice of phenomena that are considered as global. Additionally, this helps us define the perspective and conditions from which actors of the musicking of TikTok interact, and from which they inhabit, transform, and make sense of the multimedia space in which they interact. On this basis we can then examine and discuss the different strategies that the actors in the musicking of TikTok use to inhabit, transform, and make sense of the musical geography of TikTok, in my case from an Austrian context.

Performances

The practices of the musicking of TikTok are strongly connected to the local realities that TikTokers experience. On the one hand, these practices are embedded in embodiments, infrastructures, laws, and regulations, as already mentioned, but on the other hand, TikTokers use their musicking, especially their performances, also to deal and negotiate with situations that affect their daily lives, thematizing their feelings, identity, and collectivity, as well as the problems and challenges they experience. A clear example of this is the local crisis unleashed with the COVID-19 pandemic. The negotiating of the actors on daily situations through their performances helps them to create a feeling of locality and community as well, that at the same time has become one of the most common strategies used by TikTokers to make sense of the phantasmagoric geography of TikTok. In these performances, TikTokers position their own physical locality through (1) the presentation of a physical place and (2) through the thematizing of this locality.

On the one hand, recalling that performances take place on a particular location, TikTokers position their performance on a specific physical location. Some of these locations end up being places in the private lives of TikTokers, like their homes or bedrooms. In contrast, other locations seem like places in their public lives, like parks, squares, and streets. The preference of one of these places, either private or public, obey the specific aims that TikTokers develop during their creation and negotiation process of their TikTok persona. Following my observations, when TikTokers choose to present places from their private sphere in their performances, they pursue to produce a growing sensation of intimacy and authenticity between them and their followers in an attempt to creating a sense of community through partaking in their intimate daily lives, a way of personally and authentically sharing their lives. In contrast, the predilection toward presenting places in the public sphere attempts to creating a sentiment of remembrance and longing, which can be directly related with our own experiences and/or embodied desires, a sense of community through the desire/possibility of bodily sharing a specific locality.

It is interesting to observe that some TikTokers can keep a constant preference toward a public or private physical location for their performances throughout the development of their TikTok persona. Most of them prefer the presentation of private places during their performances, while others usually perform in public spaces. Other TikTokers instead vary this preference continuously or by phases along this same development. Another way in which TikTokers enunciate their physical locality by thematizing their own locality is through their performance. This thematizing can be directly or indirectly through language. A direct way in which TikTokers thematize their physical locality is, for example, the case of *#steckbrief*,[30] a challenge that started on June 2020 by @simonwill. In this challenge, TikTokers are invited to share with the TikTok community their name, age, city in which they live, favorite color, height, and languages they speak. Here TikTokers directly thematize their physical location, positioning their performance through the language of a specific geographical location. In this example, the physical location seen during the performance can or cannot correspond to a place in the public or private life in the thematized geographical location through language used by TikTokers. The locality of the performance is mainly marked by the act of naming a certain city instead of the location presented in the TikTok video by itself.

In contrast, an indirect way of this kind of thematizing can be observed in the performances that TikTokers make of *Oachkatzlschwoaf*[31] from @martyaustria. In this example, the thematization of locality is directly done, on the one hand, through the text "*Oachkatzlschwoaf, jede Österreicher kennt den Oachkatzlschwoaf*" [squirrel's tail, every Austrian knows the squirrel's tail], but on the other through the dialect used in the song that this locality is thematized. "*Oachkatzlschwoaf*" refers to "squirrel's tail" in Austrian German. What is

[30] @simonwill, "original sound," TikTok sound, https://www.tiktok.com/music/original-sound-6842300809875639046?is_from_webapp=1&sender_device=pc.

[31] @martyaustria, "MartyAustria Oachkatzlschoaf official," TikTok sound, https://www.tiktok.com/music/MartyAustria-Oachkatzlschwoaf-official-6867543265806142213?is_from_webapp=1&sender_device=pc.

particularly interesting here is not the word by itself but the use and importance that this word received in Austria to indicate a particular sense of *true* belonging. According to the generalized discourse, only *true* Austrians can *correctly* say "*Oachkatzlschwoaf*," and therefore "*Oachkatzlschwoaf*" is used as a symbol for *true* Austrian identity.[32] This idea is reinforced by the "*Oachkatzlschwoaf*" text, which provides a particular sentimental and erotic value to this emic knowledge: "*Jeden tåg und jeden nåcht mågst du mi richtig schoaf weil du sågst Oachkatzlschwoaf*" [Every day and every night you turn me on (this could be also understood as "you make me horny") because you say squirrel's tail]. In this example, it is not necessary to use the text fragment where the TikToker is an "*Österreicher*" [Austrian] to position his/her/themselves as such, but just by understanding what this dialect implies, specifically this word, TikTokers are able to be in an emic position: "*Österreicher*" *are the only ones* able to correctly say (and thematize) "*Oachkatzlschwoaf*." In this example, the thematization of the locality, and belonging, of the TikTokers is developed in a much more subtle manner.

Algorithms

The second aspect that allows TikTokers to create a sense of locality and community through TikTok goes beyond their own strategy; it involves the algorithms within the application itself. Although TikTok is an application with wide presence around the world, based on my observations, there are some factors that seem particularly important for the algorithms of TikTok, which tend to place the physical location of users/TikTokers on a high rank of priority. These factors are engagement rate, viewing time, and replay-quote. These three factors reflect the different forms TikTokers interact with the application. The engagement rate reflects the proportion between the number of visits a TikTok video has and the number of likes, comments, and repostings. At the same time, viewing time and replay-quote reflect the amount of time and intensity that a TikToker interacts with a video. The more often and longer a TikToker watches a video, the bigger chance that the video is perceived as valuable by the algorithms. However, what does this have to do with the locality of TikTokers?

32 These statements are based on my own experiences and confrontations with these aspects of *authenticity* and belonging after more than fifteen years living and researching in Austria.

TikTok algorithms aim to keep TikTokers using the application as much as possible. Based on my observations, I dare to say that this is mostly done by evoking of a local/regional sensation of *togetherness* among TikTokers, together with other resources like related topics. When you start using the application, you will notice that soon after, the performances displayed in the feed start to reflect the geographic region from which you are accessing it. Although it cannot be denied that personal aesthetic or gender preferences, age, and other sociocultural factors, as well as those regarding connectivity and infrastructure have an influence on the material the algorithm decides to show, the case of TikTok stands out because of the strong role for the physical location of its users. The algorithms of TikTok prioritize physical location, showing performances that reinforce a local and embodied experience. This favoring of the local is quite divergent in comparison with other applications where this factor plays a subaltern role. In Instagram, for example, it is possible to observe that algorithms greatly prioritize the sociocultural preferences of its users (e.g., personal aesthetic and gender preferences, age, etc.), while the physical location and/or connection point does not seem to affect the feed.

TikTok algorithms emphasizing the local stimulate and strengthen the embodied experience and sense of belonging of TikTokers. Additionally, this favors TikTokers who openly incorporate this sense of locality and community in their performances, positioning their own physical locality by presenting a physical place and/or thematizing this location, as previously mentioned. Besides providing the possibility for corporal interaction beyond the interface of the application, TikTok algorithms stimulate and reinforce the embodied experience and sense of belonging by giving visibility to the local places and experiences of TikTokers. This allows them to create relationships of *empathic co-presence* with other TikTokers, creating much stronger community ties and bonds of belonging among them, which in turn contributes to the fact that the musicking of TikTok is not lived as a global and deterritorialized experience.

These community and corporal belonging bonds allow TikTokers to create a sense of locality and community through TikTok, taking it from a purely global phenomenon to an openly glocal one. This locality sensation additionally enhances interactions and interrelations between TikTokers beyond the interface. This leads to negotiating friendships that are much more intense and lasting, which intensify with reciprocity expectations between TikTokers during their musicking in TikTok. The number of visits, likes, comments, and/or shares [repostings] a TikTok video receives is not simple anonymous interactions for TikTokers anymore, but they become a necessary action of active support for maintaining their own community. For this, algorithms favoring the local promotes an increase in engagement rate, viewing time, and replay-quote for longer time among TikTokers.

Interactions

TikTok is a social practice, and as such, it needs the physical and digital interactions of its actors to be created, maintained, and transformed by its musicking. TikTokers interact through the application by creating *faceless commitments*: they dialogue with each other, exchange information, show their aesthetic and belonging preferences, and interact with performances by observing, commenting, and liking them. Through these faceless interactions, TikTokers create and negotiate a sense of community by positioning their own physical locality through the presentation of a physical place and thematizing this locality. This way, they make sense of the phantasmagoric reality of TikTok. This way, the musicking of TikTok becomes a multimedia practice that is not exclusively experienced in a global and digital way, but it is strongly entwined with the realities and facework commitments of TikTokers. The facework interactions between TikTokers become part of the different strategies that the actors of this musicking use to inhabit, transform, and make sense of the musical geography of TikTok, in this case, from an Austrian perspective.

In the musicking of TikTok there is a strong physical interaction between TikTokers. The example of the teenagers on the train at the beginning of this chapter is a good example of this. TikTokers get together to make, watch, comment, and analyze TikTok videos. Complex physical interactions are normal components of the practices outside the interface of TikTok. These presence relations cannot be observed from the application, yet they make up an indisputable part of TikTok musicking. Some of these interactions can be easily observed throughout different public spaces: teenagers grouped around a smartphone in some park, doing some movements that resemble TikTok performances in a mall, or discussing aesthetic preferences on the train. These interactions can also happen in much more private spaces and moments in the life of TikTokers. These presence relations existing among TikTokers are shown to be important in TikTok musicking by creating embodied feelings of locality and community among TikTokers and allowing them to inhabit and make sense of the multimedia space of TikTok.

For obvious reasons these physical interactions have diminished in intensity during the COVID-19 pandemic. TikTokers, like the rest of the population, have been required to reduce physical contact to the minimum. The Austrian government was no exception for issuing several lockdowns with diverse intensities, therefore restricting the physical interaction between TikTokers. However, COVID-19 pandemic interfered with my observation and participation in these interactions. Nevertheless, it is possible to observe that this need of physically relating has not lost importance for TikTokers. TikTokers continue musicking and physically getting together, even if in a more restricted way. All these physical interactions reinforce articulating and negotiating cohorts and embodied social spaces among TikTokers, which renew their empathic co-presence relations as well. This allows the experiencing of an ontological security, making sense of the deterritorialized world we seem to live in.

Meetups

Following this, I would like to briefly discuss the last strategy for creating a sense of locality and community used by TikTokers—and making sense of the musical geography of TikTok with it. This strategy is the Meetups. TikTokers keep a very close relationship with their followers. Therefore, getting together physically with them is a very important practice in TikTok musicking. Meetups are physical gatherings organized by TikTokers who already hold certain popularity.[33] These gatherings have the purpose, among others, of intensifying the community and embodying reciprocity bonds with followers. Some of these encounters end up being quite improvised and spontaneous, while others are professionally organized and aim to incentivize economical processes.

Less formal Meetups are made by TikTokers who are on the way for having a professional career in TikTok, whose TikTok persona is already recognized by a reasonable amount of fellow TikTokers. A good example of this is the first Meetup of @anna_strigl in Vienna. During the Meetup in October 2019, @anna_strigl was making her first steps toward the consolidation of her career

[33] These MeetUps are as important for TikTokers as it is for TikTok—the company. TikTok organizes these kinds of gatherings in their offices around the world. Many TikTokers are invited by TikTok to these MeetUps with the purpose of enhancing/boosting friendships, campaigns, alliances, and so on, and therefore a "TikTok Community." This is emphasized with gifts and goodies that TikTok constantly gives its creators/TikTokers to foster a relationship beyond a simple service.

as a professional TikToker.[34] Her visibility in the application was already over a hundred thousand followers, and her TikTok persona began to be visible outside the application, making appearances in newspapers and local magazines (see Goldenberg 2019). After pausing her TikTok activities for personal reasons, this gathering marked the beginning of a new phase in her development as TikToker, in which she was mainly looking for contact with her followers as well as the application in her own career of some of the knowledge she would have gained through her experience during the practice of the musicking of TikTok, as well as during her undergraduate studies in Business & Management (@anna_strigl, pers. comm., October 15, 2019).

This Meetup was developed in a very spontaneous and improvised way. The date, time, and place of encounter (October 15 at 4:30 pm in Prater) was announced a couple of days earlier on a *story* in her Instagram account. The day of the encounter, the Instagram activities of @anna_strigl were crucial for coordinating and communication with people participating in the Meetup. Throughout the day, @anna_strigl presented with photos in her *IG stories* her location, and with it, she anticipated and coordinated the exact time and place for the gathering. As soon as a place was fixed, the Meetup was developed by just a few people, and almost exclusively in a physical manner. This encounter did not follow a fixed schedule. A monetary profit plan did not play an important role either. The main purpose of this encounter was giving followers the chance to hang out a bit with @anna_strigl. This was possible in a very intense way due to the reduced number of people who participated in this Meetup, who were able to chat, drink something, walk around, ride some of the attractions in the park, and so on, in a more intense and intimate way. Shortly after the Meetup was over, the lived experiences during this encounter were shared with the rest of her followers through TikTok and Instagram. The following year @anna_stringl repeated this Meetup on July 31st with the same group of teenagers who participated in the first encounter.

In contrast, Meetups by @lisamarie_schiffner or @lisaandlena in February 2020 show us a much more professional and clearly economic-orientated version of these kind of encounters. These kinds of "professional" Meetups are organized by TikTokers who already have a consolidated career as TikTokers.

[34] In the last couple of years, @anna_strigl has consolidated a professional career as TikToker, reaching two million followers by the beginning of 2022, and has done several cooperation agreements with various companies.

This is reflected in the level of visibility and the infrastructures and resources that these TikTokers have at their disposal for making these Meetups, which show a great contrast with the gatherings organized by TikTokers whose career is not yet consolidated. The Meetup by @lisamarie_schiffner—who at that time had over two million TikTok followers and about a million on Instagram—took place at a drugstore in Shopping City Süd mall in Vösendorf and the event had already been advertised through different media. Around three hundred people participated in this encounter, and they had to wait about an hour for taking a picture with @lisamarie_schiffner and buy the cereal and photo album she was promoting. However, this Meetup seemed small compared with the one by @lisaandlena in February 2020 in Vienna. Although both TikTokers have an established TikTok career, @lisaandlena[35]—with over twelve million TikTok followers, fifteen million on Instagram, and about a million on YouTube by the beginning of 2022—are on top of the German-speaking TikTok landscape.

The Meetup by @lisaandlena in Vienna in February 2020 was part of a series of Meetups that @lisaandlena did throughout German-speaking countries to promote their new line of shoes. This Meetup was widely promoted by many digital platforms with a professional planning and implementation. Access to the area in which the shoe store was located was only allowed to people who had previously acquired a ticket.

Three hours before the gathering started, around one thousand fans were already in line to get in. Besides a considerably large organizing staff, @ lisaandlena were guarded by at least four security guards and were always followed by about three camera people for documenting different aspects of this Meetup. TikTokers attending this Meetup were able to have around a minute with @lisaandlena for talking with them, hugging them, taking a photo, and having an autograph on their brand-new shoes.

Meetups allow TikTokers to create new embodied relations with their followers while they appropriate the location of the TikTok musicking to a specific physical location. Thus, articulating and negotiating corporeal social spaces between the TikTokers, who create and renew through these encounters

[35] @lisaandlena are a special case in the German-speaking history of TikTok. Starting their career on Musical.ly in 2015, the twin sisters Lisa and Lena reached international fame through their performances. After the transformation of Musical.ly to TikTok in 2018, @lisaandlena decided to delete their account (with around thirty million followers) in 2019, since they did not feel part of that community anymore. However, in the early 2020, @lisaandlena came back to TikTok, recovering after a short time their status as the most successful TikTokers in the German-speaking area.

Figure 13 Meetup by @lisaandlena in Vienna, photo by author.

their relationships of empathic co-presence, and which can be seen as ritual events (see Turner [1969] 2017), are essential. The transformative power of these Meetups lies in the power they have to convert a virtual reality into an actual, embodied reality, or in other words, by transforming a relationship of co-presence into a relationship of empathic co-presence, generating a much more bodily sense of locality and community, thus enabling the negotiation of much more intense and lasting relationships of friendship and reciprocity between them.

Dwelling in TikTok

I would like to end with a couple of words regarding the reason for these activities. All of these practices entwine the musicking of TikTok with embodied localities, embodied daily experiences, with bodies. These interactions reinforce the articulation and negotiation of cohort and conjunct and corporal social spaces between TikTokers. These practices create, negotiate, and renew relations of empathic co-presence, which allows TikTokers to experience ontological security, letting them make sense of the phantasmagorical geography of

TikTok, and therefore feel "at home." Through the practices of our embodied consciousness, we make sense of our world. We shape communities and social spaces through practice. The same way as walking, thinking, talking, or playing an instrument, the use of digital media like TikTok lets us make sense of the world we live in. Musicking in TikTok is not just about representing a physical reality in a digital environment but a practice that is experienced through our embodied consciousness in a phantasmagorical multimedia reality with the purpose of inhabiting and making sense of it. TikTok musicking is not a musical practice lived globally but one that is continuously re-embedded in the local embodied realities of TikTokers. For TikTokers, TikTok is more than just an application; TikTok becomes a part of their home. The musical geography of TikTok cannot be understood as a phantasmagoric representation lacking real existence, but rather as the embodied experience of the actors when inhabiting their multimedia world.

Having analyzed the way in which localities in TikTok musicking are articulated and negotiated, as well as some strategies that the TikTokers use for inhabiting, transforming, and making sense of the musical geography of TikTok from an Austrian context, in the next chapter I will examine and discuss different strategies of how TikTokers appropriate TikTok to develop and adapt their musical practices.

5

TikToking Musics

My journey into the world of TikTok's musical expressions was a whirlwind of curiosity and amazement. The more I immersed myself in the musicking of TikTok, the more I was astounded by the sheer scale, adaptability, and diversity of the musical expressions. TikTokers didn't just sing or play instruments; they also lip-synced while performing choreographies, framed challenges with music, and even created musical memes. The bond between TikTok and music was so strong that the absence of music in a performance was like a void, underscoring its inseparability from TikTok. This chapter is focused on the performances held within the musicking of TikTok. Here I explore and analyze some examples of the ways in which TikTokers appropriate the platform for creating musical practices in and through it. It is important to point out that this chapter is not focused on the strategies used by TikTokers for advertising their work (marketing) but on the creation of the performances.

In the first part of this chapter, I discuss how TikTok is used as a digital stage for developing performances. In this section I present how TikTokers use the performative space and visibility provided by TikTok and turn it into a place, or more specifically, a *stage* for the development of their musical practices. The second part of this chapter is focused on the way in which actors of other already established musical traditions use TikTok for performative experimentation in new formats. Drawing mainly from examples of the opera tradition, in this section I analyze how these actors adapt their musical practices to the technical possibilities, conventions, and aesthetic expectations of TikTok together with how they negotiate diverse performative circumstances in divergent occasions with the purpose of achieving a satisfactory development of their performance. At the end, in the third part of this chapter, I focus on how TikTokers develop musical practices that are characterized by their understanding of TikTok as a practice of its own and of equal performative value. In these musical practices, TikTokers look to appropriate these musics from other contexts, norms, expectations, and aesthetics of TikTok from a performative understanding particular to the platform through their performance, in other words, how TikTokers are TikToking musics.

TikTok as a Digital Stage

Understanding TikTok as a digital stage means seeing it as another performative space for developing musical practices, as a place that allows carrying out and distributing performances. Let's think of a physical stage. Although this setting frames a performance (see Chapter 3), in principle, this stage can host a wide array of performances in number and kind, and, at the same time, a performance can be hosted by an endless number of different stages. Therefore, the musical practices developed here are not necessarily specific for a location and/or a performance. This situation is equally valid if we conceptualize a digital platform as a digital stage. For example, a live stream can take place not only in multiple applications and/or digital platforms (e.g., Facebook, Instagram, YouTube, etc.) but also through other broadcasting means (e.g., television, radio, etc.). In the same way, a particular platform can host different kinds of performances that might not have much relation with another. Although the settings that frame performances are different, the practice and way of understanding the function of the device and/or setting behind it are similar in all the previously mentioned examples. Understanding TikTok as a digital stage certainly influences the way in which TikTokers use the application for developing their musical practices. But how is TikTok used by TikTokers as a digital stage for developing their performances?

Live is Live

One way in which TikTokers use the performative space and visibility by TikTok as a digital stage for their performances can be observed in the live streaming they carry out in physical locations. Either by transmitting organized events or small spontaneous presentations, TikTok is used as a platform for the distribution of a kind of performance that exists outside the platform. Here TikTokers look to increasing the number of people they reach, looking to increase the visibility of their TikTok persona, as well as their performances. It is important to notice that, in this case, the use of TikTok is not fundamental for the development of the performance, but the physical performance and that it reaches more people. For this reason, streaming can be and is developed simultaneously on other platforms, like YouTube or Instagram. That said, TikTok can be understood as one more interchangeable space that allows music to reach particular audiences, turning TikTok into one of the many infrastructures for distributing performances.

As already mentioned in previous pages, the live function is a performative tool that only becomes available when TikTokers acquire at least one thousand followers. The musicians who already have access to this tool use this option for developing live streaming of complete concerts and/or excerpts. During my research I was able to observe different contexts in which these transmissions were used for performances, as well as the different aims their producers had in mind. On the one hand, musicians who have been carrying out performances for a while and have already established a steady network of locations to play at use this function for streaming their performances in these usual locations. On the other hand, TikTokers who do not have a steady access to a stage use this space for exponentially increasing the visibility of the performances they develop in a more spontaneous way by presenting themselves on diverse locations, such as the street and/or a subway station.

In the case of already established musicians who possess a stable network of locations for performing, the live function is especially used for streaming themselves playing in these locations. Many musicians use the visibility provided by TikTok and use the platform—especially the live function—for promoting their performance and getting more people to go to their concerts. A very common way of doing this is by making short streaming sessions before the concert, where they personally invite the audience to assist. But besides this, musicians use the live function for streaming their performances right in the moment they are doing them. Musicians here develop their performance in a conventional stage, at a bar, a café, or a concert hall, to mention some examples, and use this function for streaming on TikTok the performance happening in a physical location. Usually, the smartphone streaming finds itself in a static position somewhere in the stage, though sometimes the musician is assisted by other people for transmitting from different perspectives throughout the performance.

It is interesting to observe that the interaction between musicians and their audience during the streaming of performances takes place mainly on the physical setting. The audience observing the performance through TikTok tends to receive less attention from the performing musician. Most of the time, the musician is focused on the audience that is in front of her, negotiating a satisfactory development of her musicking. The audience that participates by watching the show at home or elsewhere through the live transmission seems to stay in the background. Nevertheless, the remote audience can let the musician know if the performance pleases them or not through likes and emojis, but since the musician is usually focused on the interaction with the physical audience, she reacts less to these displays of appreciation and/or dislike. This situation can remind us of different experiences during many kinds of performances transmitted through other means of telecommunication, like television, and/or digital platforms, like YouTube.

Besides these local contexts, musicians and/or professional agencies take this possibility to make live streaming of their performances. Music labels, among others, launch campaigns and stream live converts of their artists through TikTok and other digital platforms. TikTok as a company organizes and streams exclusive concerts through its platform as well. Some clear examples of these transmissions include Ed Sheeran's concert "TikTok UEFA EURO 2020" on July 25, 2021; the presentation of the album "Familia" by Camila Cabello on April 7, 2022; and the premiere of the TikTok Musical "For You, Paige" on April 14, 2022. TikTok is used as one more stage from which a performance can be presented, widening exponentially their visibility.

On the other hand, the possibility of increasing the visibility of performances provided by TikTok is very attractive for musicians who have not yet experienced access to a stage and/or have not been able to establish a lasting network of locations to play at. TikTok, especially its live function, allows these musicians to spontaneously turn a public space, like a train station or a park, or a private space, like a bedroom or a living room, into the setting of a performance that can be watched by millions of people around the world. Even when these practices are similar to the ones carried out by the aforementioned musicians, it is possible to find some differences in the way this function is used by amateur musicians. For example, by not having a stable network of locations to play, amateur musicians are pushed to appropriate public spaces that were not originally designed for hosting a musical performance. This situation creates a contrast between the audience and the musician in this case and the situation in, for example, a bar. The setting that frames the performance, a street, a park, or a subway station, requires another kind of attention from the musician with the audience to achieve a satisfactory performance. The people who walk by do not "expect" to experience a musical performance in that setting, and therefore the musician needs to give another kind of attention to the act of engaging with these people. In this kind of setting, where the audience is constantly changing, the smartphone or device from which it is streamed turns into a continuous source throughout the performance. Following my observations, musicians give a bigger part of their attention to the relations generated from the platform, integrating the TikTok audience more consciously into the physical performance. For this reason, the interactions between the musician and the audience—both physical and digital—are a little more balanced compared to the ones carried out in spaces destined to host a musical performance. An example of this kind of public location streaming can be observed in the case of @daniliamusik, who, as I was doing my research, streamed several performances at the facilities of some subway stations across the city of Vienna.

In the same way, musicians stream their performances from private spaces as another way to gain visibility in their performances through the streaming services provided by TikTok. This kind of performances clearly show the possibilities that digital platforms like TikTok provide amateur musicians for developing a career as performers, and how these possibilities influence the development of musical practices. In this context, it is relevant to highlight live streaming set in living rooms or bedrooms. Here, musicians perform music from the safety of their homes, providing the performer with many advantages. Firstly, neither a stage nor an institutionalized infrastructure for supporting a successful performance is needed anymore, but rather just performing from the safety of their home and streaming this performance through TikTok is enough for performers to be able to reach millions of people. In the same way, the fact of performing in such a personal space helps amateur musicians feel more confident at the moment of performing and motivates them to have an audience. This situation makes it easier to "jump" into developing a public music career. Besides that, performance streaming in these private settings creates and/or reinforces authenticity ideals, as well as creating a sense of intimacy between the musician and her audience. It is interesting that, although these performances seem to be intimate, they can be seen by millions of people, creating a kind of *public intimacy* (see Pink et al. 2016), which may increase the visibility and fame of the musician without ever stepping on a traditional stage.

Thus, online streaming through TikTok has become a practice that lets amateur musicians exponentially increase the visibility of their performances in a more spontaneous way, both in private and public locations. Additionally, it is possible to observe TikToks that, although they are not live transmissions, show recordings of presentations taking place in physical locations. However, musicians also record TikToks "as if" they were live-streamed or publish excerpts of live performances as an advertisement strategy to promote future concerts and/or musical pieces. With this, we can see that some aspects of the aesthetic created by streaming influence other kinds of performative practices in the musicking of TikTok, as well as intensifying authenticity ideals.

Performing Songs and Music Pieces

Understanding TikTok as a digital stage does not reduce performative possibilities for musicians to only live-stream their performances. TikTokers can also carry out performances that can be carried out asynchronously in a presentational manner (see Turino 2008: 51–65) through the application. TikTokers who are still in the early phase of their musical careers can find this particularly beneficial since the function for live streaming requires at least one thousand followers to gain access. When talking about these asynchronous performances I specifically refer to TikToks in which musicians perform songs and/or other musical pieces. In these performances, TikTokers use TikTok as a digital stage for performing asynchronously. It is worth pointing out that in this section I focus on performances in which TikTokers create the sound themselves with their voices[1] and/or musical instruments.

Throughout my research I observed numerous TikToks where TikTokers perform their own original music. On one side, there are some TikTokers who play short cover versions of songs and/or musical pieces; on the other, there are TikTokers who prefer composing their own original songs and/or musical pieces specifically to be interpreted on TikTok. In both cases, musicians use TikTok as an asynchronous digital stage in which they can develop their performances and create small independent works[2] that can be performed, appreciated, and shared asynchronously by other users without depending on the performer.[3] Similar to

[1] It is worth highlighting that there are some performances where TikTokers sing a song where lip-syncing practices and/or playback practices can be identified. Many TikTokers record the video and the audio of their performances separately and mix them afterward in the TikTok that will be published in the application.

[2] This context creates a kind of hybrid performative state, where the performance is being performed (process) at the same time it is a work (audiovisual object).

[3] The development of an autonomous life that musical objects can experience can be seen and understood from what Julio Mendívil calls "la vida social de las canciones" (the social life of songs) (see Mendívil 2013).

live streaming, asynchronously performing songs and/or other musical pieces can also be done in other digital platforms. However, compared to performances seen through live streaming, the aesthetics and performative styles exhibited in these asynchronous performances appear to be heavily influenced by the practices characteristic of TikTok.

In the first place, TikTokers use TikTok as a stage for interpreting already existing song excerpts and/or musical pieces to demonstrate their abilities as musical interpreters and achieve more visibility for their TikTok persona. This kind of performance is not restricted to amateur music, but professionals also carry out this kind of asynchronous performance. Compared with other performative forms in TikTok, in this one, TikTokers openly seek to show their vocal and/or instrumental abilities. It is about demonstrating that they can indeed "do music." In this context, TikTokers use a very diverse repertoire in their performances. On one side, many TikTokers use famous songs and/or musical pieces, especially mainstream music from the Global North, with the purpose of increasing the visibility of their performance. This follows the logic that a famous song has a better chance of receiving a *like*. Conversely, as part of the creation process of their TikTok persona, TikTokers seek to reflect their performer identity by curating a repertoire they feel represented with, even if they are not as famous as other mainstream artists, and try to build that way a more intimate relationship with their audience. Vocal and/or instrumental performances, like those by @rachelchiu1, @frombritton, and @annamaurer_music, can serve us as reference for this kind of performances.

Beyond this, as part of the creation of a performer identity, TikTokers develop their musical practices through the platform. The creation of their own music is the most common next step in the process. Following this line, it is possible to observe that TikTokers not just play excerpts of already existing songs and/or musical pieces, but that occasionally they also compose and perform their own original music. Making their own music known and making themselves known as independent performers is a common practice among TikTokers. Vocal and/or instrumental performances, like those by @aymzoffizial, @coremyofficial, and @valeriooon.off, can provide us with clear examples of this kind of performances. Beyond these examples, there are nevertheless TikTokers who have developed a kind of performance much more particular of TikTok. These TikTokers compose their songs, especially made for being (almost) exclusively performed on TikTok. In this case, the application is not seen as a stage but rather as a practice. I will expand on this later.

Yet, despite wanting to demonstrate their abilities, TikTokers choose to limit themselves and just perform an excerpt instead of recording the whole song and/or musical piece. This seems to be a consistent decision, since TikTokers can perform a whole song and/or musical piece without any problem. TikTokers can record themselves up to three minutes long.[4] Despite that, TikTokers choose otherwise. This is also seen in the fact that these musicians occasionally publish complete performances of their songs and/or musical pieces in other digital platforms like YouTube, a situation that exposes that musicians frame their performances in some of the existing aesthetic and performative ideals in the platform. An example of this is the use of a 9:16 format and a recording time between fifteen seconds and one minute. Another interesting aspect that can be observed in these performances is that many of these TikTokers perform and record their performances at their bedrooms and/or their living rooms. Here, musicians perform their music from the safety of their home, which is not just a product of the easy and constant access to this location but also to a certain extent a consequence of some of the prevailing intimacy and authenticity ideals of TikTok. This situation is meaningful because, as previously mentioned, creating performances in these kinds of private settings generates and/or reinforces a sense of intimacy and trust between the musician and their audience, a situation that allows them to create longer-lasting reciprocity bonds.

By performing either their own songs or other musical pieces, or those by other artists, musicians essentially seek to leverage their performances through the digital stage provided by TikTok as a kind of "springboard" to jump into their musical career. Following my observations, many TikTokers aim to "be discovered" by agents of the music industry, and that way being able to develop a professional career and/or reach fame as musicians. For this reason, musicians try to show that they can indeed "make music" by themselves. Therefore, the sound quality on their TikToks becomes a fundamental aspect for demonstrating these abilities together with the conscious visual positioning of the performance. This aims to make the creation of sound visible and accentuate that they are "really" performing visually. A remarkable aspect here lies on the authenticity images that this kind of performers promote. Following these ideals, making "true" music is tightly related with the production of sound through a musical

[4] It is possible to make recordings up to ten minutes in TikTok. However, this function is not available to all users.

instrument—classically understood[5]—and/or the own voice. This position frames the conceptualization of TikTok as a digital stage.

Performing Duets

Another way in which TikTokers use the performative space and visibility offered by TikTok as a digital stage for their performances can be observed in the creation of musical duets through the duet function. Similar to other kinds of performances presented in previous chapters, TikTokers seek to publicly show their vocal and/or instrumental abilities through these duets. This has the purpose of demonstrating that they can indeed "make music" by themselves and in cooperation with other TikTokers. In a similar way to the previously presented examples, TikTokers perform excerpts of songs and/or musical pieces composed by themselves or by other authors. At the same time, the aesthetic decisions for these duets are similar to those seen in previous kinds of performances. However, compared to those other performances, these are developed by TikTokers, who develop their performance in an asynchronous and multimedia way. This means that TikTokers involved in creating the performance are not located in the same physical place nor are making their performance at the same time.

Although these practices show many similarities with each other, I decided to approach them as different phenomena because when TikTokers use the duet function, they integrate typical practices and aesthetics of TikTok in a narrower way to the performance and away from the conceptualization of TikTok as a digital stage. In contrast to the aforementioned way of performing songs and/or musical pieces, TikTokers explicitly include the tools provided by the TikTok application for carrying out their performance. Consequently, these kinds of practices will not be easy to develop on other digital platforms. The performative possibilities offered by the interface of TikTok become an essential factor for developing performances. It is worth highlighting that just like the already mentioned practices, there are duet versions that have been thought in advance to be exclusively performed on TikTok. In this case, TikTok is not seen as a stage, but rather as a practice of its own. I will go back to this topic later.

The development of a satisfactory duet is the result of a collective performance, in this case, an asynchronous performance. This might seem

[5] Here smartphones are not understood and/or considered as music instruments.

a little trivial, but it is a very interesting situation to observe considering the asynchronous and multilocal side of TikTok practices. In these duets, TikTokers play experts of songs and/or musical pieces, either composed by themselves or by other authors. To achieve this, TikTokers require the participation of other performers for developing the performance. This participation can be either planned or spontaneous. Until now, nothing seems to be new. However, the necessary interactions for creating a TikTok are not required to be in situ or synchronous, nor completely consensual. With this I mean that, compared to other musical practices in which not just a consensual agreement is required but also physical and synchronous interactions between performers, in TikTok, a duet can be carried out without having to share a specific place and time[6] nor previous organization. Additionally, a TikTok duet can be accomplished without notifying and/or directly involving the other performer.

Thanks to the performative possibilities of the platform and the relative independence it encourages its users, organizing and carrying out duets can be done in different ways. These duets can be organized in advance and jointly by performing TikTokers, but they can also be spontaneous and unilateral. In the first place, as part of the development of their musical practices, TikTokers know other performers and befriend them. These relations can lead TikTokers to make collaborations and perform together, as it is in the case of the duets. Motivated by friendship, mutual admiration, or something else, some TikTokers decide to create duets and make agreements for contextualizing and/or fixing the development of the performance. Some of the decisions they make together include choosing the song/musical piece for singing/playing, how they will play it, possible musical arrangements, and so on. Once the frame of action of the performance is organized and fixed, TikTokers perform parts of the duet asynchronously, and then they put them together for publishing.

However, not all duets are created in these circumstances. In fact, the most common way of creating a duet is following a spontaneous unilateral decision, as presented in the case of "The Wellerman,"[7] a sea shanty performed

6 A similar situation in which collective performances can be carried out without having to share a specific place and time can be found in the development of recording sessions. It is common that during these sessions the musicians are not always located in the same place nor the music is recorded at the same time.

7 @nathanevanss, "The Wellerman," December 27, 2020, TikTok video, https://www.tiktok.com/@nathanevanss/video/6910995345421962498?is_from_webapp=1&sender_device=pc&web_id=7062339902340007429.

by @nathanevanss on TikTok. "The Wellerman" was used as the base for developing many duets without previous organization between @nathanevanss and other TikTokers. This evidences the fact that it is not necessary to have explicit[8] authorization from the performer/creator of the original TikTok and/or their synchronous participation in creating a duet. Even if the original TikTok was ever made with the purpose of serving as a duet base seems irrelevant. TikTokers spontaneously react to already existing TikToks, where she or other TikTokers perform excerpts of songs and/or musical pieces to develop their own performance in the form of a duet afterward.

After listening to a TikTok performance, sometimes TikTokers suddenly have spontaneous ideas. An example of this is reflected on the comment by @MissBunPun: "When I hear something that makes me think—Oh, that's pretty cool … I mean, there are … like such inspirations, that come spontaneously, because I'm also seeing someone else … I don't know, something cool played in a guitar and I want to sing to it or something"[9] (@MissBunPun 2021). Reacting to this inspiration, as mentioned by @MissBunPun, TikTokers develop their ideas and new performances to complement the previous. That way they create countless performances from different TikTok bases, as well as different versions of the same TikTok base. These versions, which can be used to make a new duet, create an asynchronous shared creativity network through the growing overlapping of individual performances.

However, TikTokers not only react to these TikToks because they feel inspired, but they can also react to possible duet invitations that the author of the base TikTok extends through their performance. Many TikTokers record TikToks waiting for someone to react to their invitation and complement their performance through a duet. A common practice to exemplify this is when TikTokers play either the vocal or instrumental part of a song and then invite other TikTokers to complete their performance in their video or in text. Another way to do this is by composing an original musical piece and also including a verbal or text message inviting TikTokers to contribute to this composition.

[8] It is worth highlighting that in order to enable the duet function on TikTok, a TikToker must activate this function at the moment of publishing their performance, meaning that the TikToker is actually authorizing in advance the use of their performance for duet. However, this authorization does not specify a kind of performance nor a particular performer.

[9] "Wenn ich irgendwas höre, wo ich mir denk—Oh, das ist ziemlich cool. … Also, es sind … also so Inspirationen, die spontan kommen, weil ich eben irgendjemanden sehe, … weiß ich nicht auf der Gitarre was Cooles spielt und ich mag dazu singen oder so" (@MissBunPun 2021). Translated from German to English by Natalia Neira Nieto.

An example of this can be seen in the case of @binabianca89 and her TikTok "Singt mit mir! Ich bin die background vocals! Hab a #duet gebastelt! Zum #valentinstag #valentinesday"[10] (Sing with me! I'm the background vocals! Have a #duet crafted! For #valentinstag #valentinesday). Here she plays the guitar and background vocals of the song "Can't Help Falling in Love" by Elvis Presley while inviting other TikTokers to perform the main melody in a duet. Either developed spontaneously or organized, at the end performing duets through TikTok relates the participating TikTokers, creating or strengthening relations between them. This will set the base for possible future collaborations, as was the case in the previously mentioned example of bassist @caseybassy and the singer and pianist @annamaurer_music.

Through these asynchronous collaborative performances, TikTokers seek to create a process of synergy between both TikTokers with the purpose, among others, of widening their performative possibilities, as well as increasing their visibility and recognition. Either through the duet performance of songs and/or other musical pieces of their authorship or by other artists, musicians essentially seek to use the digital stage provided by TikTok as a "springboard" for jumping into their music career. Moreover, a very remarkable aspect of duets is that they not only promote an interaction between TikTokers but also allow TikTokers to widen their performative possibilities by making duets with themselves. In this case, TikTokers can, for example, complete their performances by playing different voices or sections by themselves. It is possible to observe a stronger tendency in this kind of performance of adapting musical styles to the forms, practices, aesthetics, and so on of TikTok. The aim is not to perform in a digital stage anymore, but TikTokers begin to appropriate the platform through these practices in a more intense way. In the following section I focus on musical practices in which TikTok stops being just a digital stage but as a space for performative experimentation, either by using the platform as an extension of performance or as a musical instrument.

10 @binabianca89, "Singt mit mir! Ich bin die background vocals! Hab a #duet gebastelt! Zum #valentinstag #valentinesday," February 14, 2022, TikTok video, https://www.tiktok.com/@binabianca89/video/7064585546508569862.

Adapting Musics to TikTok: The TikTok Operas by Opernloft

TikTok is usually thought as a place for enjoying trivial videos, short videos without any relation between one and the next. It is not common to perceive TikTok as a place for developing long-duration musical-dramaturgical practices and narrative extension, like those developed in opera and/or musical theater. However, there are some proposals where TikTok is understood not just as a place for presenting a performance but also as a tool and/or extended performative space through which it is possible to create new ways for playing music and performing. Opernloft in Hamburg had an attempt on adapting Wolfgang A. Mozart's "Die Entführung aus dem Serai" (1782) in 2021 and Georges Bizet's "Carmen" (1875) in 2022 to be performed in TikTok, becoming not just a novelty in the performative world of TikTok but also a multimedia sample of the performative possibilities and formats in the opera world.

Opernloft is a theater and opera house located in the German city of Hamburg. Compared to other opera houses, productions at Opernloft are characterized for having a "friendlier and more accessible" format for the audience, as stated in their slogan "Opernloft ist anders" ("Opernloft is different"). In the first place, the productions at Opernloft are never longer than ninety minutes. Operas presented there are condensed to the essential and reinterpreted in a contemporary context, no matter if it is a work by Mozart, Wagner, Verdi, or Puccini. At the same time, instrumentation is reduced to a small ensemble. Additionally, the audience at Opernloft has the opportunity to enjoy the show while having a drink from their seat, from a table inside the auditorium, or at the terrace viewing the Elbe River.[11] As dramaturgist and director of the Opernloft projects "#FREE_Constanze" and "Carmen by Carmen," Hannah Schlags mentioned: "Here [at Opernloft] we want to make opera for everyone, we want, that everyone, regardless of their background, comes by and has nice evening and that they can somehow take with them this amazement we have for opera"[12] (Schlags 2021).

[11] See https://www.opernloft.de.

[12] "Wir [im Opernloft] wollen Oper für alle machen, wir möchten, dass Alle, egal mit welchem Hintergrund zu uns kommen und einen schönen Abend haben und irgendwie diese Begeisterung, die wir für Oper haben, mitnehmen können" (Schlags 2021). Translated from German to English by Natalia Neira Nieto.

At the beginning of 2021, TikTok Germany in collaboration with betterplace lab launched the program #CreatorsForDiversity with the purpose of helping artistic and cultural institutions in Germany endure the economic struggles caused by the COVID-19 pandemic. This program was designed to support those artistic-cultural institutions "that gave a new impulse to the creative debate on the topic of inclusion and diversity." In the words of Tobias Henning, general manager of TikTok Germany:

> It's important to us to offer creators new ways of engaging with their audiences. With #CreatorsForDiversity, new formats are created that inspire and encourage TikTok users to immerse themselves in the topics of art, culture and diversity. In this way, we want to support the cultural sector, which suffers greatly from the current situation because special regulations make personal encounters impossible.[13] (TikTok 2021a)

The Opernloft team has been working for a while on opera adaptations with topics regarding diversity. Therefore, the open call published by TikTok appeared at the perfect moment. For the Opernloft team, this program marked a very good opportunity to economically overcome the lack of audiences after being forced to close their facilities to the public on several occasions for several months due to lockdowns in Germany. But, besides that, this allowed them to focus on a project they have been wanting to try for a long time without the pressure of being a financial success, in which they wanted to experiment with digital formats. As soon as Hannah Schlags and the Opernloft team knew about this program they decided to develop the project "Oper und Diversität" for adapting and producing two operas exclusively for TikTok. This project was promoted by the project #CreatorsForDiversity.

The way in which gender, class, and race are represented in opera leaves a lot of space for reinforcing stereotypes and racism, as well as different kinds of discrimination motivated by aspects related to class and/or ethnicity among others. For this reason, the topic of diversity can (and must) be worked critically from different levels. As explained by Hannah Schlags, the general conditions for the concept and staging of the two operas had from the start a clear frame

[13] Uns ist es wichtig, Kulturschaffenden neue Wege des Austauschs mit ihrem Publikum anzubieten. Mit #CreatorsForDiversity entstehen neue Formate, die TikTok-Nutzer*innen dazu inspirieren und animieren, in die Themen Kunst, Kultur und Diversität einzutauchen. Damit wollen wir den Kulturbetrieb unterstützen, der stark unter der derzeitigen Situation leidet, weil spezielle Auflagen persönliche Begegnungen unmöglich machen (TikTok 2021a). Translated from German to English by Natalia Neira Nieto.

related to diversity. The Opernloft team wanted to change these stereotypes and question existing prejudices in opera. For this, they chose two works that, on the one hand, would allow them to work on these topics broadly and profoundly, and on the other, were appealing enough to the audience. The chosen works were Mozart's "Die Entführung aus dem Serai" (1782) and Bizet's "Carmen" (1875). Both are operas by famous composers, with good audience reception, and plots in which they could approach critically and widely topics of racism, religion, class, and gender (Hannah Schlags, pers. comm., September 7, 2021).

#FREE_Constanze

For the first production, the Opernloft team sought working in collaboration with an external direction team. For this, they published a call inviting stage directors to develop "a sustainable concept for digital opera productions," in which "discrimination and racist elements" in the operatic materials were mentioned and critically approached. For Mozart's "Die Entführung aus dem Serai" it was specifically required to work critically with the representation of Muslims and Islam, as well as the figure of Osmin the guard. Beyond these thematic aspects, other technicalities included having a cast limited to three characters, total duration of the production had to be between forty-five and sixty minutes, and the production had to include a high proportion of opera music (Hannah Schlags, pers. comm., September 7, 2021). After the deadline for receiving the project, the Opernloft team chose Kollektiv Kreisquadratur, an Austrian direction team consisting of Julia Schreiner and Michael Renath, to work together on the production of the first opera for TikTok: the #FREE_Constanze project.

"#FREE_Constanze" is a free adaptation of Mozart's "Die Entführung aus dem Serai." Its plot is about the young Constanze, a TikTok influencer, who is kidnapped for ransom from her wealthy parents. As the synopsis tells us:

> Young Constanze is kidnapped on the street! Sack over her head and off to the criminals' hideout. A gang member, Adam, is supposed to guard Constanze while the leader Bossa pursues his dubious business somewhere. Bahira, Bossa's aunt, is hired to look after the prisoner. And indeed, she is quickly challenged: Adam becomes abusive towards Constanze. While Bahira and Adam argue about the safety of the hostage, Constanze manages to use her mobile phone unnoticed. She is young, she uses TikTok—and starts the challenge #FREE_Constanze. Constanze manages to communicate with her TikTok community. Under the

hashtag #FREE_Constanze, her fan community grows from hour to hour.[14] (Opernloft 2021)

"#FREE_Constanze" consists of a series of fifty-nine TikToks, each with a duration no longer than a minute. The first of these clips premiered on October 8, 2021, through the Opernloft account in TikTok. The rest of the parts of the TikTok-Opera were continuously published in the same account until November 16, 2021. The project was coordinated by Hannah Schlags and stage-directed by Julia Schreiner and Michael Renath. Amy Brinkmann-Davis was the musical director and Daniel Jamernik was the photography director. One of the most radical changes in this adaptation was reducing the cast to four characters: Constanze, Bahira, Adam, and Bossa.

Constanze is a digital native young woman from a wealthy family, who is also a TikTok influencer. During the time she is kidnapped, she meets different worlds from those she is used to, and learns to understand them. This character was cast by two people: visually by the actress Ludovica Schiariti and vocally by the soprano So Yeon Yang. Then we have Bahira, the healer and midwife of the village. This role is based on the character of Blonde but was completely rewritten. Here, Bahira is featured as the carrier of Sufism with the purpose of creating a counternarrative to the image of Islam disseminated by mass media. In the beginning, Bahira appears neutral, but as the hostage-taking continues, Bahira decides against her origins/family in favor of feminist solidarity. The role of Bahira was played by the soprano Luzie Franke. Adam, the character based on Osmin, is the guard of Constanze and the henchman of Bossa. This character received a new name to avoid a cultural attribution. Besides, compared to the character of Osmin, who is unilaterally portrayed, Adam is an ambivalent figure. This character reflects a kind of masculinity in conflict related to his position as a social subordinate in the group.[15] The role of Adam was interpreted by the baritone-bass singer Timotheus Maas. Finally, there is the character of

[14] Die junge Constanze wird auf offener Straße entführt! Sack über den Kopf und ab ins Versteck der Verbrecher. Ein Bandenmitglied, Adam, soll Constanze bewachen, während der Anführer Bossa irgendwo seine dubiosen Geschäfte verfolgt. Bahira, Bossas Tante, wird angeheuert, um sich um die Gefangene zu kümmern. Und tatsächlich wird sie schnell gefordert: Adam wird Constanze gegenüber übergriffig. Während sich Bahira und Adam um die Sicherheit der Geisel streiten, gelingt es Constanze, unbemerkt ihr Handy zu benutzen. Sie ist jung, sie nutzt—und startet die Challenge #FREE_Constanze. Constanze schafft es, mit ihrer TikTok-Community zu kommunizieren. Unter dem Hashtag #FREE_Constanze vergrößert sich ihre Fangemeinde von Stunde zu Stunde (Opernloft 2021). Translated from German to English by Natalia Neira Nieto.

[15] See Connell [1995] 2005 for an exhaustive analysis of types of masculinities.

Bossa, the boss and figure representing power relations and dominance. This character always appears with a mask and never speaks. The role of Bossa was interpreted by Nastja Freese. These characters were created and/or adapted by Julia Schreiner and Michael Renath (Julia Schreiner and Michael Renath, pers. comm., September 7, 2021).

In this adaptation, Julia Schreiner and Michael Renath sought to create a dramaturgical work of the existing power relations in the opera of Mozart from a global context without limiting themselves to cultural borders, but instead focused on highlighting gender and class aspects and its consequent inequalities. This way, they created a story in a performative space in which guilt and atonement are recognized in every moment. Besides that, the whole story and the relations between characters are approached from a Stockholm's syndrome perspective, presenting diverse ways of negotiating both dependence and power relations (Julia Schreiner & Michael Renath, pers. comm., September 7, 2021). This intersectional focus is particularly reflected in the development of the characters. On the one hand, feminine characters are much more active and independent. For example, in contrast with the original version, here Constanze actively tries to free herself from her captor, which she achieves with the help of Bahira and her TikTok community. On the other hand, the character of Adam, represented by a white privileged man, is frequently struggling to understand discrimination, even though he suffers from the impositions on gender and class mandates derived from the patriarchy (Julia Schreiner & Michael Renath, pers. comm., September 7, 2021).

Carmen by Carmen

To continue their idea of developing a sustainable concept for digital opera productions in which diverse discrimination and racist elements of operatic materials were critically mentioned and worked out, the Opernloft team decided to work with con Georges Bizet's "Carmen" (1875) for the second production. This project aims to critically reflect on the way in which Romani groups are represented, as well as gender, class, and race stereotypes related to feminine figures, particularly those portrayed by the main character, Carmen, as "a sensual and frivolous '*Femme fatale*'" (Hannah Schlags, pers. comm., September 7, 2021). This time, the Opernloft team deiced to work with their own resources, having Hanna Schlags and Jessica Maier as stage director and photography director for this project, using the experience from previous adaptations of

Carmen, as well as the lived experiences in creating "#FREE_Constanze." Just like in "#FREE_Constanze," the adaptation of "Carmen" had a reduced cast, a total duration between forty-five and sixty minutes, and opera music had to hold the higher proportion in music.

"Carmen by Carmen" is a free adaptation of Bizet's "Carmen" (1875). Its story is about Carmen, a famous moderator, who is murdered during her television show. Suddenly she wakes up and finds herself trapped in a parallel world, from which she searches for those responsible of her death, as we can see in the synopsis of the opera:

> Welcome to "Carmen by Carmen!" A new late-night show takes the audience by storm—not least because of the fascinating host Carmen. The media star is as successful as she is merciless, until someone makes short work of her on camera: a shot is fired—and Carmen awakens in an in-between world that surprisingly resembles her TV studio … Here a teleprompter is running and asks her to continue the show. One after the other, guests appear who help her to solve the crime and to encounter herself in a completely new way in the process.[16] (Opernloft 2022)

"Carmen by Carmen" consists of thirty-two TikToks, most of them with a duration between one and three minutes. The first of these clips was premiered on January 20, 2022, through Opernloft's account on TikTok. The rest of the parts of the TikTok-Opera were continuously published in that same account until February 2, 2022. This project was coordinated by Hannah Schlags. Stage and photography direction was also made by Hannah Schlags in collaboration with Jessica Maier. Amy Brinkmann-Davis also operated as musical director in this project.

For developing the plot, Hannah Schlags and Jessica Maier focus on four characters: Carmen, Micaëla, Jo, and Escamillo. Carmen is the moderator in a television show called "Carmen by Carmen." This character was played by mezzosoprano Alina Behning. Micaëla is the fiancé of Jo and the antagonist of Carmen. This character represents a kind of femininity that contrasts with

[16] Herzlich Willkommen zu "Carmen by Carmen!" Eine neue Late-Night-Show erobert das Publikum im Sturm - nicht zuletzt wegen der faszinierenden Moderatorin Carmen. Der Medienstar ist ebenso erfolgreich wie gnadenlos, bis vor laufender Kamera jemand kurzen Prozess macht: Es fällt ein Schuss—und Carmen erwacht in einer Zwischenwelt, die erstaunlicherweise ihrem Fernsehstudio gleicht … Hier läuft ein Teleprompter und fordert sie auf, die Show fortzuführen. Nacheinander erscheinen nun Gäste, die ihr helfen, das Verbrechen aufzuklären und sich selbst dabei ganz neu zu begegnen (Opernloft 2022). Translated from German to English by Natalia Neira Nieto.

the one represented by Carmen. Through the conflict of these two characters different gender mandates are represented and worked during the opera. The role of Micaëla was interpreted by soprano Sophia Keiler. Escamillo is the ex-boyfriend of Carmen. Through his character, they explain different aspects of the plot, while introducing toxic masculinity elements. This character was played by tenor Richard Neugebauer. Finally, there is Jo, who is based on Bizet's José. Jo is the fiancé of Micaëla and ex-lover of Carmen. After being rejected by Carmen, Jo tries to force her to love him again. Jo represents a typical case of toxic masculinity. This character was played by baritone Peter Kubik. Besides the characters inspired on the opera by Bizet, the TikTok Opera Carmen by Carmen features Krystyna Lipska, a member of the activist group "Identitaeter_innen" as a character that unites the operatic and real world.

In this adaptation, Hannah Schlags and Jessica Maier decided to focus the plot on the character of Carmen and the process of self-reflection she experiences as she faces arguments and claims by Micaëla, Jo, and Escamillo. The original plot was taken to the backseat, focusing the dramaturgy of the production on the criticism of gender, class, and race stereotypes in Bizet's "Carmen." Approaching opera as a topic allowed the Schlags-Maier duo to create a meta-level for the narrative, in which the character Carmen can critically reflect on her own behavior in relation to the other characters and the gender and class mandates she is subject to. Carmen lives through tense moments as she is forced to negotiate and reinterpret expectations about her behavior to the ends of and in opposition to certain gender mandates. Similarly, diverse aspects of the origin of Carmen are approached. For this, it is worth highlighting the participation of Krystyna Lipska, who talks with Carmen about discrimination against Sinti and Romani, as well as the way in which the figure of Carmen represents these stereotypes and its corresponding gender and class mandates, thus exercising a critique that goes beyond the work itself, and that cries out to be heard by the opera world as a whole.

Adapting Opera

The biggest challenge the Opernloft team had to face during the project "Oper und Diversität" was adapting the music and stage of both operas to the performative context of TikTok. Although summarizing the story and the characters was not the true challenge for the production team, the way of telling and developing the plot surely did, as well as the way in which music could or could not be used and/or performed in this format. In both projects, the Opernloft team wanted to go beyond a simple representation and/or live streaming of the operas through TikTok. As mentioned by Hanna Schlags, they were looking to create a new way of making opera, they wanted to create a TikTok-Opera (Hannah Schlags, pers. comm., September 7, 2021). Therefore, it was fundamental to create a new performative concept in which the contexts, norms, expectations, and aesthetics of TikTok were combined with those of the performative world of opera.

From the beginning, some of the performative and stage possibilities provided by TikTok for music theater were clear for the Opernloft team. In the words of Hannah Schlags:

> [You can] tell with it what you might not be able to tell on stage. It's [something that is] very strong in TikTok. What you can tell and change through effects or filters alone. [… for example] if you take a slow-motion effect or if you put a red filter over a person who is just angry or having a violent emotion, it just amplifies it. You can [also do that in] a play on stage, you can light the stage red, but it will always be different. Or a multiplication effect like that; what does that mean? Is that many versions of the person, or is that different sides, or what's going on. I think … it's already super exciting to work with that.[17] (Schlags 2021)

However, while some of the possibilities emerging from TikTok for stage experimentation were clear, the way in which these could be implemented and/or exploited was not as obvious as one might think, since the members of the production team were not TikTokers, nor were they fluent or acquainted to the practices and aesthetics of TikTok. As in the practice of any other performative tool, performers needed to get acquainted with certain knowledge and practices for satisfactorily developing their musicking. Performers—including the production and direction team—did not just need to know the technical and/or performative repertoire possible on TikTok, but it was also necessary to have certain experience and control of their practice. Besides, an intense negotiation between the contexts, norms, expectations, and aesthetics of the

[17] [Man kann] damit erzählen, was man vielleicht auf der Bühne nicht erzählen kann. Es ist [etwas, dass bei] TikTok ganz stark ist. Was man durch Effekte oder Filter allein erzählen kann und verändern kann. [… z.B.] wenn du ein Slow-Motion-Effekt nimmst oder wenn du einen roten Filter über eine Person legst, die gerade wütend oder eine heftige Emotion hat, dann verstärkt es einfach. Das kannst du [auch in] ein Stück auf der Bühne machen, du kannst die Bühne rot einleuchten, aber es wird immer anders sein. Oder so ein Vervielfältigungseffekt; Was bedeutet das? Sind das viele Versionen der Person, oder sind das verschiedene Seiten oder was ist da los. Ich glaube, … dass es schon superspannend ist damit zu arbeiten (Schlags 2021). Translated from German to English by Natalia Neira Nieto.

operatic performative world and those of TikTok was necessary, given the technical circumstances of the platform, as well as the already existing aesthetic and performative expectations. The stage direction teams participating in this project approached this creation and negotiation process in a different way in each of the adaptations.

First, it is possible to observe that this adaptation process was carried out focusing on two performative levels: the stage narration and the musical. On the stage narration, Julia Schreiner and Michael Renath approached "#FREE_Constanze" from a cinematographic perspective. The idea guiding the adaptation was to create a new narrative, a story, a work that was identified and understood as such. The audience could recognize that the small TikTok they just watched was a part of something bigger; that every clip was recognized as part of a meta-narrative, which could (and should) be seen from its entirety (Schreiner 2021). A difficult challenge to solve involved the performative possibilities of TikTok, where the duration of each video was limited to fifteen, sixty, or 180 seconds. Another challenge was that the Opernloft team had no control on who would watch the videos and in what order, leading to a situation in which a viewer could begin to watch the opera from the last video. This situation, while problematic, fascinated Julia Schreiner and Michael Renath, who felt strongly motivated to do something new, something never done before. Even if the meta-narrative of the project did not work, they felt happy already for developing a story through a means that was not designed for that and with working in the development of new forms of storytelling and/or making opera (Julia Schreiner & Michael Renath, pers. comm., September 7, 2021).

Because of the cinematic approach that Julia Screiner and Michael Renath decided to take, it was necessary to negotiate not just with the aesthetics of TikTok but also with the technical and aesthetic possibilities of the theatrical world. As commented by Julia Schreiner: "We think everything in film sets, the configuration for a film set is not the same as for theater. There is of course a way for handling … everything is in between things, which must be re-thought about differently"[18] (Schreiner 2021). An example of this can be observed in trivial things like illumination. The illumination equipment used during Opernloft productions ended up not being adequate for working on TikTok.

[18] "Wir denken alles in Filmsets, die Ausstattung ist für Filmset nicht für Theater. Das ist natürlich eine Verhandlung … Es sind alles so zwischen Dingen, die neu durchdacht denken müssen" (Schreiner 2021). Translated from German to English by Natalia Neira Nieto.

The lights used in the theater were not suited for video recording and the need for using special equipment was evident. Additionally, spaces and/or locations in which the plot was developed did not always fit with the expectations of the production, the possibilities, and the infrastructure of Opernloft and/or the visual aesthetics of TikTok.

However, an interesting aspect that was worked in the scenic-narrative part of "#FREE_Constanze," which widened the performative possibilities of the project, was that they included TikTok and many of its practices in the same plot. As remarked by Michael Renath:

> TikTok as a target medium is of course very interesting, but we also wanted to have a self-reference, in the direction of what would happen if we told a story in TikTok about a TikToker woman who subsequently blogs in TikTok and makes certain messages, certain calls there. In other words, a kind of artificial figure who operates in TikTok between appearance and reality.[19] (Michael Renath, pers. comm., September 7, 2021)

By including TikTok and many of its practices in the plot, new ways were opened for integrating the contexts, norms, expectations, and aesthetics of TikTok more organically. Some of the clearest examples include the use and/or citation of trends throughout the TikTok-Opera, the continuous attempts to integrate the "community" throughout the plot, as well as the launching of *#TikTokDanceChallengeMozartEdition*.[20] A strategy developed more intensely by Hannah Schlags and Jessica Maier in the "Carmen by Carmen" project directly used viral trends and/or challenges during the production for portraying their characters, as well as (re)contextualizing the plot in a contemporary context. Yet, they also ended up introducing certain aesthetic and age ideals to the visual conception of the characters. This can be clearly perceived in the fact that the role of Constanze was interpreted by two different persons: visually by actress Ludovica Schiariti and vocally by soprano So Yeon Yang. The reason behind this decision lay in the fact that sopranos who could *adequately* sing the role

[19] "TikTok als Zielmedium ist natürlich sehr interessant, wir wollten aber auch eine Selbstreferenz haben, in Richtung was wäre wenn wir eine Geschichte in TikTok erzählen über eine TikTokerin, die in Folge auch ins TikTok hinein blogt und dort gewisse Botschaften, gewisse Aufrufe macht. Also, eine Art Kunstfigur, die in TikTok zwischen Schein und Wirklichkeit operiert" (Michael Renath, pers. comm., September 7, 2021). Translated from German to English by Natalia Neira Nieto.

[20] @opernloft, "Bereit für einen kleinen Tanz?," October 29, 2021, TikTok video, https://www.tiktok.com/@opernloft/video/7024568232203783430?is_from_webapp=1&sender_device=pc&web_id=7062339902340007429.

did not visually comply with the expectations attributed—either consciously or unconsciously—to the role of the young and charismatic TikToker.

On the musical side, both proposals followed similar parameters, from which they carried out this negotiation and/or adaptation. First, it is worth highlighting that even though it was already considered, perhaps even expected, that the music and/or lyrics of the opera would go through some changes in both productions, in practice it was very clear that these changes could only be fulfilled as long as the existing aesthetic ideals of the operatic world were kept. As stated by Hannah Schlags: "The music must be worked too, but this 'opera music moments' is expected to stay. Because it [is] certain that that's what we do here … [at the end] the main product to be recognized [should be] 'opera'"[21] (Schlags 2021). This expectation certainly set the point of departure from which the production teams sought to adapt the operas to the performative possibilities and contexts of TikTok. The music of Mozart and Bizet, while not completely, would be kept almost entirely intact in both projects.

Given their performative concept, the Opernloft team has plenty of experience reducing the duration of many operas. This certainly facilitated the process of selection and adaptation of the selected musical pieces and reducing the characters in the new plot. Many arias and recitatives could be easily excluded because the characters participating in them were no longer part of the "#FREE_Constanze" or "Carmen by Carmen" plot. However, some musical pieces, especially recitatives, which could be used for the plot, were not considered due to their little impact in the development of the story or because they were musically less attractive and/or recognizable. Nevertheless, the duration restrictions of TikTok would be an essential aspect for negotiating the adaptation of the operas to TikTok. As explained by Michael Renath:

> There are clear guidelines in TikTok, and that is above all the time. There is the 15-second clip, the one-minute clip, and there is now the three-minute clip. And if you take an aria with 11 minutes, yes, you have to come up with something … I had to put the arias into small, mostly minute pieces. That means, of course, that with Osmin [= Adam], for example, there is no continuous aria … For example, in the 19th aria I looked at where there were parts that were exciting,

[21] "Es darf auch an der Musik gearbeitet werden, aber es sollen trotzdem diese ‚Opernmusik-Momenten' bleiben. Weil [ist] es natürlich was wir hier machen. … [Am Ende soll] das Grundprodukt ‚Oper' trotzdem zu erkennen bleiben" (Schlags 2021). Translation from German to English by Natalia Neira Nieto.

that interested us in terms of content, and then cut out a minute musically.[22] (Michael Renath, pers. comm., September 7, 2021)

Both Julia and Michael Renath, as well as Hannah Schlags and Jessica Maier, opted for focusing on the use and adaptation of the arias to settle this. As Michael Renath explained, they allow creating a kind of "musical selfie," a narrative of singularity ("Erzählweise der Vereinzelung"). Given that, on the one hand, these are concentrated in one single act or dramaturgical act, and on the other, because of their closed form, it is easier to isolate, adapt, and recontextualize (Michael Renath, pers. comm., September 7, 2021). In the case of "#FREE_Constanze," Michael Renath made new arrangements of the selected arias, shortening them to last less than a minute and sometimes making small modifications on the text. In contrast, Hannah Schlags and Jessica Maier opted for another approach on adapting Bizet's "Carmen." In "Carmen by Carmen," Schlags and Maier took advantage of the fame that Bizet's "Carmen" already has and focused on using the most famous arias of this opera. It is interesting here that the text of the arias was not adapted to the new plot. The connection to the plot was achieved through "adapted subtitles." With this I mean that these arias were sung in with the original text while visually a new text appeared on the screen with captions. For example, while Escamillo (Richard Neugebauer) was singing the aria "Votre toast, je peu vous le rendre" with the original French text:

Toreador, en garde!	Toreador, on guard!
Toreador, Toreador!	Toreador, Toreador!
Et songe bien, oui, songe en combattant	And think well, yes, think as you fight
Qu'un oeil noir te regarde,	That a black eye is watching you
Et que l'amour t'attend,	And that love awaits you,
Toreador, L'amour L'amour t'attend!	Toreador, love, love is waiting for you!

[22] Es gibt klare Vorgaben im TikTok, und das ist vor allem die Zeit. Es gibt das Clip 15 Sekunden, das Clip eine Minute, und es gibt neu das Clip drei Minuten lang. Und wenn man eine Arie mit 11 Minuten nimmt, ja da muss man sich was einfallen lassen. … Ich musste die Arien in kleine, meistens Minute-Stücke packen. D.h. das gibt natürlich jetzt bei Osmin [= Adam] z.B. keine durchgehende Arie. … z.B. bei der 19. Arie habe ich mir angeschaut, wo sind Teile die spannend sind, die uns interessieren inhaltlich und habe dann musikalisch eine Minute rausgeschnitten" (Michael Renath, pers. comm., September 7, 2021). Translated from German to English by Natalia Neira Nieto.

TikTok subtitles would show:

Meine Zeit ist gekommen!	My time has come!
Ich wusste immer, dass	I always knew that
etwas Großes auf mich wartet.	something big was waiting for me.
Jetzt bin ich ein erfolgreicher Star	Now I'm a successful star
und feiere Partys auf meiner Yacht!	and I'm having parties on my yacht!

having no relation with each other.[23] But besides these arias in "Carmen by Carmen," different popular songs were also used throughout the plot. Not only some aspects of the character's personality were developed through these songs, but they allowed linking the plot of the opera with diverse TikTok trends and practices in a better way, like the example of the performance of "I am Woman" by Emmy Meli performed by Carmen and Micaëla.[24]

The proposals for the project "Opern und Diversität" presented by the Opernloft team within the program #CreatorsForDiversity is certainly a multimedia example of possible performances and formats in the operatic world. The Opernloft team understood TikTok as a tool and/or performative space through which it is possible to create new interpretative and performative forms for developing a performance, trying to take the operatic world to a new performative context. Although the contexts, norms, expectations, and aesthetics of TikTok were widely considered in these proposals, it is still possible to perceive a kind of performative "limitation" since the aspiration is still set on creating a multimedia format without ceasing to be considered as opera. And here, in my opinion, perhaps lies in the source of a permanent conflict in these performances: the eagerness to adapt an operatic work to TikTok without ceasing to be an opera could lead the projects to a lose-lose performative situation, neither making opera nor TikTok in a satisfactory way.

23 @opernloft, "Escamilo singt für euch den ‚Toreador,'" January 24, 2022, TikTok video, https://www.tiktok.com/@opernloft/video/7056753494384037126?is_from_webapp=1&sender_device=pc&web_id=7062339902340007429.

24 @opernloft, „May we present to you: women," January 26, 2022, TikTok video, https://www.tiktok.com/@opernloft/video/7057547482284248325?is_from_webapp=1&sender_device=pc&web_id=7062339902340007429.

To continue with this exploration and analysis of the ways in which the actors of TikTok musicking carry out and/or conceptualize their musical practices, in the next section I focus on the musical practices that are notorious for understanding TikTok as a practice of its own and of equal performative value. In these musical practices, TikTokers appropriate musics from the contexts, norms, expectations, and aesthetics of TikTok with a performative understanding of the application, instead of trying to adapt musics to TikTok. In other words, they are TikToking musics.

TikToking Musics

The normative images of what "music really is" are so deeply rooted in our cultural imaginary, especially among music researchers, that we sometimes forget how vast and diverse contemporary musical worlds can be. An example of this performative diversity can be conceptualized in and through TikTok. Over the course of this chapter, we have seen different ways in which TikTokers understand their musical activities while using TikTok in many ways during their performance: from understanding TikTok as a stage to using this platform as a space for performative experimentation. However, there is still one kind of conceptualization I observed during my research I would like to present: understanding TikTok as a practice of its own and with equal performative value. There is no doubt that this kind of conceptualization influences the way in which TikTokers use the application for developing their musical practices. However, how can performances be developed through this understanding? In the following pages, I try to answer this question by presenting some examples of this kind of performances in the immense performative world of TikTok.

TikToking Music and Music Theater

As vast as the performative world of TikTok is, so are the ways its actors conceptualize their practices. To begin with the analysis of performative projects in which performers understand TikTok as a practice of its own and of equal performative value as other existing practices in the world, I would like to first focus on examples. Though we cannot speak of TikTok-specific performances, we can observe a kind of understanding that goes beyond seeing TikTok as merely a digital stage. For this, I focus on some examples found in music theater and contemporary music.

In the fall of 2021, I was on my way back from the research stay I made in Hamburg on the production of the TikTok-Opera "#FREE_Constanze," as I was having a conversation with my colleague Barbara Babić about the Opernloft project "Oper und Diversität" and the performative possibilities that TikTok brought to the opera world. Suddenly a new project looking to combine the opera world with TikTok slipped into our conversation: "Tiger King 2—the TikTokpera."[25] The so-called TikTopera was the result of a cooperation between The English National Opera and Netflix, produced as a teaser trailer and advertisement for the launching of the second season of the Netflix Series *Tiger King* 2. This TikTopera premiered on November 15, 2021, in TikTok and YouTube in the accounts of Netflix and The English National Opera, as well as in the profiles of six participating TikTokers, @hannahlowther8, @maxandharveryofficial, @sophiaauroraa, @hellovicco, and @philwgreen.

"Tiger King 2: The TikTopera" consists of five TikToks, lasting a minute long and with a clear structure. In the first part of each of these TikToks, different TikTokers summarize parts of the first season of the show Netflix *Tiger King*, followed by the second part of the TikTok, in which the second season of this series is announced. This dual structure is also perceived in the music used during the TikToks. Although the base melody of the whole TikTopera is the aria from the opera "Carmen" by Georges Bizet "Votre toast, je peux vous le rendre"—particularly the part commonly known as the "toreador song"—, it is possible to observe that while in the first part of the TikToks the TikTokers perform this aria alone and in their personal style, in the second part of the TikTok the choir and orchestra of The English National Opera (ENO) make their appearance to perform together a specific arrangement of this aria with the TikToker. Here are the lyrics of this arrangement:

> Cool cats and kittens it's your lucky day
> It's coming back! Hip hip hooray!
> This season's got a lot
> big cats, bad teeth and murder plots and mullets
> Cool cats and kittens let the binge begin
> It's the return of the Tiger King!

[25] The English National Opera and Netflix, "Tiger King 2 The TikTopera," November 15, 2021, YouTube video, https://www.youtube.com/watch?v=lnh1UD8t_nA.

The first TikTok of the TikTopera was performed by @hannahlowther8[26] and the ENO. In this TikTok, @hannahlowther8 uses the melody of "Votre toast, je peux vous le rendre" played by the ENO and sings new lyrics on top of this melody. In the TikTok description, @hannahlowther8 invites us to continue watching the next part of the TikTopera: the TikTok performed by @maxandharveryofficial[27] and the ENO. Here Max and Harvery, finalist singers from the show X-Factor, sing a song based on the melody of the aria "Votre toast, je peux vous le rendre." In the second part of the TikTok you can hear the choir and the orchestra of the ENO playing the arrangement of this aria while Max and Harvery dance to the rhythm of the music. Just like in the video by @hannahlowther8, @maxandharveryoffical invite watchers in the TikTok description to continue watching the next part of the TikTopera: the TikTok by @sphiaauroraa[28] and the ENO.

Just like in the other TikToks, @sophiaauroraa plays a song based on the melody of the main theme of the aria. In this TikTok, the aria is modulated to minor mode to give this section a more dramatic touch and for highlighting the lyrics. In the second part of this TikTok, the ENO choir and orchestra appear again playing the aria. Like in previous examples, an invitation to watch the fourth TikTok is extended in the description. The TikTopera continues with the performance of @hellovicco[29] and the ENO. In this performance, @hellovicco raps to the harmonic base of the aria "Votre toas, je peux vous le rendre," played by the ENO. In the second part of the TikTok, just like all others, the ENO choir and orchestra perform the aria again. During this section, @hellovicco appears sitting on a sofa pretending to watch television, where the choir and the orchestra are broadcasted while they are playing the music of the TikTok video. To wrap

[26] @hannahlowther8 and The English National Opera, "Casually singing in The @Netflix Tiger King #TikTopera with @ENO Over to @Max and Harvey next," November 15, 2021, TikTok video, https://www.tiktok.com/@hannahlowther8/video/7030875251206524166.

[27] @maxandharveryofficial and The English National Opera, "So excited for @netflix Tiger King series 2 we sang a lil verse about it with the @ENO (as you do). Up next @sophiaauroraa," November 15, 2021, TikTok video, https://www.tiktok.com/@maxandharveyofficial/video/7030874956695178501.

[28] @sophiaauroraa and The English National Opera, "My verse of the @Netflix tiger king 2 #tiktopera with @ENO! @hellovicco you're next!," November 15, 2021, TikTok video, https://www.tiktok.com/@sophiaauroraa/video/7030874010179194117.

[29] @hellovicco and The English National Opera, "I wrote a verse for the @Netflix Tiger King #Tiktopera with the @ENO. Next verse by @Philip Green," November 15, 2021, TikTok video, https://www.tiktok.com/@hellovicco/video/7030877366020869382.

the TikTopera up, we now have the TikTok by @philwgreen[30] and the ENO. In this TikTok, @philwgreen performs the aria "Votre toast, je peux vous le rendre" with a similar aesthetic to the first TikTok of the TikTopera series—the one by @hannahlowther8. This way, the TikTopera cycle closes in a more recognizable manner.

Compared to the TikTok-Operas "#FREE_Constanze" and "Carmen by Carmen," where the purpose was to create a TikTok adaptation of both Wolfgang A. Mozart's "Die Entführung aus dem Serai" (1782) and Georges Bizet's "Carmen" (1875), in "Tiger King 2: The TikTopera" the performative aim is not adapting Bizet's opera to TikTok, but—besides advertising the new season of the series—rather that of making TikToks. There was no attempt of adapting and/or performing the music or the plot through the context, aesthetics, and expectations of the operatic world. Besides, the TikToks constituting the TikTopera were done according to the visual and acoustic aesthetics usually performed in the musicking of the featured TikTokers. In the way music is used in this production we can observe a different understanding of TikTok compared to the TikTok operas by Opernloft.

Compared with the previously mentioned projects "#FREE_Conztanze" and "Carmen by Carmen," the TikTopera is not and did not seek to be an opera, strictly speaking. By having the project, a different performative purpose, and not committing to the operatic expectations, "Tiger King 2: The TikTopera" could focus on developing short TikToks with semi-closed plots performed from the context and aesthetic of the featured TikTokers. This allowed TikTokers and the production team to see these performances not as an adaptation of something that already existed but as a new kind of performance that can be understood as a TikTopera, a new performative possibility in the extensive world of TikTok, and from which a new way of storytelling is reimagined. There was no practice and aesthetics that had to be adapted to TikTok, but it was the TikTok practices and aesthetics that determined the context of the performance.

As published on the website of The English National Opera: "historically, opera told dramatic stories as a form of pure entertainment to the masses across Europe and eventually the world. Over time, as musical tastes have changed, so have the mediums in which these stories are enjoyed, the latest being TikTok" (ENO 2021). It

[30] @philwgreen and The English National Opera, "Mixing 2 of my favourite things…@Netflix and Opera! The Tiger King #Tiktopera w/ @englishnationalopera," November 15, 2021, TikTok video, https://www.tiktok.com/@philwgreen/video/7030873897302019334.

is perhaps from this point of view that the opera and its performative worlds can be understood from TikTok and reflect a new contemporary reality. As said in a Tweet by The English National Opera regarding the premiere of the TikTopera: "TikTok felt like the perfect place to re-imagine epic stories for the social media age and bring opera to a new audience" (@E_N_O, November 17, 2021).

"Tiger King 2: The TikTopera" illustrates without any doubt a particular example of the way in which musical performances can be conceptualized and practiced from the contexts, norms, expectations, and aesthetics of TikTok. Yet, this is not the only example of this kind of performance. A kind of performative understanding similar to "Tiger King 2: The TikTokpera" can be observed in other music theater projects, like the ones by @danieljmertzlufft on TikTok. @danieljmertzlufft is a composer who began developing many TikTok musicals, like "Grocery Store Musical-Trend" based on the viral song "New York Summer" by Louisa Melcher, and "Ratatouille: The TikTok Musical" based on the song by Emily Jacobson, as well as being the creator behind the TikTok Musical "For You, Paige." In these projects, Daniel Mertzlufft (@danieljmertzlufft) has taken different trends and other TikTok functions for creating and performing musicals in and through TikTok together with the TikToker community, placing the participation of the community and the practices and aesthetics of TikTok in the center of the creation process. This creates and/or reaffirms the many kinds of networked creativity existing on the platform. Just like in the example of "Tiger King 2: The TikTokpera," the performance on these projects is guided by the contexts, norms, expectations, and aesthetics of TikTok.

This kind of participative creation can be clearly observed in the development of "Ratatouille: The TikTok Musical." The idea behind "Ratatouille: The TikTok Musical" began with a TikTok by @danieljmertzlufft about Remy, the main character of the Pixar movie *Ratatouille* (2007). This video gained much popularity among the TikTok community, and many reinterpretations were created with the hashtag *#ratatouille*. The growing popularity and visibility of this hashtag inspired Daniel Mertzlufft to create the account @ratatouillemusical, from which he posted a TikTok asking the community to become part of the creation of the musical about Remy. Mertzlufft asked TikTokers to send their own TikToks with ideas to build the plot of musical, with dance routines, songs, possible stories, and so on. These TikToks were published with the hashtag *#RatatouilleMusical*. This way, a new kind of performance was created in which the networked creativity of TikTok was represented, while keeping in mind and carrying out the contexts, norms, expectations, and aesthetics of TikTok.

But beyond these examples, there are some attempts of using TikTok as a musical instrument and/or a musical-performative extension in contemporary music. One example of this possibility can be observed in some of the works by the composer Karel Stulens, such as "SWIPERZ: Swipe-study for Smartphone Quartet" (2020) or "As You Like It, Like it! For Smartphone Quartet, String Trio & E. Guitar" (2021). In these works, Karel Stulens explores different performative possibilities provided by TikTok, understanding the application as a musical instrument. In "SWIPERZ: Swipe-study for Smartphone Quartet," Karel Stulens uses the For-You-Page of the performers for creating a personalized piece, using the performative ability of TikTok for developing their own performative and aesthetic worlds in the moment of performing. This piece reflects the many performative worlds of TikTok in which the performers partake. In this piece, the performers are requested to explore the existing performative world of TikTok through swipes. Different TikToks appear in the For-You-Page of each performer, consequently merging and creating a unique and contextualized sound piece in the TikToks of the performers, creating a performative dialogue, a mixture of highly personal performances. In the piece "As You Like it, Like it! For Smartphone Quartet, String Trio & E. Guitar," Karel Stulen continues exploring with this kind of performative dialogue, this time taking "traditional" musical instruments to the practices and aesthetics of TikTok. As stated by Karel Stulen in the description of the piece:

> In *As You Like it, Like it!* the fast, repetitive and daily gestures we produce on our smartphones (tapping, swiping…) are transferred to the traditional instruments. Only form and gestures are fixed. The smartphones, and their use of the app *TikTok*, saturate the piece with ever-changing content. Gestures are fixed, but every performance will be a non-reproducible version. Fed, with the likings of the performers. (Stulens 2021)

It is important to point out that these works are not unique; artists like post-composer Belenish Moreno-Gil and Óscar Escudero seek to integrate TikTok, along with its practices and aesthetics, to a new level within contemporary musical theater, as in the case of "Autotune para el Pueblo" (2022), or Moreno-Gil's new project "TikTopera: Small Pieces for Performer, Voice, Video, Electronics, and Social Network."[31] The musical-performative experimentation in and through TikTok is just beginning, and the results and paths that these can open will

[31] Belenish Moreno-Gil started her new compositional project on TikTok, "TikTopera," in 2024. The first piece, "#WALL," was premiered on June 20th through the TikTok account @belenishmoreno_gil.

be positioned on a central place in our reflections about multimedia musical phenomena for sure. To continue with the analysis of performative projects in which the performers understand TikTok as a practice of its own and of same performative value, in the following subsection I focus on the performance of songs conceived to be specifically performed on TikTok.

TikToking Songs

Throughout my research, I was able to observe numerous TikToks in which TikTokers perform songs. As already mentioned, TikTokers perform excerpts of already existing songs and/or musical pieces, using TikTok as an asynchronous digital stage in which they develop their performances and create small independent works. These works can be performed, appreciated, and shared asynchronously by other users of the application separate from the performer. Similarly, TikTokers compose songs and/or musical pieces keeping in mind that they will be performed in TikTok. This is the kind of performances in which I focus in this section. Here, TikTokers use TikTok not just as a musical stage for publishing their works, as seen in the previous examples, but their songs are intended to be almost[32] exclusively performed on this platform. In fact, the short duration of these songs (between fifteen and sixty seconds) does not allow a satisfactory development outside digital platforms, and, compared to the performance of pieces and popular songs, it is a top concern in these performances to have an active participation of the audience (becoming viral), as well as using the performative and aesthetic language of TikTok. Although the degree to which these contexts, norms, expectations, and aesthetics of TikTok are integrated into this kind of song varies, it is possible to observe a performative understanding that emerges from the practice of TikTok.

On the one hand, it is possible to observe the performance of songs that, though they were especially intended to be performed on TikTok, are performed by TikTokers in a presentational way and without extensively exploiting the use of performative tools of the platform. Here TikTokers perform songs composed from the contexts, norms, expectations, and aesthetics of TikTok, but regarding their performance, they use TikTok as a digital stage. This is in a very similar way

[32] Although these songs are intended for being performed in TikTok, sometimes TikTokers share these performances on other digital platforms like Instagram and YouTube.

to the previously mentioned living room and/or bedroom concerts. An example of this kind of songs and performances can be seen in the song "Schwarzes Schaf"[33] by @rian.music. "Schwarzes Schaf" is a short twenty-six—second song intended for TikTok by @rian.music. In this song, @rian.music tells the story of his encounter with a small black sheep while walking in a field. Here are the lyrics of this song:

Ich war gestern unterwegs in der Natur weil ich es liebe. Ganz alleine auf der Wiese doch plötzlich stand da eine Ziege; eine fiese.	Yesterday I was taking a walk on the countryside, because I love it, completely alone in the field suddenly there was a goat; a nasty one.
und sie so: mähhh! und ich so: was?? und sie so: määähhh!! und ich so: wtf?? und sie so: määäääähhhh!!! und ich so: WAS? Und sie so: Das ist meine Wiese, hau ab du Sack!	and she went: meeeh! and I said: what?? and she went: meeeh! and I said: wtf? and she went: meeeeeehhh!! and I said: WHAT? and she said: this is my field, get out you sack!

In this performance, @rian.music sings the song with his guitar from home. Both the lyrics and the performance resemble a performative aesthetic that is very common in TikTok, which seeks to reflect spontaneity and authenticity, but also a kind of attitude in which the performer does not want to be taken seriously. In this sense, the song seems to be composed part as a joke and part as a spontaneous act, creating a feeling that it has the purpose of entertaining. "Schwarzes Schaf" was well received by the TikTok community, and numerous TikToks were created taking this one as a base. At the same time, TikTokers like @julinamusic took the original song and created new verses with possible outcomes and/or from different perspectives of the same story. @rian.music would not stay behind in the process of creating and performing different verses

[33] @rian.music, "Ihr habt ihn euch gewünscht," August 31, 2022, TikTok video, https://www.tiktok.com/@rian.music/video/7138105269321583877.

with variations on the story of the goat.[34] This process shows the potential these kinds of songs have for establishing creativity networks.

Another example of TikTokers that perform these kinds of songs is @ok.danke.tschuess. @ok.danke.tschuess plays short self-written songs with her guitar. Similar to @rian.music, the songs by @ok.danke.tschuess have a duration of around forty seconds and are played in a presentational way from her bedroom using the common aesthetics and sense of authenticity of TikTok. The short songs by @ok.danke.tschuess talk about diverse everyday topics, like "Es ist zu teuer in der Disko!" (The Club is too expensive!),[35] "Red flags in Beziehungen"[36] (Red flags in relationships), and "Es wird laut aufm Konzert!"[37] (It gets too loud in a concert!), but also about her own day-to-day experiences in hospitals after being diagnosed with and treated for leukemia, as narrated in the song "Leukämie du Bitch"[38] (leukemia, you bitch). Like in "Schwarzes Schaf" by @rian.music, the songs by @ok.danke.tschuess have been taken as a basis by other TikTokers to create duets and/or as inspiration for their own performances. One example is the song "Es ist zu teuer in der Disko!," a song that has not just been interpreted by other TikTokers but has also been the basis for many duets.

This kind of short songs written to be performed on TikTok allows TikTokers to experiment with topics and/or ideas without the stress of writing whole songs and/or without the risk of performative failure. By not seeking from the start to meet the ideals and/or expectations of a specific musical world, TikTokers concentrate on the performative contexts of TikTok, which allows them to set the attention first to

[34] After the success of "Schwarzes Schaf," @rian.music launched on his official Spotify account RIAN the song "Schwarzes Schaf," which includes the text of the TikTok song in the choir, as well as the song "Schwarzes Schaf—Akustik Session," a version in which the original choir is claimed with a variation.

[35] @ok.danke.tschuess, "Es ist zu teuer in der Disko!," June 29, 2022. TikTok video, https://www.tiktok.com/@ok.danke.tschuess/video/7114620787671239941.

[36] @ok.danke.tschuess, "Red flags in Beziehungen," July 21, 2022, TikTok video, https://www.tiktok.com/@ok.danke.tschuess/video/7122812805140565254?is_from_webapp=1&sender_device=pc&web_id=7062339902340007429.

[37] @ok.danke.tschuess, "Es wird laut aufm Konzert!," June 28, 2022, TikTok video, https://www.tiktok.com/@ok.danke.tschuess/video/7114176004377021701?is_from_webapp=1&sender_device=pc&web_id=7062339902340007429.

[38] @ok.danke.tschuess, "@dkms_de erklärt, wie man sich als Stammzellenspender*in registrieren lassen kann!," July 29, 2022, TikTok video, https://www.tiktok.com/@ok.danke.tschuess/video/7125743374526631173?is_from_webapp=1&sender_device=pc&web_id=7062339902340007429.

having fun performing TikToks, and therefore the musical practice of TikTok. But beyond this, it allows them to perform their own songs, and if they are successful, they can have the opportunity to widen their performances with steadiness. This situation can encourage TikTokers to write longer songs based on the ones they have already written, which can be now performed in physical concerts and/or be distributed through different digital platforms like Instagram or YouTube and streaming services, like Spotify and Apple Music.

Besides these examples, there are other types of songs written for TikTok in which TikTokers use the tools provided by the platform more extensively as part of the composition. The possibility of creating and combining performances asynchronously, as well as the duet tool are without doubt some of the most popular features of TikTok for creating music. Here, TikTokers use these tools for performing different vocal and instrumental parts and/or sections by themselves, and then putting them together for completing the performance of the song. In this case the song is not just planned as a TikTok performance, but by using the performative tools of the application during the creation process, the TikToker is able to blend more organically the contexts, norms, expectations, and aesthetics of the application in their performance. Some examples of these kinds of songs can be seen in the performances of @soundslikemichal. It is worth pointing out that, although these songs are intended as TikToks, this does not revoke the possibility of them becoming the basis of future songs purposed for being performed in a physical context.

Similar to @ok.danke.tschuess, @soundslikemichal performs her own songs written specifically for TikTok. These songs talk about different topics in the everyday life of @soundslikemichal, like "Multivitaminsaft"[39] (multivitamin juice), "Ich war beim Friseur"[40] (I went to the hairdresser), or "CORONA,"[41] where she talks about some of her experiences while being sick with COVID-19

39 @soundslikemichal, "Trink kein Kaffee oder Tee, auch zu Wasser sag ich Nee, aber Multivitaminsaft is ok," June 22, 2021, TikTok video, https://www.tiktok.com/@soundslikemichal/video/6976546007790144774?is_from_webapp=1&sender_device=pc&web_id=7062339902340007429.

40 @soundslikemichal, "Ich war heute beim Friseur," April 16, 2021, TikTok video, https://www.tiktok.com/@soundslikemichal/video/6951834595805465862?is_from_webapp=1&sender_device=pc&web_id=7062339902340007429.

41 @soundslikemichal, "Wenn ich und @sebastian.bassplayer gleichzeitig in Quarantäna sind," June 11, 2022, TikTok video, https://www.tiktok.com/@soundslikemichal/video/7108016404992920838?is_from_webapp=1&sender_device=pc&web_id=7062339902340007429.

and having to quarantine. In these songs, @soundslikemichal not just sings and performs different instruments but also physically performs aspects of the contents of the song with her body. Besides, she uses some of the technical possibilities of TikTok to make her performance visually attractive, as well as for asynchronously performing different parts of the song. We can find a very peculiar case in the use of the performative tools of TikTok in the song "Prokrastination."[42] "Prokrastination" is a short song about the procrastination problem @soundslikemichal says to have. In this song, @soundslikemichal uses the performative possibilities of TikTok to create an asynchronous performance in which she performs the different parts of the song (piano, first voice, and second voice). Three @soundslikemichal appear simultaneously on the screen of this TikTok performing the different parts of the song, creating a kind of performance that would be impossible to do in an exclusively physical context.

There is a wide variety in the types and intensity for using the performative tools of TikTok. By just using different recording modes or using camera changes, by recording different parts asynchronously, and/or by using the duet function, these performances show different ways in which TikTokers use the performative language of TikTok for creating short songs. However, some TikTokers have explored these performative possibilities in their songs in a more intense manner, creating their own performative formats in which the contexts, norms, expectations, and aesthetics of TikTok and the use of performative possibilities of the platform are much clearer. The performances by @binabianca89 are without doubt a clear example of these own performative explorations and formats.

The songs by @binabianca89 show a performative understanding that is derived completely from TikTok. Through her performances, @binabianca89 developed her own performative aesthetic and style for performing songs on TikTok. Starting as a project of FUNK[43] in TikTok, @binabianca89 performed for three years this kind of songs with the name @kopfstimme, developing through these years a performative style that deeply reflects the practices and aesthetics of TikTok. Due to personal reasons, the @kopfstimme project ended in 2022, creating a new account with new songs with the username @binabianca89. Just

42 @soundslikemichal, "'Guten Tag, mein Name ist Michal und ich leide unter Prokrastination," July 1, 2021, TikTok video, https://www.tiktok.com/@soundslikemichal/video/6980048452352806149?is_from_webapp=1&sender_device=pc&web_id=7062339902340007429.

43 Funk is the content network of the German broadcasting agencies ARD and ZDF.

like @ok.danke.tschuess and @soundslikemichal, the topics of the songs by @binabianca89 are usually about everyday life. However, the performances appear to be different to the previously presented examples. The songs by @binabianca89 are not just written to be performed on TikTok, but the performative aesthetics and style are supported by the performative tools and possibilities that TikTok provides for creating TikToks that reflect the identity of @binabianca89 as a TikToker, showing a deep understanding of the contexts, norms, expectations, and aesthetics of TikTok in these performances. An example can be observed in the song "Feedback."[44] The lyrics are:

Hey, Ich finde scheiße was du machst	Hey, I think what you do is shitty
Ist aber nur Feedback!	but it's just feedback!
Haben andere besser gemacht	Other have done better
Ist aber nur Feedback!	but it's just feedback!
Hab hierfür gar nichts bezahlt	I did not pay for this
trotzdem hast Du keine Wahl.	however, you have no choice.
Du musst auch gar nicht danach fragen,	You don't even have to ask for it,
kannst mein Feedback einfach haben.	you can just have my feedback
Ist es zu Simpel	It is too simple
Aber das ist nur mein Feedback	but its just my feedback.
Wieso ist das hier denn nicht so wie	Why is it not the way I
Ich's gern mag?	like it?
Würde meine Zeit gern investieren,	I would rather invest my time
um fremde Kunst zu kritisieren	to criticize foreign art
und auch wenn Du es gar nicht brauchst	and even if you don't need it
ich geb mein Feedback gerne raus.	I'd like to give my feedback.
Und wenn du kein Feedback	And if you don't want any
willst	feedback
dann stellt die Kunst hier nicht zu schau.	then don't present your art.
Du musst das aushalten denn Du	You must endure this because you
wusstest ja genau	knew exactly
Worauf Du dich einlässt als Du	what you are getting into when you
beschlaßt	decided
Online zu sein.	to be online.

[44] @binabianca89, "iSt aBeR NuR FeEdBaCk," April 6, 2022, TikTok video, https://www.tiktok.com/@binabianca89/video/7083526970583108870?is_from_webapp=1&sender_device=pc&web_id=7062339902340007429.

Ich kann's selber nicht	I can't do it myself
Aber Ich hab Feedback.	but I have feedback.
Lern mit Kritik umzugehen	Learn to deal with criticism
Ist nur mein Feedback.	it's just my feedback.
Und wenn Du mein Feedback nicht verträgst	And if you can't take my feedback
Ist's wohl besser wenn Du gehst	it's probably better that you leave
denn Ich war als erster hier und bevor Ich's vergess…	because I was here first and before I forget!

In this short fifty-two-second song, @binabianca89 talks in an amusing and eloquent manner about the criticism TikTokers are exposed to throughout the development of their musicking. Just like the previous examples, the performative aesthetics reflects a kind of spontaneity and authenticity frequently used in TikTok. @binabianca89 performs from her bedroom directly singing to the camera. Additionally, she enters and exits the scene on each verse to highlight a change in personality/perspective. She also uses captions during the performance to present the lyrics of the song. However, the most outstanding aspect in this performance is the loop @binabianca89 creates using the default auto play of TikTok. In "Feedback," the text and the music of the song are planned in a way in which the end connects with the beginning, creating an infinite performance. This aspect is highlighted by the performative quality with which @binabianca89 created this loop: the synchronization of the end and the beginning of this TikTok is so precise that it is barely noticeable when the song begins and ends unless enough attention is put on the lyrics. The way @binabianca89 uses this performative possibility of TikTok and the way the song is conceived and performed reflect a deep understanding of the performative contexts and possibilities of TikTok, while providing us an example of how TikTokers take advantage of the contexts, norms, expectations, and aesthetics of TikTok for developing their music effectively.

The examples presented in this section show us some of the many ways in which TikTokers create their songs and/or musical pieces through their performance. Either through performance or the development of their own songs and performative formats, TikTokers appropriate these musics from the contexts, norms, expectations, and aesthetics of TikTok, said differently: they are TikToking musics. TikToks goes from being a simple digital stage for presenting their performances to being a performative practice of its own, to become a performative space in between, where conceptions, aesthetics, and musical-performative contexts are renegotiated to create new hybrid formats, which may in the future come to be recognized as performative culture in its own right. As we have been able to observe throughout this chapter, the way in which TikTokers appropriate the platform for their musical practices in and through it are as vast as the number of performances. TikTok is and can be a place, a practice, and a performative context in which musicians can explore their identity as musicians and TikTokers simultaneously: a place, a practice, and a performative context for making and remaking music.

Conclusions

Some stories change our lives in one way or another; one that would change my life would start on a day like any other. The warm sunlight streams into an ordinary living room while a little child, full of energy, darts around an old couch. The child settles next to his grandfather, and then they turn the pages of a color book together. The child's face lights up, his tiny finger pointing to an image, and then he tries to "zoom" it with his thumb and index finger. On the other side of the room, his parents exchange knowing looks, their smiles ready to burst out into laughter. Disconcerted by the reaction, the grandfather asks with a stern tone of voice: "What is there to laugh about?" For a short moment, a slight breather, these words freeze in the air, and a second later, laughter fills the air. The child keeps trying, but he is upset and crying …

As you may still remember from the beginning of this book, this is one of many personal experiences that have made me aware of the role that new technologies and media play in shaping our children's everyday life. Years after this experience and countless adventures and misfortunes, the research project born from the thoughts provoked by this and other stories had come to an end. Time kept passing and throughout my research I had been able to observe other experiences, other realities. But my presumption that even though we share a specific lifeworld we perceive realities differently was confirmed, just like this work confirmed (again) that the realities of our current ethnographies are different to those experienced in their origins.

As I began this project at the beginning of 2018, there was very little research about the musicking of Musical.ly. Musical.ly seemed to be almost nonexistent in the (ethno)musicological literature; my research was moving on a field that was little explored by ethnomusicology and other discipline. Today, scholarship on TikTok[1] is growing rapidly and diversifying. Without doubt TikTok has gained

[1] For a detailed exposition about the current state of scholarship on TikTok, as well as Short Video Studies see: Kaye et al. (2021) and Kaye et al. (2022).

visibility, and though initiatives like TikTok Cultures Research Network and works by Crystal Abidin (among others: 2021, forthcoming), Trevor Boffone (2021, 2022, 2023), and Bondy Kaye et al. (2022) have provided access for approaching this phenomenon, there is still much to learn from the performative world of TikTok.[2] My work adds up to the search for a deeper understanding of TikTok as a glocal phenomenon from an ethnographic perspective (see 2020, 2022, 2023a, 2023b, 2024a). I embarked on this project with a broad question: how and why is the musicking of the smartphone application TikTok, formerly Musical.ly, historically constructed, socially maintained, and individually created and experienced by diverse actors from a glocal context? Based on my research, I have identified several key points worth considering for future musicological research. While I cannot claim to have found a definitive answer to this question, these points will prove valuable in advancing our understanding of the hows of multimedia human musicking.

The ways in which TikTokers appropriate the platform for creating musical practices in and through it are very wide and diverse, and are in constant change. However, during the last years I could observe the presence of some general ways/modes from which TikTokers use and/or conceptualize TikTok for developing their musical practices, which can be grouped in the following: (1) TikTok as a digital stage for developing performances; (2) TikTok as a tool and/or extended performative space through which it is possible to adapt and create new ways for playing music and performing; and (3) TikTok as a practice of its own and of equal performative value.

First, understanding TikTok as a digital stage means seeing it as another performative space for developing musical practices, a place that allows performing and distributing performances. One example can be observed in the live streaming TikTokers carry out. Either by transmitting organized events or small spontaneous presentations, TikTok is used as a platform for distributing a performance beyond a specific physical place. It is important to highlight that, in this particular situation, it is crucial that the performance reaches a broader audience. TikTok is not a mandatory component for performance development. Therefore, streaming can co-occur on other platforms, including YouTube or Instagram.

[2] The special issue "TikTok-Music-Cultures: Perspectives on the Study of Musicking Practices On & Through TikTok" (Bermúdez, 2024b) will add to these efforts from a musicological perspective.

Understanding TikTok as a digital stage does not reduce, however, the performative possibilities for musicians to live streaming their performances. TikTokers can also carry out performances that can be presented asynchronously in a presentational manner through the application. On one side, there are some TikTokers who play excerpts of already existing songs and/or musical pieces; on the other, there are TikTokers who prefer composing their own songs and/or musical pieces specifically to be interpreted on TikTok. TikTok has become a powerful tool for musicians to showcase their talent and jump-start their careers. By performing songs, either their own or those by other artists, musicians leverage the digital stage provided by TikTok to reach a global audience. Compared to other forms of performance on TikTok, musicians openly and confidently display their vocal and/or instrumental abilities. The sound quality of their TikToks plays here a vital role in demonstrating their abilities, along with the visual positioning of the performance to make it evident how sound is produced.

Besides that, thanks to the performative possibilities of the platform and the relative independence it encourages its users, organizing and carrying out duets can be done in different ways. These duets can be organized in advance and jointly by performing TikTokers, but they can also be spontaneous and unilateral. A very remarkable aspect of duets is that they not only promote an interaction between TikTokers but also allow TikTokers to widen their performative possibilities by making duets with themselves. In this case, TikTokers can, for example, complete their performances by playing different voices or instrumental sections by themselves.

In addition to these examples, there are some proposals where TikTok is understood not just as a place for presenting a performance but also as a tool and/or extended performative space through which it is possible to create new ways for playing music and performing. An example is the attempt by Opernloft in the framework of the program #CreatorsForDiversity, to adapt Wolfgang A. Mozart's "Die Entführung aus dem Serai" (1782) in 2021 as "#FREE_Constanze" and Georges Bizet's "Carmen" (1875) in 2022 as "Carmen by Carmen" to be performed in TikTok. In "#FREE_Constanze," Julia Schreiner and Michael Renath sought to create a dramaturgical work of the existing power relations in the opera of Mozart from a global context without limiting themselves to cultural borders, but rather highlighting gender and class aspects, as well as its consequent inequalities. On the other side, in "Carmen by Carmen," Hannah Schlags and Jessica Maier decided to focus the plot on the character of

Carmen and the process of self-reflection she experiences as she faces arguments and claims by Micaëla, Jo, and Escamillo. The original plot was taken to the backseat, focusing the dramaturgy of the production on the criticism about gender, class, and race stereotypes on Bizet's "Carmen." Approaching opera as a topic from Carmen's perspective allowed the Schlags-Maier duo to create a meta-level for the narrative, from which the character of Carmen can critically reflect by herself about her behavior in relation to the other characters and the gender and class mandates she is subject to.

The biggest challenge the Opernloft team had to face during these projects was adapting the music and stage of both operas to the performative context of TikTok. The Opernloft team understood TikTok as a tool and/or performative space through which it is possible to create new interpretative and performative forms for developing a performance, trying to take the operatic world to a new performative context. Although the contexts, norms, expectations, and aesthetics of TikTok were widely considered in these proposals, it is still possible to perceive a kind of performative "limitation" since the aspiration is still set on creating a multimedia format without ceasing to be considered as opera. And here, in my opinion, perhaps lies the source of a permanent conflict in these performances: the eagerness to adapt an operatic work to TikTok without ceasing to be an opera, in a literal sense, could lead the projects to a lose-lose performative situation, neither making opera nor TikTok in a satisfactory way.

On the other hand, there are other performances that present another kind of conceptualization of what it means to make music on TikTok, understanding it as a practice of its own and with equal performative value. First, there are some attempts in this direction to use TikTok as a musical instrument and/or a musical-performative extension in contemporary music. Examples of this possibility can be seen in the works of composers such as Karel Stulens, who has created pieces like "SWIPERZ: Swipe-study for Smartphone Quartet" and "As You Like It, Like it! For Smartphone Quartet, String Trio & E. Guitar." Similarly, post-composers like Belenish Moreno-Gil and Óscar Escudero have also explored this possibility, like in "Autotune para el pueblo." It's exciting to note that Moreno-Gil is currently in the composition phase of her new project, "TikTopera: Small Pieces for Performer, Voice, Video, Electronics, and Social Network."

Yet, there is also the example of the so-called TikTopera, a project resulting from a collaboration between the English National Opera and Netflix, produced as a preamble and promotion to the launch of the second season of the Netflix

Series *Tiger King 2*. Compared to the TikTok-Operas "#FREE_Constanze" and "Carmen by Carmen," where the purpose was to create a TikTok adaptation of both Wolfgang A. Mozart's "Die Entführung aus dem Serai" and Georges Bizet's "Carmen," in "Tiger King 2: The TikTopera" the performative aim is not adapting Bizet's opera to TikTok, but—besides advertising the new season of the series—making TikToks. There was no attempt to adapt and/or perform the music or the plot through the context, aesthetics, and expectations of the operatic world. This allowed TikTokers and the production team to see these performances not as an adaptation of something that already existed but as a new kind of performance that can be understood as a TikTopera, a new performative possibility in the extensive world of TikTok, and from which a new way of storytelling is reimagined. The TikToks constituting the TikTopera were done according to the visual and acoustic aesthetics usually performed in the musicking of the featured TikTokers. There was no practice and aesthetics that had to be adapted to TikTok, but it was the TikTok practices and aesthetics that determined the context of the performance.

On top of that, TikTokers compose songs and/or musical pieces keeping in mind that they will be almost exclusively performed on this platform. In fact, the short duration of these songs (between fifteen and sixty seconds) does not allow a satisfactory development outside digital platforms, and compared to the performance of pieces and popular songs, it is a top concern in these performances to have an active participation of the audience (becoming viral), as well as using the performative and aesthetic language of TikTok. There is a wide variety in the types and intensity of using the performative tools of TikTok. By just using different recording modes or using camera changes, by recording different parts asynchronously, and/or by using the duet or stitch function, these performances show different ways in which TikTokers use the performative language of TikTok for creating short songs. Although the degree to which these contexts, norms, expectations, and aesthetics of TikTok are integrated into these kinds of songs varies, it is possible to observe a performative understanding that emerges from the practice of TikTok.

This kind of short song written to be performed on TikTok allows TikTokers to experiment with topics and/or ideas without the stress of writing whole songs and/or without the risk of performative failure. By not seeking from the start to meet the ideals and/or expectations of a certain musical world, TikTokers concentrate on the performative contexts of TikTok, which allows them to set the attention first to having fun performing TikToks, and therefore the musical practice of TikTok. Moreover, this allows them to perform their own songs, and if they are successful, they can have the opportunity to widen their performances with steadiness. This situation can encourage TikTokers to write longer songs based on the ones they have already written, which can be now performed in physical concerts and/or be distributed through different digital platforms like Instagram or YouTube and streaming services, like Spotify and Apple Music.

The performative world of TikTok is certainly vast and varied, but this would not be the case without the actors that keep and live their musicking. TikTokers come together to watch, analyze, learn, and practice different choreographies; Meetups between TikTokers and their followers are developed in diverse physical contexts; and friendships and partnerships are taken beyond the platform in the physical world or vice versa; among many others. In the musicking of TikTok, the physical and the digital are not only in continuous contact, but they are an inseparable part of the daily lives of the TikTokers. After the unexpected merger of Musical.ly with TikTok, the application entered a new phase of creative development. Old and new practices were combined and developed differently, resulting in a performative plurality that attracted new users. In the second half of 2019, TikTok became one of the most downloaded apps in the world. This success was further reinforced by the outbreak of the COVID-19 pandemic and the subsequent lockdowns that encouraged people to try new applications and activities. TikTok became a space where social life took place, especially for young musicians drawn to experimenting with new formats, creating new collaborations, and performing live concerts. However, although TikTokers did not have any trouble in carrying out the activities they enjoyed before this merger, their identity as performers had been damaged and/or put into negotiation.

Interestingly, at that time, the performers were already developing a specific performative identity on the platform, an identity as TikToker. Following the ideas of Philip Auslander (2006, 2021), we could then say that, the same way as musicians (in the traditional sense), TikTokers perform their TikToker identity at the moment of carrying out their musicking, and therefore are also performing or developing a performer identity which we could call TikTok persona. However, this act of performing a TikToker identity—the TikToker persona—must be understood as a process of "becoming." A person is not a TikToker just by using the application, but it is necessary to actively create, negotiate, and perform this identity as a TikTok persona. This process of becoming can be seen reflected in the two existing modes of TikTok personae I have been able to observe through my research. First, (1) a kind of TikTok personae we can observe in performers, who though they perform their identity as performers, these have not been recognized by any community as such, nor have been recognized as possessing a particular kind of "TikTok identity." On the other hand, (2) there is another TikTok persona we can observe in performers who perform an established, individual, and recognizable performer identity.

For performing their TikTok persona, similar as the case of musical persona, the performer must execute their musicking according to the conventions and expectations of a given social performative context. In this sense, they would not just have to learn to make satisfactory TikToks but also to "behave correctly" in each of the contexts of the musicking they participate in. These conventions and expectations allude to all aspects of the performance, including the setting, physical appearance of the performer, the selected music, the performative aesthetics, the way of behaving, among many others. Together with this, although the focus on authenticity is very common among TikTokers, being authentic is not a quality that TikTokers may or may not have, as we might wrongly conclude. On the contrary, just like other aspects of the TikTok persona, authenticity is a performative act that can also be learned and is tied to the conventions and expectation of the social context where the interaction is taking place. These "performances of authenticity" are created and constituted through a long dialectic process of negotiation between the actors of TikTok musicking and is framed by conventions and expectations within a given social context. This process of becoming is also framed by the body and voice of the TikToker. Just like musicians perform their identity as musicians during a performance, they also perform their gender identity, class, race, and so on, and in a similar way, their performances are also read under the already existing mandates of genre, class, race, and so on. For this reason, we can talk about musical performances and the performance of a TikTok persona as a double-performative act: on one side, this act is performed and (re)negotiates the identities of the musicking actors, both the TikTok persona and the audience. However, knowledge related to the developed musical practice are also performed and (re)negotiated.

The expectations generated by the intersectional mandates that a performer attributes or is attributed to her body/performing voice frame how the performance will be carried out or how the TikTok persona will be performed. Thus, they consciously or unconsciously reproduce existing intersectional mandates through the performance of their TikTok persona. Particularly interesting is that, although TikTokers are the ones who perform these intersectional mandates, these are reinforced by the algorithms of the application. By presenting previously curated content according to the particular sociocultural preferences of the user, the algorithms reinforce the intersectional mandates consumed and/or created by TikTokers. By doing this, the algorithms exclude performances that are different from what it perceives are the tastes of the user, consequently excluding possible divergent intersectional mandates.

Inequality and mechanisms of exclusion resulting from historical colonialism are also reflected on the application. TikTok demonstrates being a predominantly white territory. BIPOC performers have much more difficulties for establishing themselves as professional TikTokers, besides the fact that credit for their work has been (and continues being) robbed mostly by white performers (see Boffone 2021). TikTok has tried to change by increasing support in their platform for BIPOC performers. This is reflected not only in support programs for BIPOC creators but also by introducing and promoting a "give credit" function for recognizing the original performance and its creator. However, there is still a long way to go. Many intersectional inequalities are still present in the application, reminding us that digital platforms are not neutral territories but rather reflect assumptions, ideals, and prejudices of a certain society, circumstances to which TikTokers are exposed.

An interesting aspect to observe, which relates with the intersectional phenomenon of the platform, is that although multimedia music practices take place through complex distribution processes in completely different spaces scattered over the world, the creation and exchange of certain knowledge, as well as several interactions between actors, occur in virtual and physical "local" situations. Therefore, these practices are embedded not just on devices but on their local contexts and infrastructures as well. On one side, the practices actors develop on TikTok are strongly framed and influenced by at least three aspects that cannot be separated from their physical location: *the device embodiment*, *the connection infrastructures*, and *the national laws and regulations*.

(1) *The device embodiment*: Like traditional musical practices, musical practices developed in multimedia environments need physical devices for their realization. In the same way as with musical instruments, these tools generate a new embodied relation that performers must acquire and maintain to effectively and satisfactorily perform their musicking. On the one hand, the embodiment generated by interacting with the device determines the way in which certain practices may or may not be developed. On the other hand, this interaction with the devices allows the creation of embodiment in the relationships between

actors, thus helping the creation of an embodied sense of locality and community in this musical practice.

(2) *The connection infrastructures*: Many of the practices developed in the musicking of TikTok require an internet connection. This might seem trivial; nonetheless, access to the necessary infrastructure influences to a great extent the way in which musicking is articulated and negotiated between actors, as well as how important these practices are. For example, although theoretically anyone can partake on the musicking of TikTok, observing this from an Austrian context may differ greatly from a Mexican one. A situation that resembles what Nick Couldry and Ulises Mejías call data colonialism (see 2019: 83–112). This can also be extended to the cost of the service itself, but also to specific needs from each device regarding, for example, the battery performance and how specific behaviors arise from this.

(3) *The national laws and regulations*: A particularly influencing aspect that cannot be completely separated from the physical location of the actors is the fact that actors find themselves framed under the conditioning of national laws and regulations. Whether the platforms are permitted or not, whether they have these certain features or not can be a clear example of this influence. In other cases, we can observe direct interventions by authorities in the musicking development, such as the case of the "Kulikitaka-Challenge," which was removed from the Austrian TikTok or the imminent banning of TikTok in the United States and other countries, including Austria.

On the other hand, there is a strong physical interaction between TikTokers taking place in this musicking. Schools and parks become meeting places for TikTokers to make, watch, comment, and analyze TikTok videos; to come together to watch, analyze, and learn different choreographies; Meetups between TikTokers and their followers are developed under different contexts. For obvious reasons these physical interactions have diminished in intensity during the COVID-19 pandemic. Nevertheless, it was possible to observe that this need for physically relating has not lost importance for TikTokers. TikTokers continue musicking and physically getting together, even if in a more restricted way. But TikTokers use their musicking, especially their performances, also to deal and negotiate with situations that affect their daily lives. A clear example of this is how they thematize their feelings, identity, and collectivity, as well as the problems and challenges they experience during the local crisis unleashed with the COVID-19 pandemic. Moreover, TikTokers thematize their own locality through their performance. This thematizing can be directly or indirectly positioning their own physical locality through the presentation of a physical place and through the thematizing of this locality. This is reinforced by the algorithms in the application itself.

TikTok algorithms aim to keep TikTokers using the application as much as possible. Based on my observations, I dare to say that this is mostly done by evoking a local/regional sensation of togetherness among TikTokers, together with other resources like related topics. Besides providing the possibility for corporal interaction beyond the interface of the application, TikTok algorithms stimulate and reinforce the embodied experience and sense of belonging by giving visibility to the local places and experiences of TikTokers. This enables them to form empathetic connections with other TikTokers, fostering stronger community bonds and a sense of belonging among them. Consequently, TikTok musicking isn't perceived as a solely global and deterritorialized experience but as a genuinely glocal one, continually reintegrating itself into the local embodied realities of TikTokers. This, in turn, enhances interactions and relationships between TikTokers beyond the platform's interface.

People around the world spend their time watching videos through the app while they go about their daily lives. They create new TikToks and appropriate and remediate existing ones. They participate in the discourse around these practices by commenting on other videos. However, some modes of engagement are carried out outside TikTok, both in physical spaces and through other digital platforms. Many of the videos created and shared on TikTok are also shared through YouTube and Instagram, and many of the discourses about these platforms are broadcast through both digital and physical magazines, as well as through web pages. Also, videos and other practices previously developed on YouTube are readapted to the aesthetic contexts and languages of digital video platforms like TikTok and Instagram. Allowing the creation and renegotiation of common multimedia practices takes advantage of the specific contexts of the original platforms to later remediate them, creating new multimedia creative practices and contexts with glocal aesthetics. The interrelationships enabled by the interoperability of platforms have fostered the development of exciting forms of networked creativity and practice, a multimedia network that emerges through the articulation of joint musical and dance practices experienced in an interlacing of physical (everyday places, e.g., school, parks) and digital interaction spaces (such as TikTok, YouTube, Instagram): a multimedia network in which we live and experience our day to day.

The examples approached through this work do not seek nor can completely represent the performative world of TikTok. These are just the first steps, a first recount, with many limitations of the many kinds of performances I noticed in the last couple of years during my research. There is no doubt that the musical-performative experimentation in and through TikTok is just beginning, and the results and paths that these can open will be positioned in a central place in our reflections about multimedia musical phenomena for sure. TikTok is and can be a place, a practice, and a performative context in which musicians can explore their identity as musicians. Simultaneously TikTok is and can be a place, a practice, a performative context for making and remaking music.

Similarly, it is important to stress that during this work I had to leave many topics and/or perspectives aside with the purpose of keeping this project in a manageable size and reach. However, this does not mean that these other topics and/or perspectives have not played an important role—even if it was indirectly—during the development of this project. Although for the moment these topics and/or perspectives could not be worked in depth, they may serve as the base for the development of future research projects.

First, there is no doubt that an (ethno)choreographic analysis of the dance practices of TikTok is very important for understanding the musicking of TikTok. This aspect, however, could not be detailed during this project. Placing the focus of my research on dance practices in the way I have done with musical practices would have required at least twice the time to carry out successfully. In addition, it is worth pointing out that, although as an ethnomusicologist I have been in contact with dance traditions during my studies and my research, ethnochoreology is an area of study in which I'm not prepared and therefore I do not have the necessary competences for developing a project of such a magnitude. Moreover, and due to similar reasons, I have also found myself in the need to reduce the depth of my research regarding the role of music and dance in challenges and trends. Conducting future investigations with colleagues trained in ethnochoreology would help clear doubts and deepen these very significant topics in the musicking of TikTok from a multidisciplinary perspective.

Furthermore, the lack of human and economic resources for executing a larger and longer project would have urged me not to go into greater detail on some of the topics covered in the book. In this context, there are four main processes that need to be approached with more detail and focused on specific case studies. In the first place, it is necessary to analyze in depth the learning processes and performance production in and through TikTok. Although these processes were mentioned in this work, I believe it is necessary to develop research about concrete cases and/or people (ethnographies of the particular) to be able to duly deepen in this subject. Also, it is equally important to make a profound examination of the existing processes of construction and performance of gender, class, and race in TikTok. The elaboration of ethnographies about specific cases and/or people is also necessary here. Additionally, it would be pertinent to carry out detailed studies (micro-ethnographies) about concrete musical worlds in and through TikTok. By analyzing the musicking surrounding specific genres or music/dance styles, this kind of specific studies is not just missing, but appear to be the next step for a greater understanding of the musical phenomenon happening in TikTok.[3]

Finally, it is significant to analyze the phenomenon approached in this book from a much more focused perspective on the processes of reception. Although this perspective was considered in methodology and topic, the development of the arguments presented in this study is from a production perspective. A focus on the reception of musics and dances in and through TikTok could benefit understanding the phenomena related with TikTok. Today, scholarship on TikTok is quickly growing and diversifying. Therefore, I am deeply convinced that soon there will be new investigations that will bring us answers to these and many other questions. For now, I hope that the results of this research serve as a starting point for interdisciplinary discussion about why and how a multimedia musicking happens, as well as a stimulus for developing new paths and points for thinking about the study of multimedia and multilocal musical phenomena.

As we have observed throughout this book, adopting an ethnographic approach is highly beneficial for studying and investigating any music culture globally from a cultural relativistic standpoint, particularly for examining multimedia musical practices such as those found on TikTok. Nevertheless, researching this type of multimedia musicking requires more than a successful ethnomusicological model, such as Merriam's (1964). Therefore, to overcome these challenges, I propose to understand internet and its (musical) practices, as embedded, embodied, and everyday, as postulated by Christine Hine (2015). This allows us, as presented in this book, to reflect on the meaning of internet in the everyday life of the actors, their musical practices, as well as the recognition

[3] A first step in this direction can be found in the special issue "TikTok-Music-Cultures. Perspectives on the Study of Musicking Practices On & Through TikTok" (Bermúdez 2024b).

of internet as an embodied experience that is influenced and determined by forms, discourses, times, objectives, and so on, and by the interactions between the human and nonhuman actors.

On this basis, I propose to take into account *concepts, behaviors, and sounds that different actors of specific musicking (musicians/dancers, audiences, producers, and other actors musicking) historically construct, socially maintain, and individually create and experience in everyday synchronous and asynchronous multimedia situations.* This model, which I call E^{3}thnography, opens up new avenues for exploring music cultures developed through physical and digital interactions. Integrating multiple modes of expression paves the way for a new era of multimodal ethnomusicology. E^{3}thnography provides an innovative approach to music research that allows us to analyze music cultures through various physical and digital mediums and navigate the contemporary world's multimedia realities.

Therefore, I propose that for exploring mediatized musical practices, it is firstly indispensable to understand digital and analog media as practices, which are created, discussed, and experienced in everyday situations and contexts synchronously or asynchronously. That is why an intensive multilocal and multimedia participatory observation in line with a hermeneutic phenomenological ethnography allows us to concentrate our focus on what people are actively doing *with* and *in* a mediatized environment and herewith against a discourse that sees media exclusively as a communication or representation channel used by physical actors. But it also means that an e^{3}thnographic approach requires a strong focus on individuals and their music-making experiences as individuals or in groups. That is why, it is important to prioritize not only the use of methods that focus on the learning of multimedia practices related to musicking but also the processes that allow the creation and negotiation of the auditory knowledge of the musicking under investigation. In addition, the focus shall also lie on the performative creation of musical personae and on the discussion of cultural behaviors related to them.

By utilizing approaches such as the one presented in this book (E^{3}thnography) and adopting a research paradigm that recognizes digital media as a practice rather than a passive representation channel or an economic product, our ethnographic work is better positioned to address the challenges presented by contemporary multimedia music practices comprehensively and effectively. An E^{3}thnography offers a unique lens to observe and experience the historical construction of concepts, behaviors, and sounds by the actors of a specific musicking. It reveals how these elements are socially maintained and individually created and experienced in everyday life, whether in synchronous or asynchronous multimedia situations. The arguments presented in this book are the foundation and result of this approach. I hope you found this piece as enjoyable to read as it was to write. Above all, I hope my ideas will prove helpful in your research pursuits.

Bibliography

Abidin, Crystal. 2018. *Internet Celebrity: Understanding Fame Online*. Bingley: Emerald.

Abidin, Crystal. 2021. "Mapping Internet Celebrity on TikTok: Exploring Attention Economies and Visibility Labours." *Cultural Science Journal* 12, no. 1: 77–103.

Abidin, Crystal. Forthcoming. *TikTok and Youth Cultures*. Bingley: Emerald Publishing.

Abidin, Crystal, and Bondy Kaye. 2021. "Audio Memes, Earworms, and Templatability: The 'Aural Turn' of Memes on TikTok." In *Critical Meme Reader: Global Mutations of the Viral Image*, edited by Chloë Arkenbout, Jack Wilson, and Daniel De Zeeuw, 58–68. Amsterdam: Institute of Network Cultures.

Abidin, Crystal, and Jin Lee. 2023. "K-pop TikTok: TikTok's Expansion into South Korea, TikTok Stage, and Platformed Glocalization." *Media International Austrialia* 188, no. 1: 86–111. https://doi.org/10.1177/1329878X231186445

Abidin, Crystal, Emily van der Nagel, Amelia Johns, Francesco Bailo, Aleesha Rodríguez, Bondy Valdovinos-Kaye, Patrik Wikström, Ysabel Gerrard, and Tama Leaver. 2020. "'Please Read the Comments': Commenting Cultures Across Platforms." AoIR Selected Papers of Internet Research. https://doi.org/10.5210/spir.v2020i0.11109.

Abu-Lughod, Lila. 1991. "Writing against Culture." In *Recapturing Anthropology: Working in the Present*, edited by Richard Fox, 137–62. Santa Fe: School of American Research Press.

Agnesmilewski [@agnesmilewski]. 2021. Interview by Stephan Steiner. September 29, 2021.

Akinbola, Bimbola. 2022. "#AfricanAunties: Performing Diasporic Digital Disbelongings on TikTok." *Text and Performance Quarterly* 42, no. 3: 284–97.

Alonso López, Nadia, Pavel Sidorenko Bautista, and Fábio Giacomelli. 2021. "Beyond Challenges and Viral Dance Moves: TikTok as a Vehicle for Disinformation and Fact-Checking in Spain, Portugal, Brazil, and the USA." *Anàlisi: Quaderns de Comunicació i Cultura* 64: 65–84.

Alvermann, Donna, Ellen Wynne, and William Wright. 2021. "Tales from TikTok: Gender and Cultural Intersectionalities." In *Genders, Cultures, and Literacies: Understanding Intersecting Identities*, edited by Barbara Guzzetti, 198–211. New York: Routledge.

Amaral, Adriana. 2022. "TikTok Doomerism: An Algorithm and the Revival of Post-Punk through Transcultural Fandom." In *Channel Power*, edited by Detlef Diederichsen and Arno Raffeiner, 5–15. Leipzig: Spector Books.

Anderson, Benedict. [1983] 2006. *Imagined Communities: Reflections on the Origin and Spread of Nationalism*. London: Verso.

Andruchowitz, Gernot. 2021. "Mit TikTok an die Spitze der Charts: Wie die Soziale-Video-App 'TikTok' die Musikindustrie beeinflusst und sich Musik-Streaming und der technologische Fortschritt auf komerzielle Musik auswirken." Bachelor's thesis. Vienna: University of Vienna.

Annamaurer_music [@annamaurer_music]. 2021. Interview by Tessa Balser-Schuhmann. June 9, 2021.

Appadurai, Arjun. 1996. *Modernity at Large: Cultural Dimensions of Globalization*. Minneapolis: University of Minnesota Press.

Ar3miss [@ar3miss]. 2021. Interview by Gernot Andruchowitz. August 6, 2021.

Augé, Marc. [1995] 2008. *Non-places: An Introduction to Supermodernity*. London: Verso.

Auslander, Philip. 2006. "Musical Personae." *The Drama Review* 50, no. 1: 100–19.

Auslander, Philip. 2018. *Reactivations: Essays on Performance and Its Documentation*. Ann Arbor: University of Michigan Press.

Auslander, Philip. 2021. *In Concert: Performing Musical Persona*. Ann Arbor: University of Michigan Press.

Avdeeff, Melissa. 2021. "TikTok, Twitter, and Platform-specific Technocultural Discourse in Response to Taylor Swift's LGBTQ+ Allyship in 'You Need to Calm Down.'" *Contemporary Music Review* 40, no. 1: 78–98.

Ayers, Michael, ed. 2006. *Cybersounds: Essays on Virtual Music Culture. Essays on Virtual Music Culture*. Bern: Peter Lang.

Baily, John. 2001. "Learning to Perform as a Research Technique in Ethnomusicology." *British Journal of Ethnomusicology* 10, no. 2: 85–98.

Baron, Jaimie, Jennifer Fleeger, and Shannon Wong Lerner, eds. 2021. *Media Ventriloquisim: How Audiovisual Technologies Transform the Voice-Body Relationship*. New York: Oxford University Press.

Barz, Gregory, and Timothy Cooley, eds. 2008. *Shadows in the Field: New Perspectives for Fieldwork in Ethnomusicology*. New York: Oxford University Press.

Baudrillard, Jean. [1981] 1994. *Simulacra and Simulation*. Ann Arbor: University of Michigan Press.

Bauman, Richard. 1986. *Story, Performance, and Event*. Cambridge: Cambridge University Press.

Ben-Atar, Ella, Smadar Ben-Asher, and Shirley Druker Shitrit. 2023. "Social Punishment by the Distribution of Aggressive TikTok Videos Against Women in a Traditional Society." *Journal of Information, Communication and Ethics in Society* 21, no. 1: 129–42. https://doi.org/10.1108/JICES-06-2022-0059.

Bench, Harmony. 2020. *Perpetual Motion: Dance, Digital Cultures, and the Common*. Minneapolis: University of Minnesota Press.

Bermúdez, Juan. 2020. "¿Qué música? Si nadie toca... si nadie sabe...: Reflexionando el etnografiar de un *musicking* digital." *Boletín Música* 52–53 (julio 2019–junio 2020): 51–60.

Bermúdez, Juan. 2021a. *Echoes of the Past: The Marimba Sencilla in Chiapas. An Exploratory Study of a Diatonic Marimba Tradition*. Vienna: Praesens.

Bermúdez, Juan. 2021b. "Ethnographing between Spaces: Researching TikTok From an E³thnomusicological Perspective." In "The in(ter)dependencies of Mobile Online and Offline Spaces: Reflections on Methods, Practices, Ethics," Katja Kaufmann, Monika Palmberger, Carolina Parreiras, Arianna Bussoletti, Francesca Belotti, Francesca Comunello, Stellamarina Donato, Welmoed Wagenaar, Juan Bermúdez, Moritz Schweiger, Jeffrey Wimmer. Panel presented at AoIR 2021. *AoIR Selected Papers of Internet Research*. https://doi.org/10.5210/spir.v2021i0.12119

Bermúdez, Juan.2022. "Virtual Musical.ly(ties): Identitites, Performances, and Meanings in a Mobile Application. An Ethnomusicological Approach to TikTok's Musicking." PhD dissertation. Vienna: University of Vienna.

Bermúdez, Juan. 2023a. "It's All About 'Being There': Rethinking Presence and Co-presence in the Ethnographic Field During and After the Covid-19 Pandemic." In "Between Memory and Knowledge–Sounding the Pandemic," edited by Maurizio Agamennone, Antonella Dicuonzo, Daniele Palma, Ludovico Peroni and Giulia Sarno. Special Issue, *Journal of World Popular Music* 10, no. 1: 19–35. https://doi.org/10.1558/jwpm.26375

Bermúdez, Juan. 2023b. "Performing Beyond the Platform – Experiencing Musicking On and through YouTube, TikTok, and Instagram." In *Remediating Sound: Repeatable Culture, YouTube and Music* edited by Holly Rogers, Joana Freitas and João Francisco Porfírio, 187–202. London: Bloomsbury Academic.

Bermúdez, Juan. 2024a. "Ethnographing TikTok: Toward an E³thnomusicological Approach to a Multimedia Musicking." In "TikTok-Music-Cultures. Perspectives on the Study of Musicking Practices On & Through TikTok," edited by Juan Bermúdez. Special Issue, *Musicologica Austriaca – Journal for Austrian Music Studies*.

Bermúdez, Juan, ed. 2024b. "TikTok-Music-Cultures. Perspectives on the Study of Musicking Practices On & Through TikTok." Special Issue, *Musicologica Austriaca – Journal for Austrian Music Studies*.

Bermúdez, Juan, Lukas Dulling, Stephanie Gmeiner, Hannes Matthäus, Markus Rogenhofer, Florian Schriebl, Lukas Auer, and Bernd Brabec de Mori. 2018. "Von Klang(-)Wissen und anderen Fischen: Auditive Wissenskulturen von Konzertfach- und Musikologiestudierenden im Vergleich." In *Auditive Wissenskulturen: Das Wissen klanglicher Praxis*, edited by Bernd Brabec de Mori and Martin Winter, 283–302. Wiesbaden: Springer VS.

Bhabha, Homi K. [1994] 2004. *The Location of Culture*. London: Routledge.

Boellstorff, Tom. 2008. *Coming of Age in Second Life: An Anthropologist Explores the Virtually Human*. Princeton, NJ: Princeton University Press.

Boellstorff, Tom, Bonnie Nardi, Celia Pearce, and T. L. Taylor. 2012. *Ethnography and Virtual Worlds*. Princeton, NJ: Princeton University Press.

Boffone, Trevor. 2021. *Renegades: Digital Dance Cultures from Dubsmash to TikTok*. New York: Oxford University Press.

Boffone, Trevor, ed. 2022. *TikTok Cultures in the United States*. New York: Routledge.

Boffone, Trevor. 2023. *Social Media in Musical Theatre*. London: Bloomsbury.

Boffone, Trevor. Forthcoming. *TikTok Broadway: Musical Theatre Fandom in the Digital Age*. New York: Oxford University Press.

Born, Georgina. ed. 2022. *Music and Digital Media: A Planetary Anthropology*. London: UCL Press.

Bossen, Christina Bucknell, and Rita Kottasz. 2020. "Uses and Gratifications Sought by Pre-adolescent and Adolescent TikTok Consumers." *Young Consumers* 21, no. 4: 463–78.

Bourdieu, Pierre. [1984] 2010. *Distinction: A Social Critique of the Judgement of Taste*. London: Routledge.

Bourdieu, Pierre. [1972] 1977. *Outline of a Theory of Practice*. Cambridge: Cambridge University Press.

Brabec de Mori, Bernd, and Martin Winter, eds. 2018. *Auditive Wissenskulturen: Das Wissen klanglicher Praxis*. Wiesbaden: Springer VS.

Brown, Kevin. 2015. *Karaoke Idols: Popular Music and the Performance of Identity*. Bristol: Intellect.

Bruns, Axel. 2008. *Blogs, Wikipedia, Second Life, And Beyond: From Production to Produsage*. New York: Peter Lang.

Bull, Michael. 2007. *Sound Moves: iPod Culture and Urban Experience*. New York: Routledge.

Butler, Judith. [1990] 2006. *Gender Trouble: Feminism and the Subversion of Identity*. London: Routledge.

Butler, Judith. [1993] 2011. *Bodies That Matter: On the Discursive Limits of "Sex."* London: Routledge.

Carson, Biz. 2016. "How a Failed Education Startup Turned into Musical.ly, the Most Popular App you've Probably Never Heard Of." Business Insider India. May 28, 2016. https://www.businessinsider.in/How-a-failed-education-startup-turned-into-Musical-ly-the-most-popular-app-youve-probably-never-heard-of/articleshow/52481258.cms.

Cervi, Laura. 2021. "TikTok and Generation Z." *Theatre, Dance and Performance Training* 12, no. 2: 198–204.

Cheng, Catherine, and Ioana Literat. 2022. "#GenZ on TikTok: The Collective Online Self-Portrait of the Social Media Generation." *Journal of Youth Studies* 26, no. 7: 925–46.

Cho, Yoonsang. 2021. "Der Einfluss der App Musical.ly auf TikTok durch deren Übernahme und ein Ausblick auf die Zukunft der Short Videos." Bachelor's thesis. Vienna: University of Vienna.

Chu, Shu-Chuan, Teo Deng, and Juan Mundel. 2022. "The Impact of Personalization on Viral Behavior Intentions on TikTok: The Role of Perceived Creativity, Authenticity, and Need for Uniqueness." *Journal of Marketing Communications* 30, no. 1: 1–20. https://doi.org/10.1080/13527266.2022.2098364

Cohen, Sara. 1991. *Rock Culture in Liverpool: Popular Music in the Making*. Oxford: Oxford University Press.

Collie, Natalie, and CarolineWilson-Barnao. 2020. "Playing with TikTok: Algorithmic Culture and the Future of Creative Work." In *The Future of Creative Work: Creativity and Digital Disruption*, edited by Greg Hearn, 172–88. Cheltenham: Edward Elgar Publishing Limited. https://doi.org/10.4337/9781839101106.00020

Connell, John, and Chris Gibson. 2003. *Sound Tracks: Popular Music, Identity and Place*. New York: Routledge.

Connell, Raewyn. [1995] 2005. *Masculinities*. Cambridge: Polity Press.

Cook, Nicholas, Monique M. Ingalls, and David Trippett, eds. 2019. *The Cambridge Companion to Music in Digital Culture*. Cambridge: Cambridge University Press.

Cooley, Timothy, Katherine Meizel, and Nasir Syed. 2008. "Virtual Fieldwork: Three Case Studies." In *Shadows in the Field. New Perspectives for Fieldwork in Ethnomusicology*, edited by Gregory Barz and Timothy Cooley, 90–107. New York: Oxford University Press.

Couldry, Nick. 2010. "Theorising Media as Practice." In *Theorising Media and Practice*, edited by Birgit Bräuchler and John Postill, 35–54. Oxford: Berghahn.

Couldry, Nick. 2020. *Media, Voice, Space and Power: Essays of Refraction*. London: Routledge.

Couldry, Nick, and Andreas Hepp. 2017. *The Mediated Construction of Reality*. Cambridge: Polity Press.

Couldry, Nick, and Ulises Mejías. 2019. *The Costs of Connection: How Data Is Colonizing Human Life and Appopriating It for Capitalism*. Stanford: Stanford University Press.

Cusick, Suzanne G. 1994. "Feminist Theory, Music Theory, and the Mind/Body Problem." *Perspectives of New Music* 32, no. 1: 8–27.

De Certeau, Michel. [1984] 1988. *The Practice of Everyday Life*. Berkeley: University of California Press.

De Leyn, Tom, Ralf De Wolf, Mariek Vanden, and Lieven De Marez. 2022. "In-Between Child's Play and Teenage Pop Culture: Tweens, TikTok & Privacy." *Journal of Youth Studies* 25, no. 8: 1108–25.

Deleuze, Gilles. [1968] 2014. *Difference and Repetition*. London: Bloomsbury Academic.

DeNora, Tia. 2000. *Music in Everyday Life*. Cambridge: Cambridge University Press.

Dornstädter, Anna. 2021. "Musikmarketing im digital Forschungsfeld TikTok: Ethnomusikologische Perspektiven auf TikTok als Marketinginstrument für Independent Artists." Bachelor's thesis. Vienna: University of Vienna.

Doubleday, Veronica. 2008. "Sounds of Power: An Overview of Musical Instruments and Gender." *Ethnomusicology Forum* 17, no. 1: 3–39.

Duguay, Stefanie. 2023. "TikTok's Queer Potential: Identity, Methods, Movements." *Social Media + Society* 9, no. 1. https://doi.org/10.1177/20563051231157594

Eidsheim, Nina Sun. 2019. *The Race of Sound: Listening, Timbre, and Vocality*. Durham, NC: Duke University Press.

Elizabeth, Tracy. 2021. "Unsere Maßnahmen, damit TikTok ein Ort für Nutzer*innen über 13 Jahren bleibt." TikTok newsroom. May 12, 2021. https://newsroom.tiktok.com/de-de/unsere-massnahmen-damit-tiktok-ein-ort-fuer-nutzer-ueber-13-jahren-bleibt.

Elliott, David. 2007. "'Socializing' Music Education." *Action, Criticism, and Theory for Music Education* 6, no. 4: 60–95.

Enders, Bernd. 2013. "Vom Idiophon zum Touchpad: Die musiktechnologische Entwicklung zum Virtuellen Musikinstrument." In *Musik/Medien/Kunst: Wissenschaftliche und künstlerische Perspektiven*, edited by Beate Flath, 55–74. Bielefeld: transcript Verlag.

ENO. 2021. "Netflix and the ENO Launch TikTopera – an Opera Based on Tiger King Created Entirely on TikTok." English National Opera newsroom. November 29, 2021. https://www.eno.org/news/netflix-and-the-eno-launch-tiktopera-an-opera-based-on-tiger-king-created-entirely-on-tiktok/.

Evans, Alexandra. 2020. "TikTok schließt sich der Allianz zum Schutz Minderjähriger im Internet an." TikTok newsroom. November 26, 2020. https://newsroom.tiktok.com/de-de/tiktok-schliesst-sich-der-allianz-zum-schutz-minderjaehriger-im-internet-an.

Finnegan, Ruth. [1989] 2007. *The Hidden Musicians: Music-Making in an English Town*. Middletown: Wesleyan University Press.

Flath, Beate. 2016. "Co-Creation-Prozesse in Livemusikkonzerten am Beispiel der Integration von Smartphones." *Zeitschrift für Kulturmanagement* 2: 67–8.

Floundwisch [@floundwisch]. 2021. Interview by Gernot Andruchowitz. August 8, 2021.

Fornäs, Johan. 1994. "Karaoke: Subjectivity, Play and Interactive Media." *Nordicom Review* 15, no. 1: 87–103.

Foster, Susan L. 2009. "'Throwing Like a Girl'? Gender in a Transnational World." In *Contemporary Choreography: A Critical Reader*, edited by Jo Butterworth and Liesbeth Wildschut, 52–64. New York: Routledge.

Foster, Susan L. 2011. *Choreographing Empathy*. London: Routledge.

Frömming, Urte, Steffen Köhn, Samantha Fox, and Mike Terry, eds. 2017. *Digital Environments: Ethnographic Perspectives across Global Online and Offline Spaces*. Bielefeld: transcript Verlag.

Gagliardi, Paige. 2022. "TikTok the Musical: Copyright Issues Raised by the 'Ratatouille' Musical." *Washington Journal of Law, Technology & Arts* 17, no. 2: 147–71.

García Quiñones, Marta, Anahid Kassabian, and Elena Boschi. 2013. *Ubiquitous Musics: The Everyday Sounds That We Don't Always Notice*. Farnham: Ashgate.

Geertz, Clifford. 1973. *The Interpretation of Cultures: Selected Essays*. New York: Basic Books.

Giddens, Anthony. 1991. *The Consequences of Modernity*. Cambridge: Polity Press.

Glotz, Peter, Stefan Bertschi, and Chris Locke, eds. 2005. *Thumb Culture. The Meaning of Mobile Phones for Society*. Bielefeld: transcript Verlag.

Goffman, Erving. 1959. *The Presentation of Self in Everyday Life*. New York: Anchor Books.

Goldenberg, Anna. 2019. "Das YouTube von morgen: Die chinesische Musikvideo-App TikTok begeistert weltweit immer mehr junge Menschen. Warum?" *Falter* 25/19, June 19, 2019.

Gopinath, Sumanth, and Jason Stanyek, eds. 2014. *The Oxford Handbook of Mobile Music Studies*, Volume 1 and 2. Oxford: Oxford University Press.

Heidegger, Martin. 1971. *Poetry, Language, Thought*. New York: Harper & Row.

Hepp, Andreas. 2010. "Medienkultur kritisch erforschen: Cultural Studies und Medienanalyse." In *Kultursoziologie: Paradigmen – Methoden – Fragestellungen*, edited by Monika Wohlrab-Sahr, 227–49. Wiesbaden: VS Verlag für Sozialwissenschaften.

Hepp, Andreas. 2020. *Deep Mediatization*. London: Routledge.

Hilder, Thomas, Henry Stobart, and Shzr Ee Tan, eds. 2017. *Music, Indigeneity, Digital Media*. Rochester: University of Rochester Press.

Hine, Christine. 2015. *Ethnography for the Internet: Embedded, Embodied and Everyday*. London: Bloomsbury.

Hintersteiner, Ylva. 2021. "'It Is Your Character!': TikTok and the Usage of Audios within the Cosplay-Community for Storytelling with a Special Focus on the My Hero Academia Fandom." Bachelor's thesis. Vienna: University of Vienna.

Hisham.tv [@hisham.tv]. 2021. Interview by Gernot Andruchowitz. August 14, 2021.

Hjorth, Larissa. 2005. "Locating Mobility: Practices of Co-presence and the Percistence of the Postal Metaphor in SMS/MMS Mobile Phone Customization in Melbourne." *Fibreculture Journal* 6. http: //six.fibreculturejournal.org/fcj-035-locating-mobility-practices-of-co-presence-and-the-persistence-of-the-postal-metaphor-in-sms-mms-mobile-phone-customization-in-melbourne/.

Horst, Heather, and Daniel Miller. [2012] 2020. *Digital Anthropology*. New York: Routledge.

Hutchinson, Andrew. 2020. "TikTok Adds New 'Stitch' Feature to Facilitate Video Responses." *Social Media Today*, September 4, 2020.

Ian.draven [@ian.draven]. 2021. Interview by Maximiliane Schrank. June 14, 2021.

Ingold, Tim. [1996a] 2005. *Key Debates in Anthropology*. London: Routledge.

Ingold, Tim. [1996b] 2005. "Human Worlds Are Culturally Constructed: Against the Motion (1)." In *Key Debates in Anthropology*, edited by Tim Ingold, 92–7. London: Routledge.

Ingold, Tim. 2000. *The Perception of the Environment: Essays on Livelihood, Dwelling and Skill*. London: Routledge.

Ingold, Tim. 2011. *Being Alive: Essays on Movement, Knowledge and Description*. London: Routledge.

Ingold, Tim. 2015. *The Life of Lines*. London: Routledge.

Jaramillo-Dent, Daniela, Paloma Contreras-Pulido, and Amor Pérez-Rodríguez. 2022. "Immigrant Influencers on TikTok: Diverse Microcelebrity Profiles and Algorithmic (In)visibility." *Media and Communication* 10, no. 1: 208–21. https://doi.org/10.17645/mac.v10i1.4743

Jauk, Werner. 2009. *Pop/music + medien/kunst: Der musikalisierte Alltag der digitale culture*. Osnabrück: Epos Music.

Jenkis, Henry, Sam Ford, and Joshua Green. 2013. *Spreadable Media: Creating Value and Meaning in a Networked Culture*. New York: New York University Press.

Johnson, Ali. 2021. "Copyrighting TikTok Dances: Choreography in the Internet Age." *Washington Law Review* 96, no. 3: 1225–74.

Kärjä, Antti-Ville. 2018. "Why Is Uncle Paintbrush So Funny? The Case of YouTube Translation of a Syrian Kurdish Wedding Song into Finnish." *Yearbook for Traditional Music* 50: 141–64.

Kassabian, Anahid. 2013. *Ubiquitous Listening: Affect, Attention, and Distributed Subjectivity*. Berkeley: University of California Press.

Kaufmann, Katja, Monika Palmberger, Carolina Parreiras, Arianna Bussoletti, Francesca Belotti, Francesca Comunello, Stellamarina Donato, Welmoed Wagenaar, Juan Bermúdez, Moritz Schweiger, and Jeffrey Wimmer. 2021. "The In(Ter) Dependencies of Mobile Online and Offline Spaces: Reflections on Methods, Practices, Ethics." *AoIR Selected Papers of Internet Research*. https://doi.org/10.5210/spir.v2021i0.12119.

Kaye, Bondy. 2020. "Make This Go Viral: Building Musical Careers through Accidental Virality on Tiktok." *Flow Journal* 27, no. 1. https://www.flowjournal.org/2020/09/make-this-go-viral/.

Kaye, Bondy. 2022. "Please Duet This: Collaborative Music Making in Lockdown on TikTok." *Networking Knowledge: Journal of the MeCCSA Postgraduate Network* 15, no. 1: 59–77.

Kaye, Bondy. Forthcoming. "#JazzTok: Creativity, Community, and Improvisation on TikTok." *Jazz and Culture*.

Kaye, Bondy, and Jean Burgess. 2021. "Algorithmic Recommender Systems and Everyday Data Cultures: The View from Jazz Tiktok." In "Everyday Data Cultures," Albury, K., et al. Panel presented at AoIR 2021. *AoIR Selected Papers of Internet Researchers*. https://doi.org/10.5210/spir.v2021i0.12088.

Kaye, Bondy, Xu Chen, and Jing Zeng. 2021. "The Co-Evolution of Two Chinese Mobile Short Video Apps: Parallel Platformization of Douyin and Tiktok." *Mobile Media & Communication* 9, no. 2: 229–53.

Kaye, Bondy, Aleesha Rodriguez, Katrin Langton, and Patrik Wikström. 2021. "You Made This? I Made This: Practices of Authorship and (Mis)attribution on TikTok." *International Journal of Communication* 15: 3195–215.

Kaye, Bondy, Jing Zeng, and Patrik Wikström. 2022. *TikTok: Creativity and Culture in Short Video*. Cambridge: Polity Press.

Kendall, Lori. 2002. *Hanging Out in the Virtual Pub: Masculinities and Relationships Online*. Berkeley: University of California Press.

Kennedy, Melanie. 2020. "'If the Rise of the Tiktok Dance And E-Girl Aesthetic has Taught us Anything, It's that Teenage Girls Rule the Internet Right Now': Tiktok Celebrity, Girls And The Coronavirus Crisis." *European Journal of Cultural Studies* 23, no. 6: 1069–76.

Kenny, Ailbhe. 2016. *Communities of Musical Practice*. London: Routledge.

König, Eva. 2021. "Konstruktion einer Selbstidentität, Gruppenidentität und kulturellen Identität." Bachelor's thesis. Vienna: University of Vienna.

Kozinets, Robert. [2009] 2015. *Netnography: Redefined*. Los Angeles: SAGE.

Lange, Patricia. 2014. *Kids on YouTube: Technical Identities and Digital Literacies*. Walnut Creek: Routledge.

Lange, Patricia. 2019. *Thanks for Watching: An Anthropological Study of Video Sharing on YouTube*. Louisville: University Press of Colorado.

Latour, Bruno. 2005. *Reassembling the Social: An Introduction to Actor-Network-Theory*. Oxford: Oxford University Press.

Lefebvre, Henri. [1974] 1991. *The Production of Space*. Oxford: Blackwell Publishing.

Lévy, Pierre. 1998. *Becoming Virtual: Reality in the Digital Age*. New York: Plenum Press.

Liamkillenmusic [@liamkillenmusic]. 2021. Interview by Maximiliane Schrank. July 19, 2021.

López Cano, Rubén. 2018. *Música Dispersa: Apropiación, Influencias, robos y remix en la era de la escucha Digital*. Barcelona: Musikeon Books.

Lysloff, René. 2003. "Musical Community on the Internet: An On-Line Ethnography." *Cultural Anthropology* 18, no. 2: 233–63.

Madrid, Alejandro L. 2008. *Nort-tec Rifa!: Electronic Dance Music From Tijuana to the World*. New York: Oxford University Press.

Malinowski, Bronislaw. 1922. *Argonauts of the West Pacific: An Account of Native Enterprise and Adventure in the Archipelagoes of Melanesian New Guinea*. New York: E.P. Dutton.

Manabe, Noriko. 2015. *The Revolution Will Not Be Televised: Protest Music after Fukoshima*. New York: Oxford University Press.

Marcus, George. 1995. "Ethnography in/of the World System: The Emergence of Multi-Sited Ethnography." *Annual Review of Anthropology* 24: 95–117.

Matamoros-Fernández, Ariadna, Aleesha Rodriguez, and Patrik Wikström. 2022. "Humor That Harms? Examining Racist Audio-Visual Memetic Media on TikTok during Covid-19." *Media and Communication* 10, no. 2: 180–91. https://doi.org/10.17645/mac.v10i2.5154

Meizel, Katherine. 2011. *Idiolized: Music, Media and Identity in American Idol*. Bloomington: Indiana University Press.

Meizel, Katherine. 2020. *Multivocality: Singing on the Borders of Identity*. New York: Oxford University Press.

Mendívil, Julio. 2008. *Ein musikalisches Stück Heimat: Ethnologische Beobachtungen zum deutschen Schlager*. Bielefeld: transcript Verlag.

Mendívil, Julio. 2013. "The Song Remains the Same? Sobre las biografías sociales y personalizadas de las canciones." *El oido pensante* 1, no. 2: 23–49.

Mendívil, Julio. 2016. "The Battle of Evermore. Music as a Never-ending Struggle for the Construction of Meaning." In *World Music Studies*, edited by Regine Allgayer-Kaufmann, 67–91. Berlin: Logos Verlag.

Merleau-Ponty, Maurice. [1945] 2014. *Phenomenology of Perception*. London: Routledge.

Merriam, Alan P. 1964. *The Anthropology of Music*. Evanston, IL: Northwestern University Press.

Miller, Kiri. 2012. *Playing Along: Digital Games, YouTube, and Virtual Performance*. New York: Oxford University.

Miller, Kiri. 2017. *Playable Bodies: Dance Games and Intimate Media*. New York: Oxford University Press.

Mintydkalu [@mintydkalu]. 2021. Interview by Yoonsang Cho. September 20, 2021.

MissBunPun [@MissBunPun]. 2021. Interview by Emma Schrott. Mai 18, 2021.

Moore, Christopher, and Philip Purvis, eds. 2018. *Music & Camp*. Middletown: Wesleyan University Press.

Moores, Shaun. 2018. *Digital Orientations: Non-Media-Centric Media Studies and Non-Representational Theories of Practice*. New York: Peter Lang.

Morley, David. 2007. *Media. Modernity and Technology: The Geography of the New*. Oxford: Routledge.

Muchitsch, Veronika. 2024. "Sad Girls on TikTok: Musical and Multimodal Participatory Practices as Affective Negotiation of Ordinary Feelings and Knowledges in Online Music Cultures." *Popular Music and Society*, March: 1–17.

Müller, L. J. 2018. *Sound und Sexismus: Geschlecht im Klang populärer Musik. Eine feministisch-musiktheoretische Annäherung*. Hamburg: Marta Press.

Müller, L. J. 2022. *Hearing Sexism: Gender in the Sound of Popular Music. A Feminist Approach*. Bielefeld: transcript Verlag.

Nettl, Bruno. 1983. *The Study of Ethnomusicology: Twenty-nine Issues and Concepts*. Urbana: University of Illinois Press.

Nettl, Bruno. 2005. *The Study of Ethnomusicology: Thirty-one Issues and Concepts*. New edition, Urbana: University of Illinois Press.

Neuwirth, Julia. "Trending Sounds: So wird mit Musik auf TikTok interagiert." Bachelor's thesis. Vienna: University of Vienna.

Nieborg, David, and Thomas Poell. 2018. "The Platformization of Cultural Production: Theorizing the Contingent Cultural Commodity." *New Media & Society* 20, no. 11: 4275–92.

Opernloft. 2021. "#FREE_Constanze." Opernlofts programme. http://opernloft.de/spielplan/_free_constanze/index.html.

Opernloft. 2022. "Carmen by Carmen." Opernlofts programme. http://opernloft.de/spielplan/carmen-by-carmen/index.html.

Pertierra, Anna. 2018. *Media Anthropology for the Digital Age*. Cambridge: Polity Press.

Petrovic, Sonja. 2022. "From Karaoke to Lip-Syncing: Performance Communities and Tiktok Use in Japan." *Media International Australia* 186, no. 1: 11–28. https://doi.org/10.1177/1329878X221106565.

Pilipets, Elena. 2023. "Hashtagging, Duetting, Sound-linking: TikTok Gestures and Methods of (In)distinction." *The Journal of Media Art Study and Theory* 4, no. 1: 109–35. https://doi.org/10.59547/26911566.4.1.07.

Pink, Sarah, Heather Horst, John Postill, Larissa Hjorth, Tania Lewis, and Jo Tacchi. 2016. *Digital Ethnography: Principles and Practice*. London: SAGE.

Przybylski, Liz. 2021. *Hybrid Ethnography: Online, Offline, and In Between*. Los Angeles: SAGE.

Rauchberg, Jessica. 2022a. "#Shadowbanned: Queer, Trans, and Disabled Creator Responses to Algorithmic Oppression on TikTok." In *LGBTQ Digital Cultures*, edited by Paromita Pain, 196–209. New York: Routledge.

Rauchberg, Jessica. 2022b. "A Different Girl, But She's Nothing New: Olivia Rodrigo and Posting Imitation Pop On Tiktok." *Feminist Media Studies*: 1–5. https://doi.org/10.1080/14680777.2022.2093251.

Rice, Timothy. 1987. "Toward the Remodeling of Ethnomusicology." *Ethnomusicology* 31, no. 3: 469–88.

Rice, Timothy. 2003. "Time, Place, and Metaphor in Musical Experience and Ethnography." *Ethnomusicology* 47, no. 2: 151–79.

Rice, Timothy. 2008. "Toward a Mediation of Field Methods and Field Experience in Ethnomusicology." In *Shadows in the Field: New Perspectives for Fieldwork in Ethnomusicology*, edited by Gregory Barz and Timothy Cooley, 42–61. New York: Oxford University Press.

Rice, Timothy. 2014. *Ethnomusicology: A Very Short Introduction*. New York: Oxford University Press.

Rice, Timothy. 2017. *Modeling Ethnomusicology*. New York: Oxford University Press.

Ryan, Kathryn, and Tileva Antoaneta. 2022. "Taking the Past Out of the Pastoral: Tiktok's Queer 'Cottagecore' Culture and Performative Placemaking." *Queer Studies in Media & Popular Culture* 7, no. 3: 165–76.

Ryan, Marie-Laure. 1999. "Cyberspace, Virtuality, and the Text." In *Cyberspace Textuality: Computer Technology and Literary Theory*, edited by Marie-Laure Ryan, 78–107. Bloomington: Indiana University Press.

Ryan, Marie-Laure. 2015. *Narrative as Virtual Reality 2: Revisting Immersion and Interactivity in Literature and Electronic Media*. Baltimore, MD: John Hopkins University Press.

Sánchez-Omos, Cande, and EduardoViñuela. 2022. "The End of the Amateur Music Video Dream (as We Expected It): From YouTube to TikTok." In *Music in the Disruptive Era*, edited by David Hurwitz and Pedro Ordoñez, 3–22. Turnhout: Brepols.

Sarahnakya [@sarahnakya]. 2021. Interview by Yoonsang Cho. August 9, 2021.

Savage.hersi [@savage.hersi]. 2021. Interview by Tessa Balser-Schuhmann. July 7, 2021.

Savic, Milovan. 2021. "From Musical.ly to TikTok: Social Construction of 2020's Most Downloaded Short-video App." *International Journal of Communication*,15: 1–21.

Schellewald, Andreas. 2021. "Communicative Forms on Tiktok: Perspectives from Digital Ethnography." *International Journal of Communication* 15: 1437–57.

Schlags, Hannah. 2021. Interview by Juan Bermúdez and Nora Geroldinger. September 9, 2021.

Schrank, Maximiliane. 2021. "#Synthtok: Eine Netnographie zwischen Analog und Digital." Bachelor's thesis. Vienna: University of Vienna.

Schreiner, Julia. 2021. Interview by Juan Bermúdez and Nora Geroldinger, September 08, 2021.

Schrödinger, Erwin. 1935. "Die gegenwärtige Situation in der Quantenmechanik." *Die Naturwissenschaften* 23, no. 48: 807–12.

Schrott, Emma. 2021. "Performing Politics on TikTok: Activism without Activists." Bachelor's thesis. Vienna: University of Vienna.

Seeger, Anthony. 2006. "Lost Lineages and Neglected Peers: Ethnomusicologists outside Academia." *Ethnomusicology* 50, no. 2: 214–35.

Slobin, Mark. 1993. *Subcultural Sounds: Micromusics of the West*. Middletown: Wesleyan University Press.

Small, Christopher. 1998. *Musicking: The Meanings of Performing and Listening*. Middletown: Wesleyan University Press.

Smudits, Alfred. 2002. *Mediamorphosen des Kulturschaffens: Kunst und Kommunikationstechnologien in Wandel*. Vienna: Braumüller.

Şot, İrem. 2022. "Fostering Intimacy on Tiktok: A Platform that 'Listens' and 'Creates a Safe Space.'" *Media, Culture & Society* 44, no. 8: 1490–1507. https://doi.org/10.1177/01634437221104709

Stahl, Catherine, and Ioana Literat. 2022. "#GenZ on Tiktok: The Collective Online Self-Portrait of the Social Media Generation." *Journal of Youth Studies* 26: 925–46. https://doi.org/10.1080/13676261.2022.2053671

Steele, Catherine. 2021. "Black Feminist Pleasure on TikTok: An Ode to Hurston's Characteristics of Negro Expression." *Women's Studies in Communication* 44, no. 4: 463–9. https://doi.org/10.1080/07491409.2021.1987822

Stein, Krysten. 2023. "You Better Work! Drag Queen Performativity and Visibility on #dragqueen TikTok." *Queer Studies in Media & Popular Culture* 8, no. 2: 139–57. https://doi.org/10.1386/qsmpc_00095_1.

Steputtat, Kendra. 2020. "Tango Musicality and Tango Danceability: Reconnecting Strategies in Current Cosmopolitan Tango Argentino Practice." In Choreomusicology II: Translocality | Local Ontology," edited by Elina Seye and Kendra Steputtat. Special Issue, *The World of Music (new series)* 9, nr. 2: 5–30.

Stoever, Jennifer. 2016. *The Sonic Color Line: Race and the Cultural Politics of Listening.* New York: New York University Press.

Stulens, Karel. 2021. "As You Like It, Like it! For Smartphone Quartet, String Trio & E. Guitar." Score.

TikTok. 2021a. "TikTok startet Förderprogramm für Kunst und Kultur." TikTok newsroom. February 24, 2021. https://newsroom.tiktok.com/de-de/tiktok-startet-foerderprogramm-fuer-kunst-und-kultur.

TikTok. 2021b. " 'Wir sind mehr als du denkst': TikTok neue Marken-Kampagne." TikTok newsroom. March 12, 2021. https://newsroom.tiktok.com/de-de/wir-sind-mehr-als-du-denkst-tiktoks-neue-marken-kampagne?lang=de.

Tschmuck, Peter, Beate Flath, and Martin Lücke, eds. 2018. *Musikwirtschaftsforschung: Die Grundlagen einer neuen Disziplin.* Wiesbaden: Springer.

Turino, Thomas. 2008. *Music as Social Life: The Politics of Participations.* Chicago: University of Chicago Press.

Turner, Victor. [1969] 2017. *The Ritual Process: Structure and Anti-Structure.* New York: Routledge.

Van Dijck, José. 2013. *The Culture of Connectivity: A Critical History of Social Media.* Oxford: Oxford University Press.

Vernallis, Carol, Holly Roger, and Lisa Perrott, eds. 2020. *Transmedia Directors. Artistry, Industry and New Audivisual Aesthetics.* London: Bloomsbury Academic.

Vernallis, Carol. 2013. *Unruly Media: YouTube, Music Video, and the New Digital Cinema.* Oxford: Oxford University Press.

Vizcaíno-Verdú, Arantxa, and Crystal Abidin. 2022. "Music Challenge Memes on TikTok: Understanding In-Group Storytelling Videos." *International Journal of Communication* 16: 883–908.

Vizcaíno-Verdú, Arantxa, and Ignacio Aguaded. 2022. "#ThisIsMeChallenge and Music for Empowerment of Marginalized Groups on TikTok." *Media and Communication* 10, no. 1: 157–72.

Vizcaíno-Verdú, Arantxa, and Simona Tirocchi. 2021. "Tiktokers y objetivación sexual de género en retos musicales." *Media Education* 12, no. 1: 7–16.

Vizcaíno-Verdú, Arantxa, Patricia De-Casas-Moreno, and Simona Tirocchi. 2023. "Online Prosumer Convergence: Listening, Creating and Sharing Music On Youtube and Tiktok." *Communication & Society* 36, no. 1: 151–66. https://doi.org/10.15581/003.36.1.151-166.

Voithofer, Monika. 2024. *'DENKEN, HÖREN, DA CAPO': Konzeptuelle Musik im 20. und 21. Jahrhundert*. Stuttgart: Franz Steiner.

Warfield, Katie, Crystal Abidin, and Carolina Cambre, eds. 2020. *Mediated Interfaces: The Body on Social Media*. New York: Bloomsbury Academic.

Wei, Tao, and Xiaohong Wang. 2022. "A Historical Review and Theoretical Mapping on Short Video Studies 2005–2021." *Online Media and Global Communication* 1, no. 2: 247–86.

Weidman, Amanda. 2021. *Brought to Life by the Voice: Playback Singing and Cultural Politics in South India*. Oakland: University of California Press.

Wicke, Peter. 2001. *Von Mozart zu Madonna: Eine Kulturgeschichte der Popmusik*. Baden: Suhrkamp.

Willenig, Christoph. 2021. "TikTok und Subkulturen im 21. Jahrhundert." Bachelor's thesis. Vienna: University of Vienna.

Winocur, Rosalia. 2009. "Digital Convergence as the Symbolic Medium of New Practices and Meanings in Young People's Lives." *Popular Communication* 7, no. 1: 179–87.

Wood, Abigail. 2008. "E-Fieldwork: A Paradigm for the Twenty-first Century?" In *The New (Ethno)musicologies*, edited by Henry Stobart, 170–87. Lanham: Scarecrow Press.

Zeng, Jing, Crystal Abidin, and Mike Schäfer. 2021. "Research Perspectives on TikTok and Its Legacy Apps." *International Journal of Communication* 15: 3161–72.

Zulli, Diana, and David Zulli. 2022. "Extending the Internet Meme: Conceptualizing Technological Mimesis and Imitation Publics on the Tiktok Platform." *New Media & Society* 24, no. 8: 1872–90.

Index

www.ingramcontent.com/pod-product-compliance
Ingram Content Group UK Ltd.
Pitfield, Milton Keynes, MK11 3LW, UK
UKHW020211290926
15470UKWH00001B/118

9 798765 112182